PASSAGES

FROM

THE ENGLISH NOTE-BOOKS.

VOL. II.

KENILWORTH CASTLE, LEICESTER'S BUILDING. See page 337.

PASSAGES

FROM

HAWTHORNE'S ENGLISH NOTE-BOOKS.

LONDON.—MILTON-CLUB DINNER.

April 4th, 1856.—On Tuesday I went to No. 14 Ludgate Hill, to dine with Bennoch at the Milton Club; a club recently founded for dissenters, nonconformists, and people whose ideas, religious or political, are not precisely in train with the establishment in church and state. I was shown into a large reading-room, well provided with periodicals and newspapers, and found two or three persons there; but Bennoch had not yet arrived. In a few moments, a tall gentleman with white hair came in,—a fine and intelligent-looking man, whom I guessed to be one of those who were to meet me. He walked about, glancing at the periodicals; and soon entered Mr. Tupper, and, without seeing me, exchanged warm greetings with the white-haired gentleman. "I suppose," began Mr. Tupper, "you have come to meet"— Now, conscious that my name was going to be spoken, and not knowing but the excellent Mr. Tupper might say something which he would not quite like me to overhear, I advanced at once, with outstretched hand, and saluted him. He expressed great joy at the recognition, and immediately introduced me to Mr. Hall.

The dining-room was pretty large and lofty, and there were sixteen guests at table, most of them authors, or people connected with the press; so that the party represented a great deal of the working intellect of London at this present day and moment, — the men whose plays, whose songs, whose articles, are just now in vogue. Mr. Tom Taylor was one of the very few whose writings I had known anything about. He is a tall, slender, dark young man, not English-looking, and wearing colored spectacles, so that I should readily have taken him for an American literary man. I did not have much opportunity of talking with him, nor with anybody else, except Dr. ——, who seemed a shrewd, sensible man, with a certain slight acerbity of thought. Mr. Herbert Ingram, recently elected member of Parliament, was likewise present, and sat on Bennoch's left.

It was a very good dinner, with an abundance of wine, which Bennoch sent round faster than was for the next day's comfort of his guests. It is singular that I should thus far have quite forgotten W—— H——, whose books I know better than those of any other person there. He is a white-headed, stout, firm-looking, and rather wrinkled-faced old gentleman, whose temper, I should imagine, was not the very sweetest in the world. There is an abruptness, a kind of sub-acidity, if not bitterness, in his address; he seemed not to be, in short, so genial as I should have anticipated from his books.

As soon as the cloth was removed, Bennoch, without rising from his chair, made a speech in honor of his eminent and distinguished guest, which illustrious person happened to be sitting in the self-same chair that I myself occupied. I have no recollection of what he said, nor of what I said in reply, but I remember that both of us were cheered and applauded much more than the occasion deserved. Then followed about fifty other speeches; for every single individual at table was called up (as Tupper said, "toasted and roasted"), and, for my part, I was done entirely brown (to continue T——'s figure). Everybody said something kind, not a word or idea of which can I find in my memory. Certainly, if I never get any more praise in my life, I have had enough of it for once. I made another little bit of a speech, too, in response to something that was said in reference to the present difficulties between England and America, and ended, as a proof that I deemed war impossible, with drinking success to the British army, and calling on Lieutenant Shaw, of the Aldershott Camp, to reply. I am afraid I must have said something very wrong, for the applause was vociferous, and I could hear the gentlemen whispering about the table, "Good!" "Good!" "Yes, he is a fine fellow," — and other such ill-earned praises; and I took shame to myself, and held my tongue (publicly) the rest of the evening. But in such cases something must be allowed to the excitement of the moment, and to the effect of kindness and good-will, so broadly and warmly displayed; and even a sincere man must not be held to speak as if he were under oath.

We separated, in a blessed state of contentment with one another, at about eleven; and (lest I should starve before morning) I went with Mr. D—— to take supper at his house in Park Lane. Mr. D—— is a pale young gentleman, of American aspect, being a West-Indian by birth. He is one of the principal writers of editorials for the Times. We were accompanied in the carriage by another gentleman, Mr. M——, who is connected with the management of the same paper. He wrote the letters from Scutari, which drew so much attention to the state of the hospitals. Mr. D—— is the husband of the former Miss ——, the actress, and when we reached his house, we found that she had just come home from the theatre, and was taking off her stage-dress. Anon she came down to the drawing-room, — a seemingly good, simple, and intelligent lady, not at all pretty, and I should think, older than her husband. She was very kind to me, and told me that she had read one of my books — The House of the Seven Gables — thirteen years ago; which I thought remarkable, because I did not write it till eight or nine years afterwards.

The principal talk during supper (which consisted of welsh-rabbit and biscuits, with champagne and soda-water) was about the Times, and the two contributors expressed vast admiration of Mr. ——, who has the chief editorial management of the paper. It is odd to find how little we outsiders know of men who really exercise a vast influence on affairs, for this Mr. —— is certainly of far more importance in the world than a minister of state. He writes nothing himself; but the character of the Times seems to depend upon his intuitive, unerring judgment; and if ever he is absent from his post, even for a day or two, they say that the paper immediately shows it. In reply to my questions, they appeared to acknowledge that he was a man of expediency, but of a very high expediency, and that he gave the public the very best principles which it was capable of receiving. Perhaps it may be so: the Times's articles are certainly not written in so high a moral vein as might be wished; but what they lack in height they gain in breadth. Every sensible man in England finds his own best common sense there; and, in effect, I think its influence is wholesome.

Apropos of public speaking, Dr. —— said that Sir Lytton Bulwer asked him (I think the anecdote was personal to himself) whether he felt his heart beat when he was going to speak. "Yes." "Does your voice frighten you?" "Yes." "Do all your ideas forsake you?" "Yes." "Do you wish the floor to open and swallow you?" "Yes." "Why, then, you'll make an orator!" Dr. —— told of Canning, too, how once, before rising to speak in the House of Commons, he bade his friend feel his pulse, which was throbbing terrifically. "I know I shall make one of my best speeches," said Canning, "because I 'm in such an awful funk!" President Pierce, who has a great deal of oratorical power, is subject to a similar horror and reluctance.

REFORM-CLUB DINNER.

April 5th. — On Thursday, at eight o'clock, I went to the Reform Club, to dine with Dr. ——. The waiter admitted me into a great basement hall, with a tessellated or mosaic or somehow figured floor of stone, and lighted from a dome of lofty height. In a few minutes Dr. —— appeared, and showed me about the edifice, which is very noble and of a substantial magnificence that was most satisfactory to behold, — no wood-work imitating better materials, but pillars and balustrades of marble, and everything what it purports to be. The reading-room is very large, and luxuriously comfortable, and contains an admirable library: there are rooms and conveniences for every possible purpose; and whatever material for enjoyment a bachelor may need, or ought to have, he can surely find it here, and on such reasonable terms that a small income will do as much for him as a far greater one on any other system.

In a colonnade, on the first floor, surrounding the great basement hall, there are portraits of distinguished reformers, and black niches for others yet to come. Joseph Hume, I believe, is destined to fill one of these blanks; but I remarked that the larger part of the portraits, already hung up, are of men of high rank, — the Duke of Sussex, for instance; Lord Durham, Lord Grey; and, indeed, I remember no commoner. In one room, I saw on the wall the fac-simile, so common in the United States, of our Declaration of Independence.

Descending again to the basement hall, an elderly gentleman came in, and was warmly welcomed by Dr. ——. He was a very short man, but with breadth enough, and a back excessively bent, — bowed almost to deformity; very gray hair, and a face and expression of remarkable briskness and intelligence. His profile came out pretty boldly, and his eyes had the prominence that indicates, I believe, volubility of speech, nor did he fail to talk from the instant of his appearance; and in the tone of his voice, and in his glance, and in the whole man, there was something racy, — a flavor of the humorist. His step was that of an aged man, and he put his stick down very decidedly at every footfall; though as he afterwards told me that he was only fifty-two, he need not yet have been infirm. But perhaps he has had the gout; his feet, however, are by no means swollen, but unusually small. Dr. —— introduced him as Mr. Douglas Jerrold, and we went into the coffee-room to dine.

The coffee-room occupies one whole side of the edifice, and is provided with a great many tables, calculated for three or four persons to dine at; and we sat down at one of these, and Dr. —— ordered some mulligatawny soup, and a bottle of white French wine. The waiters in the coffee-room are very numerous, and most of them dressed in the livery of the Club, comprising plush breeches and white-silk stockings; for these English Reformers do not seem to include Republican simplicity of manners in their system. Neither, perhaps, is it anywise essential.

After the soup, we had turbot, and by and by a bottle of Chateau Margaux, very delectable; and then some lambs' feet, delicately done, and some cutlets of I know not what peculiar type; and finally a ptarmigan, which is of the same race of birds as the grouse, but feeds high up towards the summits of the Scotch mountains. Then some cheese, and a bottle of Chambertin. It was a very pleasant dinner, and my companions were both very agreeable men; both taking a shrewd, satirical, yet not ill-natured, view of life and people, and as for Mr. Douglas Jerrold, he often reminded me of E—— C——, in the richer veins of the latter, both by his face and expression, and by a tincture of something at once wise and humorously absurd in what he said. But I think he has a kinder, more genial, wholesomer nature than E——, and under a very thin crust of outward acerbity I grew sensible of a very warm heart, and even of much simplicity of character in this man, born in London, and accustomed always to London life.

I wish I had any faculty whatever of remembering what people say; but, though I appreciate anything good at the moment, it never stays in my memory; nor do I think, in fact, that anything definite, rounded, pointed, separable, and transferable from the general lump of conversation was said by anybody. I recollect that they laughed at Mr. ——, and at his shedding a tear into a Scottish river, on occasion of some literary festival. . . . . They spoke approvingly of Bulwer, as valuing his literary position, and holding himself one of the brotherhood of authors; and not so approvingly of Charles Dickens, who, born a plebeian, aspires to aristocratic society. But I said that it was easy to condescend, and that Bulwer knew he could not put off his rank, and that he would have all the advantages of it, in spite of his authorship. We talked about the position of men of letters in England, and they said that the aristocracy hated and despised and feared them; and I asked why it was that literary men, having really so much power in their hands, were content to live unrecognized in the State.

Douglas Jerrold talked of Thackeray and his success in America, and said that he himself purposed going and had been invited thither to lecture. I asked him whether it was pleasant to a writer of plays to see them performed; and he said it was intolerable, the presentation of the author's idea being so imperfect; and Dr. —— observed that it was excruciating to hear one of his own songs sung. Jerrold spoke of the Duke of

Devonshire with great warmth, as a true, honest, simple, most kind-hearted man, from whom he himself had received great courtesies and kindnesses (not, as I understood, in the way of patronage or essential favors); and I (Heaven forgive me!) queried within myself whether this English reforming author would have been quite so sensible of the Duke's excellence if his Grace had not been a duke. But indeed, a nobleman, who is at the same time a true and whole-hearted man, feeling his brotherhood with men, does really deserve some credit for it.

In the course of the evening, Jerrold spoke with high appreciation of Emerson; and of Longfellow, whose Hiawatha he considered a wonderful performance; and of Lowell, whose Fable for Critics he especially admired. I mentioned Thoreau, and proposed to send his works to Dr. ——, who, being connected with the Illustrated News, and otherwise a writer, might be inclined to draw attention to them. Douglas Jerrold asked why he should not have them too. I hesitated a little, but as he pressed me, and would have an answer, I said that I did not feel quite so sure of his kindly judgment on Thoreau's books; and it so chanced that I used the word "acrid," for lack of a better, in endeavoring to express my idea of Jerrold's way of looking at men and books. It was not quite what I meant; but, in fact, he often *is* acrid, and has written pages and volumes of acridity, though, no doubt, with an honest purpose, and from a manly disgust at the cant and humbug of the world. Jerrold said no more, and I went on talking with Dr. ——; but, in a minute or two, I became aware that something had gone wrong, and, looking at Douglas

Jerrold, there was an expression of pain and emotion on his face. By this time a second bottle of Burgundy had been opened (Clos Vougeot, the best the Club could produce, and far richer than the Chambertin), and that warm and potent wine may have had something to do with the depth and vivacity of Mr. Jerrold's feelings. But he was indeed greatly hurt by that little word "acrid." "He knew," he said, "that the world considered him a sour, bitter, ill-natured man; but that such a man as I should have the same opinion was almost more than he could bear." As he spoke, he threw out his arms, sank back in his seat, and I was really a little apprehensive of his actual dissolution into tears. Hereupon I spoke, as was good need, and though, as usual, I have forgotten everything I said, I am quite sure it was to the purpose, and went to this good fellow's heart, as it came warmly from my own. I do remember saying that I felt him to be as genial as the glass of Burgundy which I held in my hand; and I think that touched the very right spot; for he smiled, and said he was afraid the Burgundy was better than he, but yet he was comforted. Dr. —— said that he likewise had a reputation for bitterness; and I assured him, if I might venture to join myself to the brotherhood of two such men, that I was considered a very ill-natured person by many people in my own country. Douglas Jerrold said he was glad of it.

We were now in sweetest harmony, and Jerrold spoke more than it would become me to repeat in praise of my own books, which he said he admired, and he found the man more admirable than his books! I hope so, certainly.

We now went to the Haymarket Theatre, where Douglas Jerrold is on the free list; and after seeing a ballet by some Spanish dancers, we separated, and betook ourselves to our several homes. I like Douglas Jerrold very much.

April 8th. — On Saturday evening, at ten o'clock, I went to a supper-party at Mr. D——'s, and there met five or six people, — Mr. Faed, a young and distinguished artist; Dr. Eliotson, a dark, sombre, taciturn, powerful-looking man, with coal-black hair, and a beard as black, fringing round his face; Mr. Charles Reade, author of Christie Johnstone and other novels, and many plays, — a tall man, more than thirty, fair-haired, and of agreeable talk and demeanor.

. . . . .

FIRFIELD.

On April 6th, I went to the Waterloo Station, and there meeting Bennoch and Dr. ——, took the rail for Woking, where we found Mr. Hall's carriage waiting to convey us to Addlestone, about five miles off. On arriving we found that Mr. and Mrs. Hall had not yet returned from church. Their place is an exceedingly pretty one, and arranged in very good taste. The house is not large; but is filled, in every room, with fine engravings, statuettes, ingenious prettinesses or beautifulnesses in the way of flower-stands, cabinets, and things that seem to have bloomed naturally out of the characters of its occupants. There is a conservatory connected with the drawing-room, and enriched with lovely plants, one of which has a certain interest as being the plant on which Coleridge's eyes were fixed when he died. This conservatory is likewise beautified with several very fine casts of statues by modern sculptors, among which was the Greek Slave of Powers, which my English friends criticised as being too thin and meagre; but I defended it as in accordance with American ideas of feminine beauty. From the conservatory we passed into the garden, but did not minutely examine it, knowing that Mr. Hall would wish to lead us through it in person. So, in the mean time, we took a walk in the neighborhood, over stiles and along by-paths, for two or three miles, till we reached the old village of Chertsey. In one of its streets stands an ancient house, gabled, and with the second story projecting over the first, and bearing an inscription to the purport that the poet Cowley had once resided, and, I think, died there. Thence we passed on till we reached a bridge over the Thames, which at this point, about twenty-five miles from London, is a narrow river, but looks clean and pure, and unconscious what abominations the city sewers will pour into it anon. We were caught in two or three showers in the course of our walk; but got back to Firfield without being very much wetted.

Our host and hostess had by this time returned from church, and Mrs. Hall came frankly and heartily to the door to greet us, scolding us (kindly) for having got wet. . . . . I liked her simple, easy, gentle, quiet manners, and I liked her husband too.

. . . . .

He has a wide and quick sympathy, and expresses it freely. . . . . The world is the better for him.

The shower being now over, we went out upon the beautiful lawn before his house, where there were a good many trees of various kinds, many of which have been set out by persons of great or small distinction, and are labelled with their names. Thomas Moore's name was appended to one; Maria Edgeworth's to another; likewise Fredrika Bremer's, Jenny Lind's; also Grace Greenwood's, and I know not whose besides. This is really a pleasant method of enriching one's grounds with memorials of friends, nor is there any harm in making a shrubbery of celebrities. Three holes were already dug, and three new trees lay ready to be planted, and for me there was a sumach to plant, — a tree I never liked; but Mr. Hall said that they had tried to dig up a hawthorn, but found it clung too fast to the soil. So, since better might not be, and telling Mr. Hall that I supposed I should have a right to hang myself on this tree whenever I chose, I seized a spade, and speedily shovelled in a great deal of dirt; and there stands my sumach, an object of interest to posterity! Bennoch also and Dr. —— set out their trees, and indeed, it was in some sense a joint affair, for the rest of the party held up each tree, while its godfather shovelled in the earth; but, after all, the gardener had more to do with it than we. After this important business was over, Mr. Hall led us about his grounds, which are very nicely planned and ordered; and all this he has bought, and built, and laid out, from the profits of his own and his wife's literary exertions.

We dined early, and had a very pleasant dinner, and, after the cloth was removed, Mr. Hall was graciously pleased to drink my health, following it with a long tribute to my genius. I answered briefly; and one half of my short speech was in all probability very foolish. . . . .

After the ladies (there were three, one being a girl of seventeen, with rich auburn hair, the adopted daughter of the Halls) had retired, Dr. ——, having been toasted himself, proposed Mrs. Hall's health.

. . . . .

I did not have a great deal of conversation with Mrs. Hall; but enough to make me think her a genuine and good woman, unspoilt by a literary career, and retaining more sentiment than even most girls keep beyond seventeen. She told me that it had been the dream of her life to see Longfellow and myself! . . . . Her dream is half accomplished now, and, as they say Longfellow is coming over this summer, the remainder may soon be rounded out. On taking leave, our kind hosts presented me with some beautiful flowers, and with three volumes of a work, by themselves, on Ireland; and Dr. —— was favored also with some flowers, and a plant in a pot, and Bennoch too had his hands full, ... and we went on our way rejoicing.

[Here follows an account of the Lord Mayor's dinner, taken mostly for Our Old Home; but I think I will copy this more exact description of the lady mentioned in "Civic Banquets." — Ed.]

. . . . My eyes were mostly drawn to a young lady, who sat nearly opposite me, across the table. She was, I suppose, dark, and yet not dark, but rather seemed to be of pure white marble, yet not white; but the purest and finest complexion, without a shade of color in it, yet anything but sallow or sickly. Her hair was a wonderful deep raven-black, black as night, black as death; not raven-black, for that has a shiny gloss, and hers had not, but it was hair never to be painted nor described, — wonderful hair, Jewish hair. Her nose had a beautiful outline, though I could see that it was Jewish too; and that, and all her features, were so fine that sculpture seemed a despicable art beside her, and certainly my pen is good for nothing. If any likeness could be given, however, it must be by sculpture, not painting. She was slender and youthful, and yet had a stately and cold, though soft and womanly grace; and, looking at her, I saw what were the wives of the old patriarchs in their maiden or early-married days, — what Judith was, for, womanly as she looked, I doubt not she could have slain a man in a just cause, — what Bathsheba was, only she seemed to have no sin in her, — perhaps what Eve was, though one could hardly think her weak enough to eat the apple. . . . . Whether owing to distinctness of race, my sense that she was a Jewess, or whatever else, I felt a sort of repugnance, simultaneously with my perception that she was an admirable creature.

THE HOUSE OF COMMONS.

At ten o'clock the next day [after the Lord Mayor's dinner] I went to lunch with Bennoch, and afterwards accompanied him to one of the government offices in Downing Street. He went thither, not on official business, but on a matter connected with a monument to Miss Mitford, in which Mr. Harness, a clergyman and some sort of a government clerk, is interested. I gathered from this conversation that there is no great enthusiasm about the monumental affair among the British public. It surprised me to hear allusions indicating that Miss Mitford was not the invariably amiable person that her writings would suggest; but the whole drift of what they said tended, nevertheless, towards the idea that she was an excellent and generous person, loved most by those who knew her best.

From Downing Street we crossed over and entered Westminster Hall, and passed through it, and up the flight of steps at its farthest end, and along the avenue of statues, into the vestibule of the House of Commons. It was now somewhat past five, and we stood at the inner entrance of the House, to see the members pass in, Bennoch pointing out to me the distinguished ones. I was not much impressed with the appearance of the members generally; they seemed to me rather shabbier than English gentlemen usually, and I saw or fancied in many of them a certain self-importance, as they passed into the interior, betokening them to be very full of their dignity. Some of them looked more American — more like American politicians — than most Englishmen do. There was now and then a gray-headed country gentleman, the very type of stupidity; and two or three city members came up and spoke to Bennoch, and showed themselves quite as dull, in their aldermanic way, as the country squires. . . . . Bennoch pointed out Lord John Russell, a small, very short, elderly gentleman, in a brown coat, and so large a hat — not large of brim, but large like a peck measure — that I saw really no face beneath it. By and by came a rather tall, slender person, in a black frock-coat, buttoned up, and black pantaloons, taking long steps, but I thought rather feebly or listlessly. His shoulders were round, or else he had a habitual stoop in them. He had a prominent nose, a thin face, and a sallow, very sallow complexion; . . . . and had I seen him in America, I should have taken him for a hard-worked editor of a newspaper, weary and worn with night labor and want of exercise, — aged before his time. It was Disraeli, and I never saw any other Englishman look in the least like him; though, in America, his appearance would not attract notice as being unusual. I do not remember any other noteworthy person whom we saw enter; in fact, the House had already been some time in session, and most of the members were in their places.

We were to dine at the Refectory of the House with the new member for Boston; and, meanwhile, Bennoch obtained admittance for us into the Speaker's gallery, where we had a view of the members, and could hear what was going on. A Mr. Muntz was speaking on the Income Tax, and he was followed by Sir George Cornwall Lewis and others; but it was all very uninteresting, without the slightest animation or attempt at oratory, — which, indeed, would have been quite out of place. We saw Lord Palmerston; but at too great a distance to distinguish anything but a gray head. The House had daylight in it when we entered, and for some time afterwards; but, by and by, the roof, which I had taken to be a solid and opaque ceiling, suddenly brightened, and showed itself to be transparent; a vast expanse of tinted and figured glass, through which came down a great, mild radiance on the members below. The character of the debate, however, did not grow more luminous or vivacious; so we went down into the vestibule, and there waited for Mr. ——, who soon came and led us into the Refectory. It was very much like the coffee-room of a club. The strict rule forbids the entrance of any but members of Parliament; but it seems to be winked at, although there is another room, opening beyond this, where the law of seclusion is strictly enforced.

The dinner was good, not remarkably so, but good enough, — a soup, some turbot or salmon, cutlets, and I know not what else, and claret, sherry, and port; for, as Mr. —— said, "he did not wish to be stingy." Mr. —— is a self-made man, and a strong instance of the difference between the Englishman and the American, when self-made, and without early education. He is no more a gentleman now than when he began life, — not a whit more refined, either outwardly or inwardly; while the American would have been, after the same experience, not distinguishable outwardly, and perhaps as refined within, as nine tenths of the gentlemen born, in the House of Commons. And, besides, an American comes naturally to any distinctions to which success in life may bring him; he takes them as if they were his proper inheritance, and in no wise to be wondered at. Mr. ——, on the other hand, took evidently a childish delight in his position, and felt a childish wonder in having arrived at it; nor did it seem real to him, after all. . . . .

We again saw Disraeli, who has risen from the people by modes perhaps somewhat like those of Mr. ——. He came and stood near our table, looking at the bill of fare, and then sat down on the opposite side of the room with another gentleman, and ate his dinner. The story of his marriage does him much credit; and indeed I am inclined to like Disraeli, as a man who has made his own place good among a hostile aristocracy, and leads instead of following them.

From the House of Commons we went to Albert Smith's exhibition, or lecture, of the ascent of Mont Blanc, to which Bennoch had orders. It was very amusing, and in some degree instructive. We remained in the saloon at the conclusion of the lecture; and when the audience had dispersed, Mr. Albert Smith made his appearance. . . . .

Nothing of moment happened the next day, at least, not till two o'clock, when I went with Mr. Bowman to Birch's eating-house (it is not Birch's now, but this was the name of the original founder, who became an alderman, and has long been dead) for a basin of turtle-soup. It was very rich, very good, better than we had at the Lord Mayor's, and the best I ever ate.

In the evening Mr. J. B. Davis, formerly our Secretary of Legation, called to take us to dine at Mr. —— ——'s in Camden Town. Mr. —— calls his residence Vermont House; but it hardly has a claim to any separate title, being one of the centre houses of a block. I forget whether I mentioned his calling on me. He is a Vermonter, a graduate of Yale College, who has been here several years, and has established a sort of book brokerage, buying libraries for those who want them, and rare works and editions for American collectors. His business naturally brings him into relations with literary people; and he is himself a kindly and pleasant man. On our arrival we found Mr. D—— and one of his sisters already there; and soon came a Mr. Peabody, who, if I mistake not, is one of the Salem Peabodys, and has some connection with the present eminent London Mr. Peabody. At any rate, he is a very sensible, well-instructed, and widely and long travelled man. Mr. Tom Taylor was also expected; but, owing to some accident or mistake, he did not come for above an hour, all which time our host waited. . . . . But Mr. Tom Taylor, a wit, a satirist, and a famous diner out, is too formidable and too valuable a personage to be treated cavalierly.

In the interim Mr. —— showed us some rare old books, which he has in his private collection, a black-letter edition of Chaucer, and other specimens of the early English printers; and I was impressed, as I have often been, with the idea that we have made few, if any, improvements in the art of printing, though we have greatly facilitated the modes of it. He showed us Dryden's translation of Virgil, with Dr. Johnson's autograph in it; and a large collection of Bibles, of all dates,— church Bibles, family Bibles of the common translation, and older ones. He says he has written or is writing a history of the Bible (as a printed work, I presume). Many of these Bibles had, no doubt, been in actual and daily use from generation to generation; but they were now all splendidly bound, and were likewise very clean and smooth, — in fact, every leaf had been cleansed by a delicate process, a part of which consisted in soaking the whole book in a tub of water, during several days. Mr. —— is likewise rich in manuscripts, having a Spanish document with the signature of the son of Columbus; a whole little volume in Franklin's handwriting, being the first specimen of it; and the original manuscripts of many of the songs of Burns. Among these I saw "Auld Lang Syne," and "Bruce's Address to his Army." We amused ourselves with these matters as long as we could; but at last, as there was to be a party in the evening, dinner could no longer be put off; so we took our seats at table, and immediately afterwards Mr. Taylor made his appearance with his wife and another lady.

Mr. Taylor is reckoned a brilliant conversationist; but I suppose he requires somebody to draw him out and assist him; for I could hear nothing that I thought very remarkable on this occasion. He is not a kind of man whom I can talk with, or greatly help to talk; so, though I sat next to him, nothing came of it. He told me some stories of his life in the Temple, — little funny incidents, that he afterwards wrought into his dramas; in short, a sensible, active-minded, clearly perceptive man, with a humorous way of showing up men and matters. . . . . I wish I could know exactly what the English style good conversation. Probably it is something like plum-pudding, — as heavy, but seldom so rich.

After dinner Mr. Tom Taylor and Mr. D——, with their respective ladies, took their leave; but when we returned to the drawing-room, we found it thronged with a good many people. Mr. S. C. Hall was there with his wife, whom I was glad to see again, for this was the third time of meeting her, and, in this whirl of new acquaintances, I felt quite as if she were an old friend. Mr. William Howitt was also there, and introduced me to his wife, — a very natural, kind, and pleasant lady;

and she presented me to one or two daughters. Mr. Marston, the dramatist, was also introduced to me; and Mr. Helps, a thin, scholarly, cold sort of a man. Dr. Mackay and his wife were there, too; and a certain Mr. Jones, a sculptor, — a jolly, large, elderly person, with a twinkle in his eye. Also a Mr. Godwin, who impressed me as quite a superior person, gentlemanly, cultivated, a man of sensibility; but it is quite impossible to take a clear imprint from any one character, where so many are stamped upon one's notice at once. This Mr. Godwin, as we were discussing Thackeray, said that he is most beautifully tender and devoted to his wife, whenever she can be sensible of his attentions. He says that Thackeray, in his real self, is a sweet, sad man. I grew weary of so many people, especially of the ladies, who were rather superfluous in their oblations, quite stifling me, indeed, with the incense that they burnt under my nose. So far as I could judge, they had all been invited there to see me. It is ungracious, even hoggish, not to be gratified with the interest they expressed in me; but then it is really a bore, and one does not know what to do or say. I felt like the hippopotamus, or — to use a more modest illustration — like some strange insect imprisoned under a tumbler, with a dozen eyes watching whatever I did. By and by, Mr. Jones, the sculptor, relieved me by standing up against the mantel-piece, and telling an Irish story, not to two or three auditors, but to the whole drawing-room, all attentive as to a set exhibition. It was very funny.

The next day after this I went with Mr. Bowman to call on our minister, and found that he, and four of the ladies of his family, with his son, had gone to the

Queen's Drawing-room. We lunched at the Wellington; and spent an hour or more in looking out of the window of that establishment at the carriages, with their pompous coachmen and footmen, driving to and from the Palace of St. James, and at the Horse Guards, with their bright cuirasses, stationed along the street. . . . . Then I took the rail for Liverpool. . . . . While I was still at breakfast at the Waterloo, J—— came in, ruddy-cheeked, smiling, very glad to see me, and looking, I thought, a good deal taller than when I left him. And so ended my London excursion, which has certainly been rich in incident and character, though my account of it be but meagre.

SCOTLAND. — GLASGOW.

May 10*th.* — Last Friday, May 2d, I took the rail, with Mr. Bowman, from the Lime Street station, for Glasgow. There was nothing of much interest along the road, except that, when we got beyond Penrith, we saw snow on the tops of some of the hills. Twilight came on as we were entering Scotland; and I have only a recollection of bleak and bare hills and villages dimly seen, until, nearing Glasgow, we saw the red blaze of furnace-lights at frequent iron-founderies. We put up at the Queen's Hotel, where we arrived about ten o'clock; a better hotel than I have anywhere found in England, — new, well arranged, and with brisk attendance.

In the morning I rambled largely about Glasgow, and found it to be chiefly a modern-built city, with streets mostly wide and regular, and handsome houses and public edifices of a dark gray stone. In front of our hotel, in an enclosed green space, stands a tall column surmounted by a statue of Sir Walter Scott, — a good statue, I should think, as conveying the air and personal aspect of the man. There is a bronze equestrian statue of the Queen in one of the streets, and one or two more equestrian or other statues of eminent persons. I passed through the Trongate and the Gallow-Gate, and visited the Salt-Market, and saw the steeple of the Tolbooth, all of which Scott has made interesting; and I went through the gate of the University, and penetrated into its enclosed courts, round which the College edifices are built. They are not Gothic, but of the age, I suppose, of James I., — with odd-looking, conical-roofed towers, and here and there the bust of a benefactor in niches round the courts, and heavy stone staircases ascending from the pavement, outside the buildings, all of dark gray granite, cold, hard, and venerable. The University stands in High Street, in a dense part of the town, and a very old and shabby part, too. I think the poorer classes of Glasgow excel even those in Liverpool in the bad eminence of filth, uncombed and unwashed children, drunkenness, disorderly deportment, evil smell, and all that makes city poverty disgusting. In my opinion, however, they are a better-looking people than the English (and this is true of all classes), more intelligent of aspect, with more regular features. I looked for the high cheek-bones, which have been attributed, as a characteristic feature, to the Scotch, but could not find them. What most distinguishes them from the English is the regularity of the nose, which is straight, or sometimes a little curved inward; whereas the English nose has no law whatever, but disports itself in all manner of irregularity. I very soon learned to recognize the Scotch face, and when not too Scotch, it is a handsome one.

. . . . .

In another part of the High Street, up a pretty steep slope, and on one side of a public green, near an edifice which I think is a medical college, stands St. Mungo's Cathedral. It is hardly of cathedral dimensions, though a large and fine old church. The price of a ticket of admittance is twopence; so small that it might be as well to make the entrance free. The interior is in excellent repair, with the nave and side aisles, and clustered pillars, and intersecting arches, that belong to all these old churches; and a few monuments along the walls. I was going away without seeing any more than this; but the verger, a friendly old gentleman, with a hearty Scotch way of speaking, told me that the crypts were what chiefly interested strangers; and so he guided me down into the foundation-story of the church, where there is an intricacy and entanglement of immensely massive and heavy arches, supporting the structure above. The view through these arches, among the great shafts of the columns, was very striking. In the central part is a monument; a recumbent figure, if I remember rightly, but it is not known whom it commemorates. There is also a monument to a Scotch prelate, which seems to have been purposely defaced, probably in Covenant times. These intricate arches were the locality of one of the scenes in "Rob Roy," when Rob gives Frank Osbaldistone some message or warning, and then escapes from him into the obscurity behind. In one corner is St. Mungo's well, secured with a wooden cover; but I should not care to drink water that comes from among so many old graves.

After viewing the cathedral, I got back to the hotel just in time to go from thence to the steamer wharf, and take passage up the Clyde. There was nothing very interesting in this little voyage. We passed many small iron steamers, and some large ones; and green fields along the river-shores, villas, villages, and all such suburban objects; neither am I quite sure of the name of the place we landed at, though I think it was Bowling. Here we took the railway for Balloch; and the only place or thing I remember during this transit was a huge bluff or crag, rising abruptly from a river-side, and looking, in connection with its vicinity to the Highlands, just such a site as would be taken for the foundation of a castle. On inquiry it turned out that this abrupt and double-headed hill (for it has two summits, with a cleft between) is the site of Dumbarton Castle, for ages one of the strongest fortresses in Scotland, and still kept up as a garrisoned place. At the distance and point of view at which we passed it, the castle made no show.

Arriving at Balloch, we found it a small village, with no marked features, and a hotel, where we got some lunch, and then we took a stroll over the bridge across the Leven, while waiting for the steamer to take us up Loch Lomond. It was a beautiful afternoon, warm and sunny; and after walking about a mile, we had a fine view of Loch Lomond, and of the mountains around and beyond it, — Ben Lomond among the rest. It is vain, at a week's distance, to try to remember the shapes of mountains; so I shall attempt no description of them, and content myself with saying that they did not quite come up to my anticipations. In due time we returned to our hotel, and found in the coffee-room a tall, white-haired, venerable gentleman, and a pleasant-looking young lady, his daughter. They had been eating lunch, and the young lady helped her father on with his outside garment, and his comforter, and gave him his stick, just as any other daughter might do, — all of which I mention because he was a nobleman; and, moreover, had engaged all the post-horses at the inn, so that we could not continue our travels by land, along the side of Loch Lomond, as we had first intended. At four o'clock the railway train arrived again, with a very moderate number of passengers, who (and we among them) immediately embarked on board a neat little steamer which was waiting for us.

The day was bright and cloudless; but there was a strong, cold breeze blowing down the lake, so that it was impossible, without vast discomfort, to stand in the bow of the steamer and look at the scenery. I looked at it, indeed, along the sides, as we passed, and on our track behind; and no doubt it was very fine; but from all the experience I have had, I do not think scenery can be well seen from the water. At any rate, the shores of Loch Lomond have faded completely out of my memory; nor can I conceive that they really were very striking. At a year's interval, I can recollect the cluster of hills around the head of Lake Windermere; at twenty years' interval, I remember the shores of Lake Champlain; but of the shores of this Scottish lake I remember nothing except some oddly shaped rocks, called "The Cobbler and his Daughter," on a mountain-top, just before we landed. But, indeed, we had very imperfect glimpses of the hills along the latter part of the course because, the wind had grown so very cold that we took shelter below, and merely peeped at Loch Lomond's sublimities from the cabin windows.

The whole voyage up Loch Lomond is, I think, about thirty-two miles; but we landed at a place called Tarbet, much short of the ultimate point. There is here a large hotel; but we passed it, and walked onward a mile or two to Arroquhar, a secluded glen among the hills, where is a new hotel, built in the old manor-house style, and occupying the site of what was once a castle of the chief of the MacFarlanes. Over the portal is a stone taken from the former house, bearing the date 1697. There is a little lake near the house, and the hills shut in the whole visible scene so closely that there appears no outlet nor communication with the external world; but in reality this little lake is connected with Loch Long, and Loch Long is an arm of the sea; so that there is water communication between Arroquhar and Glasgow. We found this a very beautiful place; and being quite sheltered from all winds that blew, we strolled about late into the prolonged twilight, and admired the outlines of the surrounding hills, and fancied resemblances to various objects in the shapes of the crags against the evening sky. The sun had not set till nearly, if not quite, eight o'clock; and before the daylight had quite gone, the northern lights streamed out, and I do not think that there was much darkness over the glen of Arroquhar that night. At all events, before the darkness came, we withdrew into the coffee-room.

We had excellent beds and sleeping-rooms in this new hotel, and I remember nothing more till morning, when we were astir betimes, and had some chops for breakfast. Then our host, Mr. Macregor, who is also the host of our hotel at Glasgow, and has many of the characteristics of an American landlord, claiming to be a gentleman and the equal of his guests, took us in a drosky, and drove us to the shore of Loch Lomond, at a point about four miles from Arroquhar. The lake is here a mile and a half wide, and it was our object to cross to Inversnaid, on the opposite shore; so first we waved a handkerchief, and then kindled some straw on the beach, in order to attract the notice of the ferryman at Inversnaid. It was half an hour before our signals and shoutings resulted in the putting off of a boat, with two oarsmen, who made the transit pretty speedily; and thus we got across Loch Lomond. At Inversnaid there is a small hotel, and over the rock on which it stands a little waterfall tumbles into the lake, — a very little one, though I believe it is reckoned among the other picturesque features of the scene.

We were now in Rob Roy's country, and at the distance of a mile or so, along the shore of the lake, is Rob Roy's cave, where he and his followers are supposed to have made their abode in troublous times. While lunch was getting ready, we again took the boat, and went thither. Landing beneath a precipitous, though not very lofty crag, we clambered up a rude pathway, and came to the mouth of the cave, which is nothing but a fissure or fissures among some great rocks that have tumbled confusedly together. There is hardly anywhere space enough for half a dozen persons to crowd themselves together, nor room to stand upright. On the whole, it is no cave at all, but only a crevice; and, in the deepest and darkest part, you can look up and see the sky. It may have sheltered Rob Roy for a night, and might partially shelter any Christian during a shower.

Returning to the hotel, we started in a drosky (I do not know whether this is the right name of the vehicle, or whether it has a right name, but it is a carriage in which four persons sit back to back, two before and two behind) for Aberfoyle. The mountain-side ascends very steeply from the inn door, and, not to damp the horse's courage in the outset, we went up on foot. The guide-book says that the prospect from the summit of the ascent is very fine; but I really believe we forgot to turn round and look at it. All through our drive, however, we had mountain views in plenty, especially of great Ben Lomond, with his snow-covered head, round which, since our entrance into the Highlands, we had been making a circuit. Nothing can possibly be drearier than the mountains at this season; bare, barren, and bleak, with black patches of withered heath variegating the dead brown of the herbage on their sides; and as regards trees the hills are perfectly naked. There were no frightful precipices, no boldly picturesque features, along our road; but high, weary slopes, showing miles and miles of heavy solitude, with here and there a highland hut, built of stone and thatched; and, in one place, an old gray, ruinous fortress, a station of the English troops after the rebellion of 1745; and once or twice a village of huts, the inhabitants of which, old and young, ran to their doors to stare at us. For several miles after we left Inversnaid, the mountain-stream which makes the waterfall brawled along the roadside. All the hills are sheep-pastures, and I never saw such wild, rough, ragged-looking creatures as the sheep, with their black faces and tattered wool. The little lambs were very numerous, poor things, coming so early in the season into this inclement region; and it was laughable to see how invariably, when startled by our approach, they scampered to their mothers, and immediately began to suck. It would seem as if they sought a draught from the maternal udder, wherewith to fortify and encourage their poor little hearts; but I suppose their instinct merely drove them close to their dams, and, being there, they took advantage of their opportunity. These sheep must lead a hard life during the winter; for they are never fed nor sheltered.

The day was sunless, and very uncomfortably cold; and we were not sorry to walk whenever the steepness of the road gave us cause. I do not remember what o'clock it was, but not far into the afternoon, when we reached the Baillie Nicol-Jarvie Inn at Aberfoyle; a scene which is much more interesting in the pages of Rob Roy than we found it in reality. Here we got into a sort of cart, and set out, over another hill-path, as dreary as or drearier than the last, for the Trosachs. On our way, we saw Ben Venue, and a good many other famous Bens, and two or three lochs; and when we reached the Trosachs, we should probably have been very much enraptured if our eyes had not already been weary with other mountain shapes. But, in truth, I doubt if anybody ever does really see a mountain, who goes for the set and sole purpose of seeing it. Nature will not let herself be seen in such cases. You must patiently bide her time; and by and by, at some unforeseen moment, she will quietly and suddenly unveil herself, and for a brief space allow you to look right into the heart of her mystery. But if you call out to her peremptorily, "Nature! unveil yourself this very moment!" she only draws her veil the closer; and you may look with all your eyes, and imagine that you see all that she can show, and yet see nothing. Thus, I saw a wild and confused assemblage of heights, crags, precipices, which they call the Trosachs, but I saw them calmly and coldly, and was glad when the drosky was ready to take us on to Callender. The hotel at the Trosachs, by the by, is a very splendid one, in the form of an old feudal castle, with towers and turrets. All among these wild hills there is set preparation for enraptured visitants; and it seems strange that the savage features do not subside of their own accord, and that there should still be cold winds and snow on the top of Ben Lomond, and rocks and heather, and ragged sheep, now that there are so many avenues by which the common-place world is sluiced in among the Highlands. I think that this fashion of the picturesque will pass away.

We drove along the shore of Lake Vennachar, and onward to Callender, which I believe is either the first point in the Lowlands or the last in the Highlands. It is a large village on the river Teith. We stopped here to dine, and were some time in getting any warmth into our benumbed bodies; for, as I said before, it was a very cold day. Looking from the window of the hotel, I saw a young man in Highland dress, with bare thighs, marching through the village street towards the Lowlands, with a martial and elastic step, as if he were going forth to conquer and occupy the world. I suppose he was a soldier who had been absent on leave, returning to the garrison at Stirling. I pitied his poor thighs, though he certainly did not look uncomfortable.

After dinner, as dusk was coming on and we had still a long drive before us (eighteen miles, I believe), we took a close carriage and two horses, and set off for Stirling. The twilight was too obscure to show many things along the road, and by the time we drove into Stirling we could but dimly see the houses in the long street in which stood our hotel. There was a good fire in the coffee-room, which looked like a drawing-room in a large old-fashioned mansion, and was hung round with engravings of the portraits of the county members, and a master of fox-hounds, and other pictures. We made ourselves comfortable with some tea, and retired early.

In the morning we were stirring betimes, and found Stirling to be a pretty large town, of rather ancient aspect, with many gray stone houses, the gables of which are notched on either side, like a flight of stairs. The town stands on the slope of a hill, at the summit of which, crowning a long ascent, up which the paved street reaches all the way to its gate, is Stirling Castle. Of course we went thither, and found free entrance, although the castle is garrisoned by five or six hundred men, among whom are barelegged Highlanders (I must say that this costume is very fine and becoming, though their thighs did look blue and frost-bitten) and also some soldiers of other Scotch regiments, with tartan trousers. Almost immediately on passing the gate, we found an old artillery-man, who undertook to show us round the castle. Only a small portion of it seems to be of great antiquity. The principal edifice within the castle wall is a palace, that was either built or renewed by James VI.; and it is ornamented with strange old statues, one of which is his own. The old Scottish Parliament House is also here. The most ancient part of the castle is the tower, where one of the Earls of Douglas was stabbed by a king, and afterwards thrown out of the window. In reading this story, one imagines a lofty turret, and the dead man tumbling headlong from a great height; but, in reality, the window is not more than fifteen or twenty feet from the garden into which he fell. This part of the castle was burned last autumn; but is now under repair, and the wall of the tower is still stanch and strong. We went up into the chamber where the murder took place, and looked through the historic window.

Then we mounted the castle wall, where it broods over a precipice of many hundred feet perpendicular, looking down upon a level plain below, and forth upon a landscape, every foot of which is richly studded with historic events. There is a small peep-hole in the wall, which Queen Mary is said to have been in the habit of looking through. It is a most splendid view; in the distance, the blue Highlands, with a variety of mountain outlines that I could have studied unweariably; and in another direction, beginning almost at the foot of the Castle Hill, were the Links of Forth, where, over a plain of miles in extent the river meandered, and circled about, and returned upon itself again and again and again, as if knotted into a silver chain, which it was difficult to imagine to be all one stream. The history of Scotland might be read from this castle wall, as on a book of mighty page; for here, within the compass of a few miles, we see the field where Wallace won the battle of Stirling, and likewise the battle-field of Bannockburn, and that of Falkirk, and Sheriffmuir, and I know not how many besides.

Around the Castle Hill there is a walk, with seats for old and infirm persons, at points sheltered from the wind. We followed it downward, and I think we passed over the site where the games used to be held, and where, this morning, some of the soldiers of the garrison were going through their exercises. I ought to have mentioned, that, passing through the inner gateway of the castle, we saw the round tower, and glanced into the dungeon, where the Roderic Dhu of Scott's poem was left to die. It is one of the two round towers, between which the portcullis rose and fell.

EDINBURGH.—THE PALACE OF HOLYROOD.

At eleven o'clock we took the rail for Edinburgh, and I remember nothing more, except that the cultivation and verdure of the country were very agreeable, after our experience of Highland barrenness and desolation, until we found the train passing close at the base of the rugged crag of Edinburgh Castle. We established ourselves at Queen's Hotel, in Prince's Street, and then went out to view the city. The monument to Sir Walter Scott—a rather fantastic and not very impressive affair, I thought—stands almost directly in front of a hotel. We went along Prince's Street, and thence, by what turns I know not, to the Palace of Holyrood, which stands on a low and sheltered site, and is a venerable edifice. Arthur's Seat rises behind it, — a high hill, with a plain between. As we drew near the Palace, Mr. Bowman, who has been here before, pointed out the windows of Queen Mary's apartments, in a circular tower on the left of the gateway. On entering the enclosed quadrangle, we bought tickets for sixpence each, admitting us to all parts of the Palace that are shown to visitors; and first we went into a noble hall or gallery, — a long and stately room, hung with pictures of ancient Scottish kings; and though the pictures were none of them authentic, they, at least, answer an excellent purpose in the way of upholstery. It was here that the young Pretender gave the ball which makes one of the scenes in Waverley.

Thence we passed into the old historic rooms of the Palace, — Darnley's and Queen Mary's apartments, which everybody has seen and described. They are very dreary and shabby-looking rooms, with bare floors, and here and there a piece of tapestry, faded into a neutral tint; and carved and ornamented ceilings, looking shabbier than plain whitewash. We saw Queen Mary's old bedstead, low, with four tall posts, — and her looking-glass, which she brought with her from France, and which has often reflected the beauty that set everybody mad, — and some needlework and other womanly matters of hers; and we went into the little closet, where she was having such a cosey supper-party with two or three friends, when the conspirators broke in, and stabbed Rizzio before her face. We saw, too, the blood-stain at the threshold of the door in the next room, opening upon the stairs. The body of Rizzio was flung down here, and the attendant told us that it lay in that spot all night. The blood-stain covers a large space, — much larger than I supposed, — and it gives the impression that there must have been a great pool and sop of blood on all the spot covered by Rizzio's body, staining the floor deeply enough never to be washed out. It is now of a dark brown hue; and I do not see why it may not be the genuine, veritable stain. The floor, thereabouts, appears not to have been scrubbed much; for I touched it with my finger, and found it slightly rough; but it is strange that the many footsteps should not have smoothed it, in three hundred years.

One of the articles shown us in Queen Mary's apartments was the breastplate supposed to have been worn by Lord Ruthven at the murder, a heavy plate of iron, and doubtless a very uncomfortable waistcoat.

HOLYROOD ABBEY.

From the Palace, we passed into the contiguous ruin of Holyrood Abbey; which is roofless, although the front, and some broken columns along the nave, and fragments of architecture here and there, afford hints of a magnificent Gothic church in bygone times. It deserved to be magnificent; for here have been stately ceremonials, marriages of kings, coronations, investitures, before the high altar, which has now been overthrown or crumbled away; and the floor — so far as there is any floor — consists of tombstones of the old Scottish nobility. There are likewise monuments, bearing the names of illustrious Scotch families; and inscriptions, in the Scotch dialect, on the walls.

In one of the front towers, — the only remaining one, indeed, — we saw the marble tomb of a nobleman, Lord Belhaven, who is represented reclining on the top, — with a bruised nose, of course. Except in Westminster Abbey, I do not remember ever to have seen an old monumental statue with the nose entire. In all political or religious outbreaks, the mob's first impulse is to hit the illustrious dead on their noses.

At the other end of the Abbey, near the high altar, is the vault where the old Scottish kings used to be buried; but, looking in through the window, I saw only a vacant space, — no skull, nor bone, nor the least fragment of a coffin. In fact, I believe the royal dead were turned out of their last home, on occasion of the Revolutionary movements, at the accession of William III.

HIGH STREET AND THE GRASS-MARKET.

Quitting the Abbey and the Palace, we turned into the Canongate, and passed thence into High Street, which, I think, is a continuation of the Canongate; and being now in the old town of Edinburgh, we saw those immensely tall houses, seven stories high, where the people live in tiers, all the way from earth to middle air. They were not so quaint and strange looking as I expected; but there were some houses of very antique individuality, and among them that of John Knox, which looks still in good repair. One thing did not in the least fall short of my expectations, — the evil odor, for which Edinburgh has an immemorial renown, — nor the dirt of the inhabitants, old and young. The town, to say the truth, when you are in the midst of it, has a very sordid, grimy, shabby, unswept, unwashen aspect, grievously at variance with all poetic and romantic associations.

From the High Street we turned aside into the Grass-Market, the scene of the Porteous Mob; and we found in the pavement a cross on the site where the execution of Porteous is supposed to have taken place.

THE CASTLE.

Returning then to the High Street, we followed it up to the Castle, which is nearer the town, and of more easy access from it, than I had supposed. There is a large court or parade before the castle gate, with a parapet on the abrupt side of the hill, looking towards Arthur's Seat and Salisbury Crags, and overhanging a portion of the old town. As we leaned over this parapet, my nose was conscious of the bad odor of Edinburgh, although the streets, whence it must have come, were hundreds of feet below. I have had some experience of this ugly smell in the poor streets of Liverpool; but I think I never perceived it before crossing the Atlantic. It is the odor of an old system of life; the scent of the pine forests is still too recent with us for it to be known in America.

The Castle of Edinburgh is free (as appears to be the case with all garrisoned places in Great Britain) to the entrance of any peaceable person. So we went in, and found a large space enclosed within the walls, and dwellings for officers, and accommodation for soldiers, who were being drilled, or loitering about; and as the hill still ascends within the external wall of the castle, we climbed to the summit, and there found an old soldier, whom we engaged to be our guide. He showed us Mons Meg, a great old cannon, broken at the breech, but still aimed threateningly from the highest ramparts; and then he admitted us into an old chapel, said to have been built by a Queen of Scotland, the sister of Harold, King of England, and occupying the very highest part of the hill. It is the smallest place of worship I ever saw, but of venerable architecture, and of very solid construction. The old soldier had not much more to show us; but he pointed out the window whence one of the kings of Scotland is said, when a baby, to have been lowered down, the whole height of the castle, to the bottom of the precipice on which it stands, — a distance of seven hundred feet.

After the soldier had shown us to the extent of his jurisdiction, we went into a suite of rooms, in one of which I saw a portrait of Queen Mary, which gave me, for the first time, an idea that she was really a very beautiful woman. In this picture she is wonderfully so, — a tender womanly grace, which was none the less tender and graceful for being equally imbued with queenly dignity and spirit. It was too lovely a head to be cut off. I should be glad to know the authenticity of this picture.

I do not know that we did anything else worthy of note, before leaving Edinburgh. There is matter enough, in and about the town, to interest the visitor for a very long time; but when the visit is calculated on such brevity as ours was, we get weary of the place, before even these few hours come to an end. Thus, for my part, I was not sorry when, in the course of the afternoon, we took the rail for Melrose, where we duly arrived, and put up at the George Inn.

MELROSE.

Melrose is a village of rather antique aspect, situated on the slope and at the bottom of the Eildon Hills, which, from this point of view, appear like one hill, with a double summit. The village, as I said, has an old look, though many of the houses have at least been refronted at some recent date; but others are as ancient, I suppose, as the days when the Abbey was in its splendor, — a rustic and peasant-like antiquity, however, low-roofed, and straw-thatched. There is an aged cross of stone in the centre of the town.

Our first object, of course, was to see the Abbey, which stands just on the outskirts of the village, and is attainable only by applying at a neighboring house, the inhabitant of which probably supports himself, and most comfortably, too, as a showman of the ruin. He unlocked the wooden gate, and admitted us into what is left of the Abbey, comprising only the ruins of the church, although the refectory, the dormitories, and the other parts of the establishment, formerly covered the space now occupied by a dozen village houses. Melrose Abbey is a very satisfactory ruin, all carpeted along its nave and transepts with green grass; and there are some well-grown trees within the walls. We saw the window, now empty, through which the tints of the painted glass fell on the tombstone of Michael Scott, and the tombstone itself, broken in three pieces, but with a cross engraven along its whole length. It must have been the monument of an old monk or abbot, rather than a wizard. There, too, is still the "marble stone" on which the monk and warrior sat them down, and which is supposed to mark the resting-place of Alexander of Scotland. There are remains, both without and within the Abbey, of most curious and wonderfully minute old sculpture, — foliage, in places where it is almost impossible to see them, and where the sculptor could not have supposed that they would be seen, but which yet are finished faithfully, to the very veins of each leaf, in stone; and there is a continual variety of this accurate toil. On the exterior of the edifice there is equal minuteness of finish, and a great many niches for statues; all of which, I believe, are now gone, although there are carved faces at some points and angles. The graveyard around the Abbey is still the only one which the village has, and is crowded with gravestones, among which I read the inscription of one erected by Sir Walter Scott to the memory of Thomas Pardy, one of his servants. Some sable birds — either rooks or jackdaws — were flitting about the ruins, inside and out.

Mr. Bowman and I talked about revisiting Melrose by moonlight; but, luckily, there was to be no moon that evening. I do not myself think that daylight and sunshine make a ruin less effective than twilight or moonshine. In reference to Scott's description, I think he deplorably diminishes the impressiveness of the scene by saying that the alternate buttresses, seen by moonlight, look as if made of ebon and ivory. It suggests a small and very pretty piece of cabinet-work; not these gray, rough walls, which Time has gnawed upon for a thousand years, without eating them away.

Leaving the Abbey, we took a path or a road which led us to the river Tweed, perhaps a quarter of a mile off; and we crossed it by a foot-bridge, — a pretty wide stream, a dimpling breadth of transparent water flowing between low banks, with a margin of pebbles. We then returned to our inn, and had tea, and passed a quiet evening by the fireside. This is a good, unpretentious inn; and its visitors' book indicates that it affords general satisfaction to those who come here.

In the morning we breakfasted on broiled salmon, taken, no doubt, in the neighboring Tweed. There was a very coarse-looking man at table with us, who informed us that he owned the best horse anywhere round the Eildon Hills, and could make the best cast for a salmon, and catch a bigger fish than anybody, — with other self-laudation of the same kind. The waiter afterwards told us that he was the son of an Admiral in the neighborhood; and soon, his horse being brought to the door, we saw him mount and ride away. He sat on horseback with ease and grace, though I rather suspect, early as it was, that he was already in his cups. The Scotch seem to me to get drunk at very unseasonable hours. I have seen more drunken people here than during all my residence in England, and, generally, early in the day. Their liquor, so far as I have observed, makes them good-natured and sociable, imparting a perhaps needed geniality to their cold natures.

After breakfast we took a drosky, or whatever these fore-and-aft-seated vehicles are called, and set out for

DRYBURGH ABBEY,

three miles distant. It was a cold though rather bright morning, with a most shrewd and bitter wind, which blew directly in my face as I sat beside the driver.

An English wind is bad enough, but methinks a Scotch one is rather worse; at any rate, I was half frozen, and wished Dryburgh Abbey in Tophet, where it would have been warmer work to go and see it. Some of the border hills were striking, especially the Cowden Knowe, which ascends into a prominent and lofty peak. Such villages as we passed did not greatly differ from English villages. By and by we came to the banks of the Tweed, at a point where there is a ferry. A carriage was on the river-bank, the driver waiting beside it; for the people who came in it had already been ferried across to see the Abbey.

The ferryman here is a young girl; and, stepping into the boat, she shoved off, and so skilfully took advantage of the eddies of the stream, which is here deep and rapid, that we were soon on the other side. She was by no means an uncomely maiden, with pleasant Scotch features, and a quiet intelligence of aspect, gleaming into a smile when spoken to; much tanned with all kinds of weather, and, though slender, yet so agile and muscular that it was no shame for a man to let himself be rowed by her.

From the ferry we had a walk of half a mile, more or less, to a cottage, where we found another young girl, whose business it is to show the Abbey. She was of another mould than the ferry-maiden, — a queer, shy plaintive sort of a body, — and answered all our questions in a low, wailing tone. Passing through an apple-orchard, we were not long in reaching the Abbey, the ruins of which are much more extensive and more picturesque than those of Melrose, being overrun with bushes and shrubbery, and twined about with ivy, and all such vegetation as belongs, naturally, to old walls. There are the remains of the refectory, and other domestic parts of the Abbey, as well as the church, and all in delightful state of decay, — not so far gone but that we had bits of its former grandeur in the columns and broken arches, and in some portions of the edifice that still retain a roof.

In the chapter-house we saw a marble statue of Newton, wofully maltreated by damps and weather; and though it had no sort of business there, it fitted into the ruins picturesquely enough. There is another statue, equally unauthorized; both having been placed here by a former Earl of Buchan, who seems to have been a little astray in his wits.

On one side of the church, within an arched recess, are the monuments of Sir Walter Scott and his family, — three ponderous tombstones of Aberdeen granite, polished, but already dimmed and dulled by the weather. The whole floor of the recess is covered by these monuments, that of Sir Walter being the middle one, with Lady (or, as the inscription calls her, Dame) Scott beyond him, next to the church wall, and some one of his sons or daughters on the hither side. The effect of his being buried here is to make the whole of Dryburgh Abbey his monument. There is another arched recess, twin to the Scott burial-place, and contiguous to it, in which are buried a Pringle family; it being their ancient place of sepulture. The spectator almost inevitably feels as if they were intruders, although their rights here are of far older date than those of Scott.

Dryburgh Abbey must be a most beautiful spot of a summer afternoon; and it was beautiful even on this not very genial morning, especially when the sun blinked out upon the ivy, and upon the shrubberied paths that wound about the ruins. I think I recollect the birds chirruping in this neighborhood of it. After viewing it sufficiently, — sufficiently for this one time, — we went back to the ferry, and, being set across by the same Undine, we drove back to Melrose. No longer riding against the wind, I found it not nearly so cold as before. I now noticed that the Eildon Hills, seen from this direction, rise from one base into three distinct summits, ranged in a line. According to "The Lay of the Last Minstrel," they were cleft into this shape by the magic of Michael Scott. Reaching Melrose . . . . without alighting, we set off for

ABBOTSFORD,

three miles off. The neighborhood of Melrose, leading to Abbotsford, has many handsome residences of modern build and very recent date, — suburban villas, each with its little lawn and garden ground, such as we see in the vicinity of Liverpool. I noticed, too, one castellated house, of no great size, but old, and looking as if its tower were built, not for show, but for actual defence in the old border warfare.

We were not long in reaching Abbotsford. The house, which is more compact, and of considerably less extent than I anticipated, stands in full view from the road, and at only a short distance from it, lower down towards the river. Its aspect disappointed me; but so does everything. It is but a villa, after all; no castle, nor even a large manor-house, and very unsatisfactory when you consider it in that light. Indeed, it impressed me, not as a real house, intended for the home of human beings, — a house to die in or to be born in, — but as a plaything, — something in the same category as Horace Walpole's Strawberry Hill. The present owner seems to have found it insufficient for the actual purposes of life; for he is adding a wing, which promises to be as extensive as the original structure.

We rang at the front door (the family being now absent), and were speedily admitted by a middle-aged or somewhat elderly man, — the butler, I suppose, or some upper servant, — who at once acceded to our request to be permitted to see the house. We stepped from the porch immediately into the entrance-hall; and having the great Hall of Battle Abbey in my memory, and the ideal of a baronial hall in my mind, I was quite taken aback at the smallness and narrowness and lowness of this; which, however, is a very fine one, on its own little scale. In truth, it is not much more than a vestibule. The ceiling is carved; and every inch of the walls is covered with claymores, targets, and other weapons and armor, or old-time curiosities, tastefully arranged, many of which, no doubt, have a history attached to them, — or had, in Sir Walter's own mind. Our attendant was a very intelligent person, and pointed out much that was interesting; but in such a multitudinous variety it was almost impossible to fix the eye upon any one thing. Probably the apartment looked smaller than it really was, on account of being so wainscoted and festooned with curiosities. I remember nothing particularly, unless it be the coal-grate in the fireplace, which was one formerly used by Archbishop Sharpe, the prelate whom Balfour of Burley murdered. Either in this room or the next one, there was a glass case containing the suit of clothes last worn by Scott, — a short green coat, somewhat worn, with silvered buttons, a pair of gray tartan trousers, and a white hat. It was in the hall that we saw these things; for there too, I recollect, were a good many walking-sticks that had been used by Scott, and the hatchet with which he was in the habit of lopping branches from his trees, as he walked among them.

From the hall we passed into the study, — a small room, lined with the books which Sir Walter, no doubt, was most frequently accustomed to refer to; and our guide pointed out some volumes of the *Moniteur*, which he used while writing the history of Napoleon. Probably these were the driest and dullest volumes in his whole library. About mid-height of the walls of the study there is a gallery, with a short flight of steps for the convenience of getting at the upper books. A study-table occupied the centre of the room, and at one end of the table stands an easy-chair, covered with morocco, and with ample space to fling one's self back. The servant told me that I might sit down in this chair, for that Sir Walter sat there while writing his romances, "and perhaps," quoth the man, smiling, "you may catch some inspiration." What a bitter word this would have been if he had known me to be a romance-writer! "No, I never shall be inspired to write romances!" I answered, as if such an idea had never occurred to me. I sat down, however. This study quite satisfied me, being planned on principles of common sense, and made to work in, and without any fantastic adaptation of old forms to modern uses.

Next to the study is the library, an apartment of

respectable size, and containing as many books as it can hold, all protected by wire-work. I did not observe what or whose works were here; but the attendant showed us one whole compartment full of volumes having reference to ghosts, witchcraft, and the supernatural generally. It is remarkable that Scott should have felt interested in such subjects, being such a worldly and earthly man as he was; but then, indeed, almost all forms of popular superstition do clothe the ethereal with earthly attributes, and so make it grossly perceptible.

The library, like the study, suited me well, — merely the fashion of the apartment, I mean, — and I doubt not it contains as many curious volumes as are anywhere to be met with within a similar space. The drawing-room adjoins it; and here we saw a beautiful ebony cabinet, which was presented to Sir Walter by George IV.; and some pictures of much interest, — one of Scott himself at thirty-five, rather portly, with a heavy face, but shrewd eyes, which seem to observe you closely. There is a full-length of his eldest son, an officer of dragoons, leaning on his charger; and a portrait of Lady Scott, — a brunette, with black hair and eyes, very pretty, warm, vivacious, and un-English in her aspect. I am not quite sure whether I saw all these pictures in the drawing-room, or some of them in the dining-room; but the one that struck me most — and very much indeed — was the head of Mary, Queen of Scots, literally the head cut off, and lying on a dish. It is said to have been painted by an Italian or French artist, two days after her death. The hair curls or flows all about it; the face is of a death-like hue, but has an expression of quiet, after much pain and trouble, — very beautiful, very sweet and sad; and it affected me strongly with the horror and strangeness of such a head being severed from its body. Methinks I should not like to have it always in the room with me. I thought of the lovely picture of Mary that I had seen at Edinburgh Castle, and reflected what a symbol it would be, — how expressive of a human being having her destiny in her own hands, — if that beautiful young Queen were painted as carrying this dish, containing her own woful head, and perhaps casting a curious and pitiful glance down upon it, as if it were not her own.

Also, in the drawing-room, there was a plaster cast of Sir Walter's face, taken after death; the only one in existence, as our guide assured us. It is not often that one sees a homelier set of features than this; no elevation, no dignity, whether bestowed by nature or thrown over them by age or death; sunken cheeks, the bridge of the nose depressed, and the end turned up; the mouth puckered, and no chin whatever, or hardly any. The expression was not calm and happy; but rather as if he were in a perturbed slumber, perhaps nothing short of nightmare. I wonder that the family allow this cast to be shown, — the last record that there is of Scott's personal reality, and conveying such a wretched and unworthy idea of it.

Adjoining the drawing-room is the dining-room, in one corner of which, between two windows, Scott died. It was now a quarter of a century since his death; but it seemed to me that we spoke with a sort of hush in our voices, as if he were still dying here, or had but just departed. I remember nothing else in this room.

The next one is the armory, which is the smallest of all that we had passed through; but its walls gleam with the steel blades of swords, and the barrels of pistols, matchlocks, firelocks, and all manner of deadly weapons, whether European or Oriental; for there are many trophies here of East-Indian warfare. I saw Rob Roy's gun, rifled and of very large bore; and a beautiful pistol, formerly Claverhouse's; and the sword of Montrose, given him by King Charles, the silver hilt of which I grasped. There was also a superb claymore, in an elaborately wrought silver sheath, made for Sir Walter Scott, and presented to him by the Highland Society, for his services in marshalling the clans when George IV. came to Scotland. There were a thousand other things, which I knew must be most curious, yet did not ask nor care about them, because so many curiosities drive one crazy, and fret one's heart to death. On the whole, there is no simple and great impression left by Abbotsford; and I felt angry and dissatisfied with myself for not feeling something which I did not and could not feel. But it is just like going to a museum, if you look into particulars; and one learns from it, too, that Scott could not have been really a wise man, nor an earnest one, nor one that grasped the truth of life; he did but play, and the play grew very sad toward its close. In a certain way, however, I understand his romances the better for having seen his house; and his house the better for having read his romances. They throw light on one another.

We had now gone through all the show-rooms; and the next door admitted us again into the entrance-hall, where we recorded our names in the visitors' book. It contains more names of Americans, I should judge, from casting my eyes back over last year's record, than of all other people in the world, including Great Britain.

Bidding farewell to Abbotsford, I cannot but confess a sentiment of remorse for having visited the dwelling-place — as just before I visited the grave — of the mighty minstrel and romancer with so cold a heart and in so critical a mood, — *his* dwelling-place and *his* grave whom I had so admired and loved, and who had done so much for my happiness when I was young. But I, and the world generally, now look at him from a different point of view; and, besides, these visits to the actual haunts of famous people, though long dead, have the effect of making us sensible, in some degree, of their human imperfections, as if we actually saw them alive. I felt this effect, to a certain extent, even with respect to Shakespeare, when I visited Stratford-on-Avon. As for Scott, I still cherish him in a warm place, and I do not know that I have any pleasanter anticipation, as regards books, than that of reading all his novels over again after we get back to the Wayside.

[This Mr. Hawthorne did, aloud to his family, the year following his return to America. — Ed.]

It was now one or two o'clock, and time for us to take the rail across the borders. Many a mile behind us, as we rushed onward, we could see the threefold Eildon Hill, and probably every pant of the engine carried us over some spot of ground which Scott has made fertile with poetry. For Scotland — cold, cloudy, barren little bit of earth that it is — owes all the interest that the world feels in it to him. Few men have done so much for their country as he. However, having no guide-book, we were none the wiser for what we saw out of the window of the rail-carriage; but, now and then, a castle appeared, on a commanding height, visible for miles round, and seemingly in good repair, — now, in some low and sheltered spot, the gray walls of an abbey; now, on a little eminence, the ruin of a border fortress, and near it the modern residence of the laird, with its trim lawn and shrubbery. We were not long in coming to

BERWICK,

a town which seems to belong both to England and Scotland, or perhaps is a kingdom by itself, for it stands on both sides of the boundary river, the Tweed, where it empties into the German Ocean. From the railway bridge we had a good view over the town, which looks ancient, with red roofs on all the gabled houses; and it being a sunny afternoon, though bleak and chill, the sea-view was very fine. The Tweed is here broad, and looks deep, flowing far beneath the bridge, between high banks. This is all that I can say of Berwick, (pronounced Berrick), for though we spent above an hour at the station waiting for the train, we were so long in getting our dinner that we had not time for anything else. I remember, however, some gray walls, that looked like the last remains of an old castle, near the railway station. We next took the train for

NEWCASTLE,

the way to which, for a considerable distance, lies within sight of the sea; and in close vicinity to the shore we saw Holy Isle, on which are the ruins of an abbey. Norham Castle must be somewhere in this neighborhood, on the English shore of the Tweed. It was pretty late in the afternoon — almost nightfall — when we reached Newcastle, over the roofs of which, as over those of Berwick, we had a view from the railway, and like Berwick, it was a congregation of mostly red roofs; but, unlike Berwick (the atmosphere over which was clear and transparent), there came a gush of smoke from every chimney, which made it the dimmest and smokiest place I ever saw. This is partly owing to the iron founderies and furnaces; but each domestic chimney, too, was smoking on its own account, — coal being so plentiful there, no doubt, that the fire is always kept freshly heaped with it, reason or none. Out of this smoke-cloud rose tall steeples; and it was discernible that the town stretched widely over an uneven surface, on the banks of the Tyne, which is navigable up hither ten miles from the sea for pretty large vessels.

We established ourselves at the Station Hotel, and then walked out to see something of the town; but I remember only a few streets of duskiness and dinginess, with a glimpse of the turrets of a castle to which we could not find our way. So, as it was getting twilightish and very cold, we went back to the hotel, which is a very good one, better than any one I have seen in the South of England, and almost or quite as good as those of Scotland. The coffee-room is a spacious and handsome apartment, adorned with a full-length portrait of Wellington, and other pictures, and in the whole establishment there was a well-ordered alacrity and liberal provision for the comfort of guests that one seldom sees in English inns. There are a good many

American guests in Newcastle, and through all the North.

An old Newcastle gentleman and his friend came into the smoking-room, and drank three glasses of hot whiskey-toddy apiece, and were still going on to drink more when we left them. These respectable persons probably went away drunk that night, yet thought none the worse of themselves or of one another for it. It is like returning to times twenty years gone by for a New-Englander to witness such simplicity of manners.

The next morning, May 8th, I rose and breakfasted early, and took the rail soon after eight o'clock, leaving Mr. Bowman behind; for he had business in Newcastle, and would not follow till some hours afterwards. There is no use in trying to make a narrative of anything that one sees along an English railway. All I remember of this tract of country is that one of the stations at which we stopped for an instant is called "Washington," and this is, no doubt, the old family place, where the De Wessyngtons, afterwards the Washingtons, were first settled in England. Before reaching York, first one old lady and then another (Quaker) lady got into the carriage along with me; and they seemed to be going to York, on occasion of some fair or celebration. This was all the company I had, and their advent the only incident. It was about eleven o'clock when I beheld York Cathedral rising huge above the old city, which stands on the river Ouse, separated by it from the railway station, but communicating by a ferry (or two) and a bridge. I wandered forth, and found my way over the latter into the ancient and irregular streets of crooked, narrow, or of unequal width, puzzling, and many of them bearing the name of the particular gate in the old walls of the city to which they lead. There were no such fine, ancient, stately houses as some of those in Shrewsbury were, nor such an aspect of antiquity as in Chester; but still York is a quaint old place, and what looks most modern is probably only something old, hiding itself behind a new front, as elsewhere in England.

I found my way by a sort of instinct, as directly as possible, to

YORK MINSTER.

It stands in the midst of a small open space, — or a space that looks small in comparison with the vast bulk of the cathedral. I was not so much impressed by its exterior as I have usually been by Gothic buildings, because it is rectangular in its general outline and in its towers, and seems to lack the complexity and mysterious plan which perplexes and wonder-strikes me in most cathedrals. Doubtless, however, if I had known better how to admire it, I should have found it wholly admirable. At all events, it has a satisfactory hugeness. Seeking my way in, I at first intruded upon the Registry of Deeds, which occupies a building patched up against the mighty side of the cathedral, and hardly discernible, so small the one and so large the other. I finally hit upon the right door, and I felt no disappointment in my first glance around at the immensity of enclosed space; — I see now in my mind's eye a dim length of nave, a breadth in the transepts like a great plain, and such an airy height beneath the central tower that a worshipper could certainly get a good way towards heaven without rising above it. I only wish that the screen, or whatever they call it, between the choir and nave, could be thrown down, so as to give us leave to take in the whole vastitude at once. I never could understand why, after building a great church, they choose to sunder it in halves by this mid-partition. But let me be thankful for what I got, and especially for the height and massiveness of the clustered pillars that support the arches on which rests the central tower. I remember at Furness Abbey I saw two tall pillars supporting a broken arch, and thought it the most majestic fragment of architecture that could possibly be. But these pillars have a nobler height, and these arches a greater sweep. What nonsense to try to write about a cathedral!

There is a great, cold bareness and bleakness about the interior; for there are very few monuments, and those seem chiefly to be of ecclesiastical people. I saw no armed knights, asleep on the tops of their tombs; but there was a curious representation of a skeleton, at full length, under the table-slab of one of the monuments. The walls are of a grayish hue, not so agreeable as the rich dark tint of the inside of Westminster Abbey; but a great many of the windows are still filled with ancient painted glass, the very small squares and pieces of which are composed into splendid designs of saints and angels, and scenes from Scripture.

There were a few watery blinks of sunshine out-of-doors, and whenever these came through the old painted windows, some of the more vivid colors were faintly thrown upon the pavement of the cathedral, — very faintly, it is true; for, in the first place, the sunshine was not brilliant; and painted glass, too, fades in the course of the ages, perhaps, like all man's other works. There were two or three windows of modern manufacture, and far more magnificent, as to brightness of color and material beauty, than the ancient ones; but yet they looked vulgar, glaring, and impertinent in comparison, because such revivals or imitations of a long-disused art cannot have the good faith and earnestness of the originals. Indeed, in the very coloring, I felt the same difference as between heart's blood and a scarlet dye. It is a pity, however, that the old windows cannot be washed, both inside and out, for now they have the dust of centuries upon them.

The screen or curtain between the nave and choir has eleven carved figures, at full length, which appeared to represent kings, some of them wearing crowns, and bearing sceptres or swords. They were in wood, and wrought by some Gothic hand. These carvings, and the painted windows, and the few monuments, are all the details that the mind can catch hold of in the immensity of this cathedral; and I must say that it was a dreary place on that cold, cloudy day. I doubt whether a cathedral is a sort of edifice suited to the English climate. The first buildings of the kind were probably erected by people who had bright and constant sunshine, and who desired a shadowy awfulness — like that of a forest, with its arched wood-paths — into which to retire in their religious moments.

In America, on a hot summer's day, how delightful its

cool and solemn depths would be! The painted windows, too, were evidently contrived, in the first instance, by persons who saw how effective they would prove when a vivid sun shone through them. But in England, the interior of a cathedral, nine days out of ten, is a vast sullenness, and as chill as death and the tomb. At any rate, it was so to-day, and so thought one of the old vergers, who kept walking as briskly as he could along the width of the transepts. There were several of these old men when I first came in, but they went off, all but this one, before I departed. None of them said a word to me, nor I to them; and admission to the Minster seems to be entirely free.

After emerging from this great gloom, I wandered to and fro about York, and contrived to go astray within no very wide space. If its history be authentic, it is an exceedingly old city, having been founded about a thousand years before the Christian era. There used to be a palace of the Roman emperors here, and the Emperor Severus died here, as did some of his successors; and Constantine the Great was born here. I know not what, if any, relics of those earlier times there may be; but York is still partly surrounded with a wall, and has several gates, which the city authorities take pains to keep in repair. I grew weary in my endeavor to find my way back to the railway, and inquired it of one of the good people of York, — a respectable, courteous, gentlemanly person, — and he told me to walk along the walls. Then he went on a considerable distance; but seemed to repent of not doing more for me; so he waited till I came up, and, walking along by my side, pointed out the castle, now the jail, and the place of execution, and directed me to the principal gateway of the city, and instructed me how to reach the ferry. The path along the wall leads, in one place, through a room over the arch of a gateway, — a low, thick-walled, stone apartment, where doubtless the gatekeeper used to lodge, and to parley with those who desired entrance.

I found my way to the ferry over the Ouse, according to this kind Yorkist's instructions. The ferryman told me that the fee for crossing was a halfpenny, which seemed so ridiculously small that I offered him more; but this unparalleled Englishman declined taking anything beyond his rightful halfpenny. This seems so wonderful to me that I can hardly trust my own memory.

Reaching the station, I got some dinner, and at four o'clock, just as I was starting, came Mr. Bowman, my very agreeable and sensible travelling companion. Our journeying together was ended here; for he was to keep on to London, and I to return to Liverpool. So we parted, and I took the rail westward across England, through a very beautiful, and in some degree picturesque, tract of country, diversified with hills, through the valleys and vistas of which goes the railroad, with dells diverging from it on either hand, and streams and arched bridges, and old villages, and a hundred pleasant English sights. After passing Rochdale, however, the dreary monotony of Lancashire succeeded this variety. Between nine and ten o'clock I reached the Tithebarn station in Liverpool. Ever since until now, May 17th, I have employed my leisure moments in scribbling off the journal of my tour; but it has greatly lost by not having been written daily, as the scenes and occurrences were fresh. The most picturesque points can be seized in no other way, and the hues of the affair fade as quickly as those of a dying dolphin; or as, according to Audubon, the plumage of a dead bird.

One thing that struck me as much as anything else in the Highlands I had forgotten to put down. In our walk at Balloch, along the road within view of Loch Lomond and the neighboring hills, it was a brilliant sunshiny afternoon, and I never saw any atmosphere so beautiful as that among the mountains. It was a clear, transparent, ethereal blue, as distinct as a vapor, and yet by no means vaporous, but a pure, crystalline medium. I have witnessed nothing like this among the Berkshire hills nor elsewhere.

York is full of old churches, some of them very antique in appearance, the stones weather-worn, their edges rounded by time, blackened, and with all the tokens of sturdy and age-long decay; and in some of them I noticed windows quite full of old painted glass, a dreary kind of minute patchwork, all of one dark and dusty hue, when seen from the outside. Yet had I seen them from the interior of the church, there doubtless would have been rich and varied apparitions of saints, with their glories round their heads, and bright-winged angels, and perhaps even the Almighty Father himself, so far as conceivable and representable by human powers. It requires light from heaven to make them visible. If the church were merely illuminated from the inside, — that is by what light a man can get from his own understanding, — the pictures would be invisible, or wear at best but a miserable aspect.

LIVERPOOL.

May 24th. — Day before yesterday I had a call at the Consulate from one of the Potentates of the Earth, — a woolly-haired negro, rather thin and spare, between forty and fifty years of age, plainly dressed; at the first glimpse of whom, I could readily have mistaken him for some ship's steward, seeking to enter a complaint of his captain. However, this was President Roberts, of Liberia, introduced by a note from Mrs. O'Sullivan, whom he has recently met in Madeira. I was rather favorably impressed with him; for his deportment was very simple, and without any of the flourish and embroidery which a negro might be likely to assume on finding himself elevated from slavery to power. He is rather shy, — reserved, at least, and undemonstrative, yet not harshly so, — in fine, with manners that offer no prominent points for notice or criticism; although I felt, or thought I felt, that his color was continually before his mind, and that he walks cautiously among men, as conscious that every new introduction is a new experiment. He is not in the slightest degree an interesting man (so far as I discovered in a very brief interview), apart from his position and history; his face is not striking, nor so agreeable as if it were jet black; but there may be miles and miles of depth in him which I know nothing of. Our conversation was of the most unimportant character; for he had called merely to deliver the note, and sat only a few minutes, during which he merely responded to my observations, and originated no remarks. Intelligence, discretion, tact, — these are probably his traits; not force of character and independence.

The same day I took the rail from the Lime Street station for

MANCHESTER,

to meet Bennoch, who had asked me thither to dine with him. I had never visited Manchester before, though now so long resident within twenty miles of it; neither is it particularly worth visiting, unless for the sake of its factories, which I did not go to see. It is a dingy and heavy town, with very much the aspect of Liverpool, being, like the latter, built almost entirely within the present century. I stopped at the Albion Hotel, and, as Bennoch was out, I walked forth to view the city, and made only such observations as are recorded above. Opposite the hotel stands the Infirmary, — a very large edifice, which, when erected, was on the outskirts, or perhaps in the rural suburbs, of the town, but it is now almost in its centre. In the enclosed space before it stands the statue of Peel, and sits a statue of Dr. Dalton, the celebrated chemist, who was a native of Manchester.

Returning to the hotel, I sat down in the room where we were to dine, and in due time Bennoch made his appearance, with the same glow and friendly warmth in his face that I had left burning there when we parted in London. If this man has not a heart, then no man ever had. I like him inexpressibly for his heart and for his intellect, and for his flesh and blood; and if he has faults, I do not know them, nor care to know them, nor value him the less if I did know them. He went to his room to dress; and in the mean time a middle-aged, dark man, of pleasant aspect, with black hair, black eyebrows, and bright, dark eyes came in, limping a little, but not much. He seemed not quite a man of the world, a little shy in manner, yet he addressed me kindly and sociably. I guessed him to be Mr. Charles Swain, the poet, whom Mr. Bennoch had invited to dinner. Soon came another guest whom Mr. Swain introduced to me as Mr. ——, editor of the Manchester Examiner. Then came Bennoch, who made us all regularly acquainted, or took for granted that we were so; and lastly appeared a Mr. W——, a merchant in Manchester, and a very intelligent man; and the party was then complete. Mr. Swain, the poet, is not a man of fluent conversation; he said, indeed, very little, but gave me the impression of amiability and simplicity of character, with much feeling.

. . . . .

Mr. W—— is a very sensible man. He has spent two or three years in America, and seems to have formed juster conclusions about us than most of his countrymen do. He is the only Englishman, I think, whom I have met, who fairly acknowledges that the English do cherish doubt, jealousy, suspicion, in short, an unfriendly feeling, towards the Americans. It is wonderful how every American, whatever class of the English he mingles with, is conscious of this feeling, and how no Englishman, except this sole Mr. W——, will confess it. He expressed some very good ideas, too, about the English and American press, and the reasons why the Times may fairly be taken as the exponent of British feeling towards us, while the New York Herald, immense as its circulation is, can be considered, in no similar degree or kind, the American exponent.

We sat late at table, and after the other guests had

retired, Bennoch and I had some very friendly talk, and he proposed that on my wife's return we should take up our residence in his house at Blackheath, while Mrs. Bennoch and himself were absent for two months on a trip to Germany. If his wife and mine ratify the idea, we will do so.

The next morning we went out to see the Exchange, and whatever was noticeable about the town. Time being brief, I did not visit the cathedral, which, I believe, is a thousand years old. There are many handsome shops in Manchester; and we went into one establishment, devoted to pictures, engravings, and decorative art generally, which is most perfect and extensive. The firm, if I remember, is that of the Messrs. Agnew, and, though originating here, they have now a house in London. Here I saw some interesting objects, purchased by them at the recent sale of the Rogers' collection; among other things, a slight pencil and water-color sketch by Raphael. An unfinished affair, done in a moment, as this must have been, seems to bring us closer to the hand that did it than the most elaborately painted picture can. Were I to see the Transfiguration, Raphael would still be at the distance of centuries. Seeing this little sketch, I had him very near me. I know not why, — perhaps it might be fancied that he had only laid down the pencil for an instant, and would take it up again in a moment more. I likewise saw a copy of a handsome, illustrated edition of Childe Harold, presented by old John Murray to Mr. Rogers, with an inscription on the fly-leaf, purporting that it was a token of gratitude from the publisher, because, when everybody else thought him imprudent in giving four hundred guineas for the poem, Mr. Rogers told him it would turn out the best bargain he ever made.

There was a new picture by Millais, the distinguished Pre-Raphaelite artist, representing a melancholy parting between two lovers. The lady's face had a great deal of sad and ominous expression; but an old brick wall, overrun with foliage, was so exquisitely and elaborately wrought that it was hardly possible to look at the personages of the picture. Every separate leaf of the climbing and clustering shrubbery was painfully made out; and the wall was reality itself, with the weather-stains, and the moss, and the crumbling lime between the bricks. It is not well to be so perfect in the inanimate, unless the artist can likewise make man and woman as lifelike, and to as great a depth, too, as the Creator does.

Bennoch left town for some place in Yorkshire, and I for Liverpool. I asked him to come and dine with me at the Adelphi, meaning to ask two or three people to meet him; but he had other engagements, and could not spare a day at present, though he promises to come before long.

Dining at Mr. Rathbone's one evening last week (May 21st), it was mentioned that

BORROW,

author of the Bible in Spain, is supposed to be of gypsy descent by the mother's side. Hereupon Mr. Martineau mentioned that he had been a schoolfellow of Borrow, and though he had never heard of his gypsy blood, he thought it probable, from Borrow's traits of character. He said that Borrow had once run away from school, and carried with him a party of other boys, meaning to lead a wandering life.

If an Englishman were individually acquainted with all our twenty-five millions of Americans, and liked every one of them, and believed that each man of those millions was a Christian, honest, upright, and kind, he would doubt, despise, and hate them in the aggregate, however he might love and honor the individuals.

Captain —— and his wife Oakum; they spent an evening at Mrs. B——'s. The Captain is a Marblehead man by birth, not far from sixty years old; very talkative and anecdotic in regard to his adventures; funny, good-humored, and full of various nautical experience. Oakum (it is a nickname which he gives his wife) is an inconceivably tall woman, — taller than he, — six feet, at least, and with a well-proportioned largeness in all respects, but looks kind and good, gentle, smiling, — and almost any other woman might sit like a baby on her lap. She does not look at all awful and belligerent, like the massive English-women one often sees. You at once feel her to be a benevolent giantess, and apprehend no harm from her. She is a lady, and perfectly well mannered, but with a sort of naturalness and simplicity that becomes her; for any the slightest affectation would be so magnified in her vast personality that it would be absolutely the height of the ridiculous. This wedded pair have no children, and Oakum has so long accompanied her husband on his voyages that I suppose by this time she could command a ship as well as he. They sat till pretty late, diffusing cheerfulness all about them, and then, "Come, Oakum," cried the Captain, "we must hoist sail!" and up rose Oakum to the ceiling, and moved tower-like to the door, looking down with a benignant smile on the poor little pygmy women about her. "Six feet," did I say? Why, she must be seven, eight, nine; and, whatever be her size, she is as good as she is big.

June 11*th.* — Monday night (9th), just as I was retiring, I received a telegraphic message announcing my wife's arrival at

SOUTHAMPTON.

So, the next day, I arranged the consular business for an absence of ten days, and set forth with J——, and reached Birmingham between eight and nine, evening. We put up at the Queen's Hotel, a very large establishment, contiguous to the railway. Next morning we left Birmingham, and made our first stage to Leamington, where we had to wait nearly an hour, which we spent in wandering through some of the streets that had been familiar to us last year. Leamington is certainly a beautiful town, new, bright, clean, and as unlike as possible to the business towns of England. However, the sun was burning hot, and I could almost have fancied myself in America. From Leamington we took tickets for Oxford, where we were obliged to make another stop of two hours; and these we employed to what advantage we could, driving up into town, and straying hither and thither, till J——'s weariness weighed upon me, and I adjourned with him to a hotel. Oxford is an ugly old town, of crooked and irregular streets, gabled houses, mostly plastered of a buff or yellow hue; some new fronts; and as for the buildings of the University, they seem to be scattered at random, without any reference to one another. I passed through an old gateway of Christ-Church, and looked at its enclosed square, and that is, in truth, pretty much all I then saw of the University of Oxford. From Christ-Church we rambled along a street that led us to a bridge across the Isis; and we saw many row-boats lying in the river, — the lightest craft imaginable, unless it were an Indian canoe. The Isis is but a narrow stream, and with a sluggish current. I believe the students of Oxford are famous for their skill in rowing.

To me as well as to J—— the hot streets were terribly oppressive; so we went into the Roebuck Hotel, where we found a cool and pleasant coffee-room. The entrance to this hotel is through an arch, opening from High Street, and giving admission into a paved court, the buildings all around being part of the establishment, — old edifices with pointed gables and old-fashioned projecting windows, but all in fine repair, and wearing a most quiet, retired, and comfortable aspect. The court was set all round with flowers, growing in pots or large pedestaled vases; on one side was the coffee-room, and all the other public apartments, and the other side seemed to be taken up by the sleeping-chambers and parlors of the guests. This arrangement of an inn, I presume, is very ancient, and it resembles what I have seen in the hospitals, free schools, and other charitable establishments in the old English towns; and, indeed, all large houses were arranged on somewhat the same principle.

By and by two or three young men came in, in wide-awake hats, and loose, blouse-like, summerish garments; and from their talk I found them to be students of the University, although their topics of conversation were almost entirely horses and boats. One of them sat down to cold beef and a tankard of ale; the other two drank a tankard of ale together, and went away without paying for it, — rather to the waiter's discontent. Students are very much alike, all the world over, and, I suppose, in all time; but I doubt whether many of my fellows at college would have gone off without paying for their beer.

We reached Southampton between seven and eight o'clock. I cannot write to-day.

June 15th. — The first day after we reached Southampton was sunny and pleasant; but we made little use of the fine weather, except that S—— and I walked once along the High Street, and J—— and I took a little ramble about town in the afternoon. The next day there was a high and disagreeable wind, and I did not once stir out of the house. The third day, too, I kept entirely within doors, it being a storm of wind and rain. The Castle Hotel stands within fifty yards of the water-side; so that this gusty day showed itself to the utmost advantage, — the vessels pitching and tossing at their moorings, the waves breaking white out of a tumultuous gray surface, the opposite shore glooming mistily at the distance of a mile or two; and on the hither side boatmen and seafaring people scudding about the pier in water-proof clothes; and in the street, before the hotel door, a cabman or two, standing drearily beside his horse. But we were sunny within doors.

Yesterday it was breezy, sunny, shadowy, showery; and we ordered a cab to take us to Clifton Villa, to call on Mrs. ——, a friend of B——'s, who called on us the day after our arrival. Just as we were ready to start, Mrs. —— again called, and accompanied us back to her house. It is in Shirley, about two miles from Southampton pier, and is a pleasant suburban villa, with a pretty ornamented lawn and shrubbery about it. Mrs. —— is an instructress of young ladies; and at B——'s suggestion, she is willing to receive us for two or three weeks, during the vacation, until we are ready to go to London. She seems to be a pleasant and sensible woman, and to-morrow we shall decide whether to go there. There was nothing very remarkable in this drive; and, indeed, my stay hereabouts thus far has been very barren of sights and incidents externally interesting, though the inner life has been rich.

Southampton is a very pretty town, and has not the dinginess to which I have been accustomed in many English towns. The High Street reminds me very much of American streets in its general effect; the houses being mostly stuccoed white or light, and cheerful in aspect, though doubtless they are centuries old at heart. The old gateway, which I presume I have mentioned in describing my former visit to Southampton, stands across High Street, about in the centre of the town, and is almost the only token of antiquity that presents itself to the eye.

SALISBURY.

June 17th. — Yesterday morning, June 16th, S——, Mrs. ——, and I took the rail for Salisbury, where we duly arrived without any accident or anything noticeable, except the usual verdure and richness of an English summer landscape. From the railway station we walked up into Salisbury, with the tall spire (four hundred feet high) of the cathedral before our eyes. Salisbury is an antique city, but with streets more regular than I have seen in most old towns, and the houses have a more picturesque aspect than those of Oxford, for instance, where almost all are mean-looking alike, — though I could hardly judge of Oxford on that hot, weary day. Through one or more of the streets there runs a swift, clear little stream, which, being close to the pavement, and bordered with stone, may be called, I suppose, a kennel, though possessing the transparent purity of a rustic rivulet. It is a brook in city garb. We passed under the pointed arch of a gateway, which stands in one of the principal streets, and soon came in front of

THE CATHEDRAL.

I do not remember any cathedral with so fine a site as this, rising up out of the centre of a beautiful green, extensive enough to show its full proportions, relieved and insulated from all other patchwork and impertinence of rusty edifices. It is of gray stone, and looks as perfect as when just finished, and with the perfection, too, that could not have come in less than six centuries of venerableness, with a view to which these edifices seem to have been built. A new cathedral would lack the last touch to its beauty and grandeur. It needs to be mellowed and ripened, like some pictures; although I suppose this awfulness of antiquity was supplied, in the minds of the generation that built cathedrals, by the sanctity which they attributed to them. Salisbury Cathedral is far more beautiful than that of York, the exterior of which was really disagreeable to my eye; but this mighty spire and these multitudinous gray pinnacles and towers ascend towards heaven with a kind of natural beauty, not as if man had contrived them. They might be fancied to have grown up, just as the spires of a tuft of grass do, at the same time that they have a law of propriety and regularity among themselves. The tall spire is of such admirable proportion that it does not seem gigantic; and indeed the effect of the whole edifice is of beauty rather than weight and massiveness. Perhaps the bright, balmy sunshine in which we saw it contributed to give it a tender glory, and to soften a little its majesty.

When we went in, we heard the organ, the forenoon service being near conclusion. If I had never seen the interior of York Cathedral, I should have been quite satisfied, no doubt, with the spaciousness of this nave and these side aisles, and the height of their arches, and the girth of these pillars; but with that recollection in my mind they fell a little short of grandeur. The interior is seen to disadvantage, and in a way the builder never meant it to be seen; because there is little or no painted glass, nor any such mystery as it makes, but only a colorless, common daylight, revealing everything without remorse. There is a general light hue, moreover, like that of whitewash, over the whole of the roof and walls of the interior, pillars, monuments, and all; whereas, originally, every pillar was polished, and the ceiling was ornamented in brilliant colors, and the light came, many-hued, through the windows, on all this elaborate beauty, in lieu of which there is nothing now but space.

Between the pillars that separate the nave from the side aisles, there are ancient tombs, most of which have recumbent statues on them. One of these is Longsword, Earl of Salisbury, son of Fair Rosamond, in chain mail; and there are many other warriors and bishops, and one cross-legged Crusader, and on one tombstone a recumbent skeleton, which I have likewise seen in two or three other cathedrals. The pavement of the aisles and nave is laid in great part with flat tombstones, the inscriptions on which are half obliterated, and on the walls, especially in the transepts, there are tablets, among which I saw one to the poet Bowles, who was a canon of this cathedral. The ecclesiastical dignitaries bury themselves and monument themselves to the exclusion of almost everybody else, in these latter times; though still, as of old, the warrior has his place. A young officer, slain in the Indian wars, was memorialized by a tablet, and may be remembered by it, six hundred years hence, as we now remember the old Knights and Crusaders. It deserves to be mentioned that I saw one or two noses still unbroken among these recumbent figures. Most of the antique statues, on close examination, proved to be almost entirely covered with names and initials, scratched over the once polished surface. The cathedral and its relics must have been far less carefully watched, at some former period, than now.

Between the nave and the choir, as usual, there is a screen that half destroys the majesty of the building, by abridging the spectator of the long vista which he might otherwise have of the whole interior at a glance. We peeped through the barrier, and saw some elaborate monuments in the chancel beyond; but the doors of the screen are kept locked, so that the vergers may raise a revenue by showing strangers through the richest part of the cathedral. By and by one of these vergers came through the screen, with a gentleman and lady whom he was taking round, and we joined ourselves to the party. He showed us into the cloisters, which had long been neglected and ruinous, until the time of Bishop Dennison, the last prelate, who has been but a few years dead. This Bishop has repaired and restored the cloisters in faithful adherence to the original plan; and they now form a most delightful walk about a pleasant and verdant enclosure, in the centre of which sleeps good Bishop Dennison, with a wife on either side of him, all three beneath broad flat stones. Most cloisters are darksome and grim; but these have a broad paved walk beneath the vista of arches, and are light, airy, and cheerful; and from one corner you can get the best possible view of the whole height and beautiful proportion of the cathedral spire. One side of this cloistered walk seems to be the length of the nave of the cathedral. There is a square of four such sides; and of places for meditation, grave, yet not too sombre, it seemed to me one of the best. While we stayed there, a jackdaw was walking to and fro across the grassy enclosure, and haunting around the good Bishop's grave. He was clad in black, and looked like a feathered ecclesiastic; but I know not whether it were Bishop Dennison's ghost, or that of some old monk.

On one side of the cloisters, and contiguous to the main body of the cathedral, stands the chapter-house. Bishop Dennison had it much at heart to repair this part of the holy edifice; and, if I mistake not, did begin the work; for it had been long ruinous, and in Cromwell's time his dragoons stationed their horses there. Little progress, however, had been made in the repairs when the Bishop died; and it was decided to restore the building in his honor, and by way of monument to him. The repairs are now nearly completed; and the interior of this chapter-house gave me the first idea, anywise adequate, of the splendor of these Gothic church edifices. The roof is sustained by one great central pillar of polished marble, — small pillars clustered about a great central column, which rises to the ceiling, and there gushes out with various beauty, that overflows all the walls; as if the fluid idea had sprung out of that fountain, and grown solid in what we see. The pavement is elaborately ornamented; the ceiling is to be brilliantly gilded and painted, as it was of yore, and the tracery and sculptures around the walls are to be faithfully renewed from what remains of the original patterns.

After viewing the chapter-house, the verger — an elderly man of grave, benign manner, clad in black and talking of the cathedral and the monuments as if he loved them — led us again into the nave of the cathedral, and thence within the screen of the choir. The screen is as poor as possible, — mere barren wood-work, without the least attempt at beauty. In the chancel there are some meagre patches of old glass, and some of modern date, not very well worth looking at. We saw several interesting monuments in this part of the cathedral, — one belonging to the ducal family of Somerset, and erected in the reign of James I.; it is of marble, and extremely splendid and elaborate, with kneeling figures and all manner of magnificence, — more than I have seen in any monument except that of Mary of Scotland in Westminster Abbey. The more ancient tombs are also very numerous, and among them that of the Bishop who founded the cathedral. Within the screen, against the wall, is erected a monument, by Chantrey, to the Earl of Malmesbury; a full-length statue of the Earl in a half-recumbent position, holding an open volume and looking upward, — a noble work, — a calm, wise, thoughtful, firm, and not unbenignant face. Beholding its expression, it really was impossible not to have faith in the high character of the individual thus represented; and I have seldom felt this effect from any monumental bust or statue, though I presume it is always aimed at.

I am weary of trying to describe cathedrals. It is utterly useless; there is no possibility of giving the general effect, or any shadow of it, and it is miserable to put down a few items of tombstones, and a bit of glass from a painted window, as if the gloom and glory of the edifice were thus to be reproduced. Cathedrals are almost the only things (if even those) that have quite filled out my ideal here in this old world; and cathedrals often make me miserable from my inadequacy to take them wholly in; and, above all, I despise myself when I sit down to describe them.

We now walked around the Close, which is surrounded by some of the quaintest and comfortablest ecclesiastical residences that can be imagined. These are the dwelling-houses of the Dean, and the canons, and whatever other high officers compose the Bishop's staff; and there was one large brick mansion, old, but not so ancient as the rest, which we took to be the Bishop's palace. I never beheld anything — I must say again — so cosey, so indicative of domestic comfort for whole centuries together, — houses so fit to live in or to die in, and where it would be so pleasant to lead a young wife beneath the antique portal, and dwell with her till husband and wife were patriarchal, — as these delectable old houses. They belong naturally to the cathedral, and have a necessary relation to it, and its sanctity is somehow thrown over them all, so that they do not quite belong to this world, though they look full to overflowing of whatever earthly things are good for man. These are places, however, in which mankind makes no progress; the rushing tumult of human life here subsides into a deep, quiet pool, with perhaps a gentle circular eddy, but no onward movement. The same identical thought, I suppose, goes round in a slow whirl from one generation to another, as I have seen a withered leaf do in the vortex of a brook. In the front of the cathedral there is a most stately and beautiful tree, which flings its verdure upward to a very lofty height; but far above it rises the tall spire, dwarfing the great tree by comparison.

When the cathedral had sufficiently oppressed us with its beauty, we returned to sublunary matters, and went wandering about Salisbury in search of a luncheon, which we finally took in a confectioner's shop. Then we inquired hither and thither, at various livery-stables, for a conveyance to Stonehenge, and at last took a fly from the Lamb Hotel. The drive was over a turnpike for the first seven miles, over a bare, ridgy country, showing little to interest us. We passed a party of seven or eight men, in a coarse uniform dress, resembling that worn by convicts, and apparently under the guardianship of a stout, authoritative, yet rather kindly-looking, man with a cane. Our driver said that they were lunatics from a neighboring asylum, out for a walk.

Seven miles from Salisbury, we turned aside from the turnpike, and drove two miles across Salisbury Plain, which is an apparently boundless extent of unenclosed land, treeless and houseless. It is not exactly a plain, but a green sea of long and gentle swells and subsidences, affording views of miles upon miles to a very far horizon. We passed large flocks of sheep, with the shepherds watching them; but the dogs seemed to take most of the care of the flocks upon their own shoulders, and would scamper to turn the sheep when they inclined to stray whither they should not; and then arose a thousand-fold bleating, not unpleasant to the ear; for it did not apparently indicate any fear or discomfort on the part of the flock. The sheep and lambs are all black-faced, and have a very funny expression. As we drove over the plain (my seat was beside the driver), I saw at a distance a cluster of large gray stones, mostly standing upright, and some of them slightly inclined towards each other, — very irregular, and so far off forming no very picturesque or noteworthy spectacle. Of course I knew at once that this was and also knew that the reality was going to dwindle wofully within my ideal, as almost everything else does. When we reached the spot, we found a picnic-party just finishing their dinner, on one of the overthrown stones of the druidical temple; and within the sacred circle an artist was painting a wretched daub of the scene, and an old shepherd — the very Shepherd of Salisbury Plain — sat erect in the centre of the ruin.

There never was a ruder thing than Stonehenge made by mortal hands. It is so very rude that it seems as if Nature and man had worked upon it with one consent, and so it is all the stranger and more impressive from its rudeness. The spectator wonders to see art and contrivance, and a regular and even somewhat intricate plan, beneath all the uncouth simplicity of this arrangement of rough stones; and certainly, whatever was the intellectual and scientific advancement of the people who built Stonehenge, no succeeding architects will ever have a right to triumph over them; for nobody's work in after times is likely to endure till it becomes a mystery as to who built it, and how, and, for what purpose. Apart from the moral considerations suggested by it, Stonehenge is not very well worth seeing. Materially, it is one of the poorest of spectacles, and when complete, it must have been even less picturesque than now, — a few huge, rough stones, very imperfectly squared, standing on end, and each group of two supporting a third large stone on their tops; other stones of the same pattern overthrown and tumbled one upon another; and the whole comprised within a circuit of about a hundred feet diameter; the short, sheep-cropped grass of Salisbury Plain growing among all these uncouth boulders. I am not sure that a misty, lowering day would not have better suited Stonehenge, as the dreary midpoint of the great, desolate, trackless plain; not literally trackless, however, for the London and Exeter Road passes within fifty yards of the ruins, and another road intersects it.

After we had been there about an hour, there came a horseman within the Druid's circle, — evidently a clerical personage by his white neckcloth, though his loose gray riding pantaloons were not quite in keeping. He looked at us rather earnestly, and at last addressed Mrs. ——, and announced himself as Mr. Hinchman, — a clergyman whom she had been trying to find in Salisbury, in order to avail herself of him as a cicerone; and he had now ridden hither to meet us. He told us that the artist whom we found here could give us more information than anybody about Stonehenge; for it seems he has spent a great many years here, painting and selling his poor sketches to visitors, and also selling a book which his father wrote about the remains. This man showed, indeed, a pretty accurate acquaintance with these old stones, and pointed out what is thought to be the altar-stone, and told us of some relation between this stone and two other stones, and the rising of the sun at midsummer, which might indicate that Stonehenge was a temple of solar worship. He pointed out, too, to how little depth the stones were planted in the earth, insomuch that I have no doubt the American frosts would overthrow Stonehenge in a single winter; and it is wonderful that it should have stood so long, even in England. I have forgotten what else he said; but I bought one of his books, and find it a very unsatisfactory performance, being chiefly taken up with an attempt to prove these remains to be an antediluvian work, constructed, I think the author says, under the superintendence of Father Adam himself! Before our departure we were requested to write our names in the album which the artist keeps for the purpose; and he pointed out Ex-President Fillmore's autograph, and those of one or two other Americans who have been here within a short time. It is a very curious life that this artist leads, in this great solitude, and haunting Stonehenge like the ghost of a Druid; but he is a brisk little man, and very communicative on his one subject.

Mr. Hinchman rode with us over the plain, and pointed out Salisbury spire, visible close to Stonehenge. Under his guidance we returned by a different road from that which brought us thither, — and a much more delightful one. I think I never saw such continued sylvan beauty as this road showed us, passing through a good deal of woodland scenery, — fine old trees, standing each within its own space, and thus having full liberty to outspread itself, and wax strong and broad for ages, instead of being crowded, and thus stifled and emaciated, as human beings are here, and forest-trees are in America. Hedges, too, and the rich, rich, verdure of England; and villages full of picturesque old houses, thatched, and ivied, or perhaps overrun with roses, — and a stately mansion in the Elizabethan style; and a quiet stream, gliding onward without a ripple from its own motion, but rippled by a large fish darting across it; and over all this scene a gentle, friendly sunshine, not ardent enough to crisp a single leaf or blade of grass. Nor must the village church be forgotten, with its square, battlemented tower, dating back to the epoch of the Normans. We called at a house where one of Mrs. ——'s pupils was residing with her aunt, — a thatched house of two stories high, built in what was originally a sand-pit, but which, in the course of a good many years, has been transformed into the most delightful and homelike little nook almost that can be found in England. A thatched cottage suggests a very rude dwelling indeed; but this had a pleasant parlor and drawing-room, and chambers with lattice-windows, opening close beneath the thatched roof; and the thatch itself gives an air to the place as if it were a bird's-nest, or some such simple and natural habitation. The occupants are an elderly clergyman, retired from professional duty, and his sister; and having nothing else to do, and sufficient means, they employ themselves in beautifying this sweet little retreat, — planting new shrubbery, laying out new walks around it, and helping Nature to add continually another charm; and Nature is certainly a more genial playfellow in England than in my own country. She is always ready to lend her aid to any beautifying purpose.

Leaving these good people, who were very hospitable, giving tea and offering wine, we reached Salisbury in time to take the train for Southampton.

June 18th. — Yesterday we left the Castle Hotel, after paying a bill of £20 for a little more than a week's board. In America we could not very well have lived so simply, but we might have lived luxuriously for half the money. This Castle Hotel was once an old Roman castle, the landlord says, and the circular sweep of the tower is still seen towards the street, although, being painted white, and built up with modern additions, it would not be taken for an ancient structure. There is a dungeon beneath it, in which the landlord keeps his wine.

J—— and I, quitting the hotel, walked towards Shirley along the water-side, leaving the rest of the family to follow in a fly. There are many traces, along the shore, of the fortifications by which Southampton was formerly defended towards the water, and very probably their foundations may be as ancient as Roman times. Our hotel was no doubt connected with this chain of defences, which seems to have consisted of a succession of round towers, with a wall extending from one to another. We saw two or three of these towers still standing, and likely to stand, though ivy-grown and ruinous at the summit, and intermixed and even amalgamated with pot-houses and mean dwellings; and often, through an antique arch, there was a narrow doorway, giving access to the house of some sailor or laborer or artisan, and his wife gossiping at it with her neighbor, or his children playing about it.

After getting beyond the precincts of Southampton our walk was not very interesting, except to J——, who kept running down to the verge of the water, looking for shells and sea insects.

June 29th. — Yesterday, 28th, I left Liverpool from the Lime Street Station; an exceedingly hot day for England, insomuch that the rail carriages were really uncomfortable. I have now passed over the London and Northwestern Railway so often that the northern part of it is very wearisome, especially as it has few features of interest even to a new observer. At Stafford — no, at Wolverhampton — we diverged to a track which I have passed over only once before. We stopped an hour and a quarter at Wolverhampton, and I walked up into the town, which is large and old, — old, at least, in its plan, or lack of plan, — the streets being irregular, and straggling over an uneven surface. Like many of the English towns, it reminds me of Boston, though dingier. The sun was so hot that I actually sought the shady sides of the streets; and this, of itself, is one long step towards establishing a resemblance between an English town and an American one.

English railway carriages seem to me more tiresome than any other; and I suppose it is owing to the greater motion, arising from their more elastic springs. A slow train, too, like that which I was now in, is more tiresome than a quick one, at least to the spirits, whatever it may be to the body. We loitered along through afternoon and evening, stopping at every little station, and nowhere getting to the top of our speed, till at last, in the late dusk, we reached

GLOUCESTER,

and I put up at the Wellington Hotel, which is but a little way from the station. I took tea and a slice or two of ham in the coffee-room, and had a little talk with two people there; one of whom, on learning that I was an American, said, "But I suppose you have now been in England some time?" He meant, finding me not absolutely a savage, that I must have been caught a good while ago. . . . .

The next morning I went into the city, the hotel being on its outskirts, and rambled along in search of the cathedral. Some church-bells were chiming and clashing for a wedding or other festal occasion, and I followed the sound, supposing that it might proceed from the cathedral, but this was not the case. It was not till I had got to a bridge over the Severn, quite out of the town, that I saw again its tower, and knew how to shape my course towards it.

I did not see much that was strange or interesting in Gloucester. It is old, with a good many of those antique Elizabethan houses with two or three peaked gables on a line together; several old churches, which always cluster about a cathedral, like chickens round a hen; a hospital for decayed tradesmen; another for blue-coat boys; a great many butcher's shops, scattered in all parts of the town, open in front, with a counter or dresser on which to display the meat, just in the old fashion of Shakespeare's house. It is a large town, and has a good deal of liveliness and bustle, in a provincial way. In short, judging by the sheep, cattle, and horses, and the people of agricultural aspect that I saw about the streets, I should think it must have been market-day. I looked here and there for the old Bell Inn, because, unless I misremember, Fielding brings Tom Jones to this inn, while he and Partridge were travelling together. It is still extant; for, on my arrival the night before, a runner from it had asked me to go thither; but I forgot its celebrity at the moment. I saw nothing of it in my rambles about Gloucester, but at last I found

THE CATHEDRAL,

though I found no point from which a good view of the exterior can be seen.

It has a very beautiful and rich outside, however, and a lofty tower, very large and ponderous, but so finished off, and adorned with pinnacles, and all manner of architectural devices, — wherewith these old builders knew how to alleviate their massive structures, — that it seems to sit lightly in the air. The porch was open, and some workmen were trundling barrows into the nave; so I followed, and found two young women sitting just within the porch, one of whom offered to show me round the cathedral. There was a great dust in the nave, arising from the operations of the workmen. They had been laying a new pavement, and scraping away the plaster, which had heretofore been laid over the pillars and walls. The pillars come out from the process as good as new, — great, round, massive columns, not clustered like those of most cathedrals; they are twenty-one feet in circumference, and support semicircular arches. I think there are seven of these columns, on each side of the nave, which did not impress me as very spacious; and the dust and racket of the work-people quite destroyed the effect which should have been produced by the aisles and arches; so that I hardly stopped to glance at this part, though I saw some mural monuments and recumbent statues along the walls.

The choir is separated from the nave by the usual

screen, and now by a sail-cloth or something of that kind, drawn across, in order to keep out the dust, while the repairs are going on. When the young woman conducted me hither, I was at once struck by the magnificent eastern window, the largest in England, which fills, or looks vast enough to fill, all that end of the cathedral, — a most splendid window, full of old painted glass, which looked as bright as sunshine, though the sun was not really shining through it. The roof of the choir is of oak and very fine, and as much as ninety feet high. There are chapels opening from the choir, and within them the monuments of the eminent people who built them, and of benefactors or prelates, or of those otherwise illustrious in their day. My recollection of what I saw here is very dim and confused; more so than I anticipated. I remember somewhere within the choir the tomb of Edward II. with his effigy upon the top of it, in a long robe, with a crown on his head, and a ball and sceptre in his hand; likewise, a statue of Robert, son of the Conqueror, carved in Irish oak and painted. He lolls in an easy posture on his tomb, with one leg crossed lightly over the other, to denote that he was a Crusader. There are several monuments of mitred abbots, who formerly presided over the cathedral. A Cavalier and his wife, with the dress of the period elaborately represented, lie side by side in excellent preservation; and it is remarkable that though their noses are very prominent, they have come down from the past without any wear and tear. The date of the Cavalier's death is 1637, and I think his statue could not have been sculptured until after the Restoration, else he and his dame would hardly have come through Cromwell's time unscathed. Here, as in all the other churches in England, Cromwell is said to have stabled his horses, and broken the windows, and belabored the old monuments.

There is one large and beautiful chapel, styled the Lady's Chapel, which is, indeed, a church by itself, being ninety feet long, and comprising everything that appertains to a place of worship. Here, too, there are monuments, and on the floor are many old bricks and tiles, with inscriptions on them, or Gothic devices, and flat tombstones, with coats of arms sculptured on them; as indeed, there are everywhere else, except in the nave, where the new pavement has obliterated them. After viewing the choir and the chapels, the young woman led me down into the crypts below, where the dead persons who are commemorated in the upper regions were buried. The low ponderous pillars and arches of these crypts are supposed to be older than the upper portions of the building. They are about as perfect, I suppose, as when new, but very damp, dreary, and darksome; and the arches intersect one another so intricately, that, if the girl had deserted me, I might easily have got lost there. These are chapels where masses used to be said for the souls of the deceased; and my guide said that a great many skulls and bones had been dug up here. No doubt a vast population has been deposited in the course of a thousand years. I saw two white skulls, in a niche, grinning as skulls always do, though it is impossible to see the joke. These crypts, or crypts like these, are doubtless what Congreve calls the "aisles and monumental caves of Death," in that passage which Dr. Johnson admired so much.

They are very singular, — something like a dark shadow or dismal repetition of the upper church below ground.

Ascending from the crypts, we went next to the cloisters, which are in a very perfect state, and form an unbroken square about the green grass plot, enclosed within. Here also it is said Cromwell stabled his horses; but if so, they were remarkably quiet beasts, for tombstones, which form the pavement, are not broken, nor cracked, nor bear any hoof-marks. All around the cloisters, too, the stone tracery that shuts them in like a closed curtain, carefully drawn, remains as it was in the days of the monks, insomuch that it is not easy to get a glimpse of the green enclosure. Probably there used to be painted glass in the larger apertures of this stone-work; otherwise it is perfect. These cloisters are very different from the free, open, and airy ones of Salisbury; but they are more in accordance with our notions of monkish habits; and even at this day, if I were a canon of Gloucester, I would put that dim ambulatory to a good use. The library is adjacent to the cloisters, and I saw some rows of folios and quartos. I have nothing else to record about the cathedral, though if I were to stay there a month, I suppose it might then begin to be understood. It is wicked to look at these solemn old churches in a hurry. By the by, it was not built in a hurry; but in full three hundred years, having been begun in 1188 and only finished in 1498, not a great many years before Papistry began to go out of vogue in England.

From Gloucester I took the rail for Basingstoke before noon. The first part of the journey was through an uncommonly beautiful tract of country, hilly, but not wild; a tender and graceful picturesqueness, — fine, single trees and clumps of trees, and sometimes wide woods, scattered over the landscape, and filling the nooks of the hills with luxuriant foliage. Old villages scattered frequently along our track, looking very peaceful, with the peace of past ages lingering about them; and a rich, rural verdure of antique cultivation everywhere. Old country-seats — specimens of the old English hall or manor-house — appeared on the hill-sides, with park-scenery surrounding the mansions; and the gray churches rose in the midst of all the little towns. The beauty of English scenery makes me desperate, it is so impossible to describe it, or in any way to record its impression, and such a pity to leave it undescribed; and, moreover, I always feel that I do not get from it a hundredth or a millionth part of the enjoyment that there really is in it, hurrying past it thus. I was really glad when we rumbled into a tunnel, piercing for a long distance through a hill; and, emerging on the other side, we found ourselves in a comparatively level and uninteresting tract of country, which lasted till we reached Southampton. English scenery, to be appreciated and to be reproduced with pen and pencil, requires to be dwelt upon long, and to be wrought out with the nicest touches. A coarse and hasty brush is not the instrument for such work.

July 6th. — Monday, June 30th, was a warm and beautiful day, and my wife and I took a cab from Southampton and drove to

NETLEY ABBEY,

about three or four miles. The remains of the Abbey stand in a sheltered place, but within view of Southampton Water; and it is a most picturesque and perfect ruin all ivy-grown, of course, and with great trees where the pillers of the nave used to stand, and also in the refectory and the cloister court; and so much soil on the summit of the broken walls, that weeds flourish abundantly there, and grass too; and there was a wild rose-bush, in full bloom, as much as thirty or forty feet from the ground. S—— and I ascended a winding stair, leading up within a round tower, the steps much foot-worn; and, reaching the top, we came forth at the height where a gallery had formerly run round the church, in the thickness of the wall. The upper portions of the edifice were now chiefly thrown down; but I followed a foot-path, on the top of the remaining wall, quite to the western entrance of the church. Since the time when the Abbey was taken from the monks, it has been private property; and the possessor, in Henry VIII.'s days, or subsequently, built a residence for himself within its precincts out of the old materials. This has now entirely disappeared, all but some unsightly old masonry, patched into the original walls. Large portions of the ruin have been removed, likewise, to be used as building-materials elsewhere; and this is the Abbey mentioned, I think, by Dr. Watts, concerning which a Mr. William Taylor had a dream while he was contemplating pulling it down. He dreamed that a part of it fell upon his head; and, sure enough, a piece of the wall did come down and crush him. In the nave I saw a large mass of conglomerated stone that had fallen from the wall between the nave and cloisters, and thought that perhaps this was the very mass that killed poor Mr. Taylor.

The ruins are extensive and very interesting; but I have put off describing them too long, and cannot make a distinct picture of them now. Moreover, except to a spectator skilled in architecture, all ruined abbeys are pretty much alike. As we came away, we noticed some women making baskets at the entrance, and one of them urged us to buy some of her handiwork; for that she was the gypsy of Netley Abbey, and had lived among the ruins these thirty years. So I bought one for a shilling. She was a woman with a prominent nose, and weather-tanned, but not very picturesque or striking.

TO BLACKHEATH.

On the 6th July, we left the Villa, with our enormous luggage, and took our departure from Southampton by the noon train. The main street of Southampton, though it looks pretty fresh and bright, must be really antique, there being a great many projecting windows, in the old-time style, and these make the vista of the street very picturesque. I have no doubt that I missed seeing many things more interesting than the few that I saw. Our journey to London was without any remarkable incident, and at the Waterloo station we found one of Mr. Bennoch's clerks, under whose guidance we took two cabs for the East Kent station at London Bridge, and there railed to Blackheath, where we arrived in the afternoon.

. . . . .

On Thursday I went into London by one of the morning trains, and wandered about all day, — visiting the Exhibition of the Royal Academy, and Westminster Abbey and St. Paul's, the two latter of which I have already written about in former journals. On Friday, S——, J——, and I walked over the heath, and through the Park to Greenwich, and spent some hours in the Hospital. The painted hall struck me much more than at my first view of it; it is very beautiful indeed, and the effect of its frescoed ceiling most rich and magnificent, the assemblage of glowing hues producing a general result of splendor. . . . .

In the evening I went with Mr. and Mrs. —— to a conversazione at Mrs. Newton Crosland's, who lives on Blackheath. . . . . I met with one person who interested me, — Mr. Bailey, the author of Festus; and I was surprised to find myself already acquainted with him. It is the same Mr. Bailey whom I met a few months ago, when I first dined at Mr. ——'s, — a dark, handsome, rather picturesque-looking man, with a gray beard, and dark hair, a little dimmed with gray. He is of quiet and very agreeable deportment, and I liked him and believed in him. . . . . There is sadness glooming out of him, but no unkindness nor asperity. Mrs. Crosland's conversazione was enriched with a supper, and terminated with a dance, in which Mr. —— joined with heart and soul, but Mrs. —— went to sleep in her chair, and I would gladly have followed her example if I could have found a chair to sit upon. In the course of the evening I had some talk with a pale, nervous young lady, who has been a noted spiritual medium.

Yesterday I went into town by the steamboat from

Greenwich to London Bridge, with a nephew of Mr. ——'s, and, calling at his place of business, he procured us an order from his wine-merchants, by means of which we were admitted into

THE WINE-VAULTS OF THE LONDON DOCKS.

We there found parties, with an acquaintance, who was going, with two French gentlemen, into the vaults. It is a good deal like going down into a mine, each visitor being provided with a lamp at the end of a stick; and following the guide along dismal passages, running beneath the streets, and extending away interminably, — roughly arched overhead with stone, from which depend festoons of a sort of black fungus, caused by the exhalations of the wine. Nothing was ever uglier than this fungus. It is strange that the most ethereal effervescence of rich wine can produce nothing better.

The first series of vaults which we entered were filled with port-wine, and occupied a space variously estimated at from eleven to sixteen acres, — which I suppose would hold more port-wine than ever was made. At any rate, the pipes and butts were so thickly piled that in some places we could hardly squeeze past them. We drank from two or three vintages; but I was not impressed with any especial excellence in the wine. We were not the only visitors, for, far in the depths of the vault, we passed a gentleman and two young ladies, wandering about like the ghosts of defunct wine-bibbers, in a Tophet specially prepared for them. People employed here sometimes go astray, and, their lamps being extinguished, they remain long in this everlasting gloom. We went likewise to the vaults of sherry-wine, which have the same characteristics as those just described, but are less extensive.

It is no guaranty for the excellence or even for the purity of the wine, that it is kept in these cellars, under the lock and key of the government; for the merchants are allowed to mix different vintages, according to their own pleasure, and to adulterate it as they like. Very little of the wine probably comes out as it goes in, or is exactly what it pretends to be. I went back to Mr. ——'s office, and we drove together to make some calls jointly and separately. I went alone to Mrs. Heywood's; afterwards with Mr. —— to the American minister's, whom we found at home; and I requested of him, on the part of the Americans at Liverpool, to tell me the facts about the American gentleman being refused admittance to the Levee. The ambassador did not seem to me to make his point good for having withdrawn with the rejected guest.

. . . . .

July 9th. (Our wedding-day.) — We were invited yesterday evening to Mrs. S. C. Hall's, where Jenny Lind was to sing; so we left Blackheath at about eight o'clock in a brougham, and reached Ashley Place, as the dusk was gathering, after nine. The Halls reside in a handsome suite of apartments, arranged on the new system of flats, each story constituting a separate tenement, and the various families having an entrance-hall in common. The plan is borrowed from the Continent, and seems rather alien to the traditionary habits of the English; though, no doubt, a good degree of seclusion is compatible with it. Mr. Hall received us with the greatest cordiality before we entered the drawing-room. Mrs. Hall, too, greeted us with most kindly warmth. Jenny Lind had not yet arrived; but I found Dr. Mackay there, and I was introduced to Miss Catherine Sinclair, who is a literary lady, though none of her works happen to be known to me. Soon the servant announced Madam Goldschmidt, and this famous lady made her appearance, looking quite different from what I expected. Mrs. Hall established her in the inner drawing-room, where was a piano and a harp; and shortly after, our hostess came to me, and said that Madam Goldschmidt wished to be introduced to me. There was a gentle peremptoriness in the summons, that made it something like being commanded into the presence of a princess; a great favor, no doubt, but yet a little humbling to the recipient. However, I acquiesced with due gratitude, and was presented accordingly. She made room for me on the sofa, and I sat down, and began to talk.

Jenny Lind is rather tall, — quite tall, for a woman, — certainly no beauty, but with sense and self-reliance in her aspect and manners. She was suffering under a severe cold, and seemed worn down besides, so probably I saw her under disadvantages. Her conversation is quite simple, and I should have great faith in her sincerity; and there is about her the manner of a person who knows the world, and has conquered it. She said something or other about The Scarlet Letter; and, on my part, I paid her such compliments as a man could pay who had never heard her sing. . . . . Her conversational voice is an agreeable one, rather deep, and not particularly smooth. She talked about America, and of our unwholesome modes of life, as to eating and exercise, and of the ill health especially of our women; but I opposed this view as far as I could with any truth, insinuating my opinion that we are about as healthy as other people, and affirming for a certainty that we live longer. In good faith, so far as I have any knowledge of the matter, the women of England are as generally out of health as those of America; always something has gone wrong with them; and as for Jenny Lind, she looks wan and worn enough to be an American herself. This charge of ill-health is almost universally brought forward against us nowadays, — and, taking the whole country together, I do not believe the statistics will bear it out.

. . . . .

The rooms, which were respectably filled when we arrived, were now getting quite full. I saw Mr. Stevens, the American man of libraries, and had some talk with him; and Durham, the sculptor; and Mr. and Mrs. Hall introduced me to various people, some of whom were of note, — for instance, Sir Emerson Tennent, a man of the world, of some parliamentary distinction, wearing a star; Mr. Samuel Lover, a most good-natured, pleasant Irishman, with a shining and twinkling visage; Miss Jewsbury, whom I found very conversable. She is known in literature, but not to me. We talked about Emerson, whom she seems to have been well acquainted with while he was in England; and she mentioned that Miss Martineau had given him a lock of hair; it was not her own hair, but a mummy's.

After our return Mrs. —— told us that Miss Jewsbury had written, among other things, three histories, and as she asked me to introduce her to S——, and means to cultivate our acquaintance, it would be well to know something of them. We were told that she is now employed in some literary undertaking of Lady Morgan's, who, at the age of ninety, is still circulating in society, and is as brisk in faculties as ever. I should like to see her ladyship, that is, I should not be sorry to see her; for distinguished people are so much on a par with others, socially, that it would be foolish to be overjoyed at seeing anybody whomsoever.

Leaving out the illustrious Jenny Lind, I suspect that I was myself the greatest lion of the evening; for a good many persons sought the felicity of knowing me, and had little or nothing to say when that honor and happiness was conferred on them. It is surely very wrong and ill-mannered in people to ask for an introduction unless they are prepared to make talk; it throws too great an expense and trouble on the wretched lion, who is compelled, on the spur of the moment, to convert a conversable substance out of thin air, perhaps for the twentieth time that evening. I am sure I did not say — and I think I did not hear said — one rememberable word in the course of this visit; though, nevertheless, it was a rather agreeable one. In due season ices and jellies were handed about; and some ladies and gentlemen — professional, perhaps — were kind enough to sing songs, and play on the piano and harp, while persons in remote corners went on with whatever conversation they had in hand. Then came supper; but there were so many people to go into the supper-room that we could not all crowd thither together, and, coming late, I got nothing but some sponge-cake and a glass of champagne, neither of which I care for. After supper, Mr. Lover sang some Irish songs, his own in music and words, with rich, humorous effect, to which the comicality of his face contributed almost as much as his voice and words. The Lord Mayor looked in for a little while, and though a hard-featured Jew enough, was the most picturesque person there.

July 10th. — Mrs. Heywood had invited me to dinner last evening. . . . . Her house is very finely situated, overlooking Hyde Park, and not a great way from where Tyburn tree used to stand. When I arrived, there were no guests but Mr. and Mrs. D——; but by and by came Mr. Monckton Milnes and lady, the Bishop of Lichfield, Mr. Tom Taylor, Mr. Ewart, M. P., Sir Somebody Somerville, Mr. and Mrs. Musgrave, and others. Mr. Milnes, whom I had not seen for more than a year, greeted me very cordially, and so did Mr. Taylor. I took Mrs. Musgrave in to dinner. She is an Irish lady, and Mrs. Heywood had recommended her to me as being very conversable; but I had a good deal more talk with Mrs. M——, with whom I was already acquainted, than with her. Mrs. M—— is of noble blood, and therefore not snobbish, — quite unaffected, gentle, sweet, and easy to get on with, reminding me of the best-mannered American women. But how can anything characteristic be said or done among a dozen people sitting at table in full dress? Speaking of full dress, the Bishop wore small-clothes and silk stockings, and entered the drawing-room with a three-cornered hat, which he kept flattened out under his arm. He asked the briefest blessing possible, and, sitting at the ultra end of the table, I heard nothing further from him till he officiated as briefly before the cloth was withdrawn. Mrs. M—— talked about Tennyson, with whom her husband was at the University, and whom he continues to know intimately. She says that he considers Maud his best poem. He now lives in the Isle of Wight, spending all the year round there, and has recently bought the place on which he resides. She was of opinion that he would have been gratified by my calling on him, which I had wished to do, while we were at Southampton; but this is a liberty which I should hardly venture upon with a shy man like Tennyson, — more especially as he might perhaps suspect me of doing it on the score of my own literary character. But I should like much to see him. . . . . Mr. Tom Taylor, during dinner, made some fun for the benefit of the ladies on either side of him. I liked him very well this evening.

. . . . .

When the ladies had not long withdrawn, and after the wine had once gone round, I asked Mr. Heywood to make my apologies to Mrs. Heywood, and took leave; all London lying betwixt me and the London Bridge station, where I was to take the rail homeward. At the station I found Mr. Bennoch, who had been dining with the Lord Mayor to meet Sir William Williams, and we railed to Greenwich, and reached home by midnight. Mr. and Mrs. Bennoch have set out on their Continental journey to-day, — leaving us, for a little space, in possession of what will be more like a home than anything that we shall hereafter find in England.

This afternoon I had taken up the fourth volume of Jerdan's Autobiography, — wretched twaddle, though it records such constant and apparently intimate intercourse with distinguished people, — and was reading it, between asleep and awake, on the sofa, when Mr. Jerdan himself was announced. I saw him, in company with Mr. Bennoch, nearly three years ago, at Rock Park, and wondered then what there was in so uncouth an individual to get him so freely into polished society. He now looks rougher than ever, — time-worn, but not reverend; a thatch of gray hair on his head; an imperfect set of false teeth; a careless apparel, checked trousers, and a stick, for he had walked a mile or two from his own dwelling.

I suspect — and long practice at the Consulate has made me keen-sighted — that Mr. Jerdan contemplated some benefit from my purse; and, to the extent of a sovereign or so, I would not mind contributing to his comfort. He spoke of a secret purpose of Mr. —— and himself to obtain me a degree or diploma in some Literary Institution, — what one I know not, and did not ask; but the honor cannot be a high one, if this poor old fellow can do aught towards it. I am afraid he is a very disreputable senior, but certainly not the less to be pitied on that account; and there was something very touching in his stiff and infirm movement, as he resumed his stick and took leave, waving me a courteous farewell, and turning upon me a smile, grim with age, as he went down the steps. In that gesture and smile I fancied some trace of the polished man of society, such as he may have once been; though time and hard weather have roughened him, as they have the once polished marble pillars which I saw so rude in aspect at Netley Abbey.

Speaking of Dickens last evening, Mr. —— mentioned his domestic tastes, — how he preferred home enjoyments to all others, and did not willingly go much into society. Mrs. ——, too, the other day told us of his taking on himself all possible trouble as regards his domestic affairs. . . . . There is a great variety of testimony, various and varied, as to the character of Dickens. I must see him before I finally leave England.

July 13th. — On Friday morning (11th), at nine o'clock, I took the rail into town to breakfast with Mr. Milnes. As he had named a little after ten as the hour, I could not immediately proceed to his house, and so walked moderately over London Bridge and into the city, meaning to take a cab from Charing Cross, or thereabouts. Passing through some street or other, contiguous to Cheapside, I saw in a court-yard the entrance to the Guildhall, and stepped in to look at it. It is a spacious hall, about one hundred and fifty feet long, and perhaps half as broad, paved with flagstones which look worn, and some of them cracked across; the roof is very lofty and was once vaulted, but has been shaped anew in modern times. There is a vast window partly filled with painted glass, extending quite along each end of the hall, and a row of arched windows on either side, throwing their light from far above downward upon the pavement. This fashion of high windows, not reaching within twenty or thirty feet of the floor, serves to give great effect to the large enclosed space of an antique hall. Against the walls are several marble monuments; one to the Earl of Chatham, a statue of white marble, with various allegorical contrivances, fronting an obelisk or pyramid of dark marble; and another to his son, William Pitt, of somewhat similar design and of equal size; each of them occupying the whole space, I believe, between pavement and ceiling. There is likewise a statue of Beckford, a famous Lord Mayor, — the most famous except Whittington, and that one who killed Wat Tyler; and like those two, his fame is perhaps somewhat mythological, though he lived and bustled within less than a century. He is said to have made a bold speech to the King; but this I will not believe of any Englishman — at least, of any plebeian Englishman — until I hear it. But there stands his statue in the Guildhall in the act of making his speech, as if the monstrous attempt had petrified him.

Lord Nelson, too, has a monument, and so, I think, has some other modern worthy. At one end of the hall, under one of the great painted windows, stand three or four old statues of mediæval kings, whose identities I forget; and in the two corners of the opposite end are two gigantic absurdities of painted wood, with grotesque visages, whom I quickly recognized as Gog and Magog. They stand each on a pillar, and seem to be about fifteen feet high, and look like enormous playthings for the children of giants; and it is strange to see them in this solemn old hall, among the memorials of dead heroes and statesmen. There is an annual banquet in the Guildhall, given by the Lord

Mayor and sheriffs, and I believe it is the very acme of civic feasting.

After viewing the hall, as it still lacked something of ten, I continued my walk through that entanglement of city streets, and quickly found myself getting beyond my reckoning. I cannot tell whither I went, but I passed through a very dirty region, and I remember a long, narrow, evil-odored street, cluttered up with stalls, in which were vegetables and little bits of meat for sale; and there was a frowzy multitude of buyers and sellers. Still I blundered on, and was getting out of the density of the city into broader streets, but still shabby ones, when, looking at my watch, I found it to be past ten, and no cab-stand within sight. It was a quarter past when I finally got into one; and the driver told me that it would take half an hour to go from thence to Upper Brook Street; so that I was likely to exceed the license implied in Mr. Milnes's invitation. Whether I was quite beyond rule I cannot say; but it did not lack more than ten minutes of eleven when I was ushered up stairs, and I found all the company assembled. However, it is of little consequence, except that if I had come early, I should have been introduced to many of the guests, whom now I could only know across the table. Mrs. Milnes greeted me very kindly, and Mr. Milnes came towards me with an elderly gentleman in a blue coat and gray pantaloons, — with a long, rather thin, homely visage, exceedingly shaggy eyebrows, though no great weight of brow, and thin gray hair, and introduced me to the Marquis of Lansdowne. The Marquis had his right hand wrapped up in a black-silk handkerchief; so he gave me his left, and from some awkwardness in meeting it, when I expected the right, I gave him only three of my fingers, — a thing I never did before to any person, and it is droll that I should have done it to a Marquis. He addressed me with great simplicity and natural kindness, complimenting me on my works, and speaking about the society of Liverpool in former days. Lord Lansdowne was the friend of Moore, and has about him the aroma communicated by the memories of many illustrious people with whom he has associated.

Mr. Ticknor, the Historian of Spanish Literature, now greeted me. Mr. Milnes introduced me to Mrs. Browning, and assigned her to me to conduct into the breakfast-room. She is a small, delicate woman, with ringlets of dark hair, a pleasant, intelligent, and sensitive face, and a low, agreeable voice. She looks youthful and comely, and is very gentle and ladylike. And so we proceeded to the breakfast-room, which is hung round with pictures; and in the middle of it stood a large round table, worthy to have been King Arthur's, and here we seated ourselves without any question of precedence or ceremony. On one side of me was an elderly lady, with a very fine countenance, and in the course of breakfast I discovered her to be the mother of Florence Nightingale. One of her daughters (not Florence) was likewise present. Mrs. Milnes, Mrs. Browning, Mrs. Nightingale, and her daughter were the only ladies at table; and I think there were as many as eight or ten gentlemen, whose names — as I came so late — I was left to find out for myself, or to leave unknown.

It was a pleasant and sociable meal, and, thanks to

my cold beef and coffee at home, I had no occasion to trouble myself much about the fare; so I just ate some delicate chicken, and a very small cutlet, and a slice of dry toast, and thereupon surceased from my labors. Mrs. Browning and I talked a good deal during breakfast, for she is of that quickly appreciative and responsive order of women with whom I can talk more freely than with any man; and she has, besides, her own originality, wherewith to help on conversation, though, I should say, not of a loquacious tendency. She introduced the subject of spiritualism, which, she says, interests her very much; indeed, she seems to be a believer. Mr. Browning, she told me, utterly rejects the subject, and will not believe even in the outward manifestations, of which there is such overwhelming evidence. We also talked of Miss Bacon; and I developed something of that lady's theory respecting Shakespeare, greatly to the horror of Mrs. Browning, and that of her next neighbor, — a nobleman, whose name I did not hear. On the whole, I like her the better for loving the man Shakespeare with a personal love. We talked, too, of Margaret Fuller, who spent her last night in Italy with the Brownings; and of William Story, with whom they have been intimate, and who, Mrs. Browning says, is much stirred about spiritualism. Really, I cannot help wondering that so fine a spirit as hers should not reject the matter, till, at least, it is forced upon her. I like her very much.

Mrs. Nightingale had been talking at first with Lord Lansdowne, who sat next her, but by and by she turned to me, and began to speak of London smoke. . . . . Then, there being a discussion about Lord Byron on the other side of the table, she spoke to me about Lady Byron, whom she knows intimately, characterizing her as a most excellent and exemplary person, high-principled, unselfish, and now devoting herself to the care of her two grandchildren, — their mother, Byron's daughter, being dead. Lady Byron, she says, writes beautiful verses. Somehow or other, all this praise, and more of the same kind, gave me an idea of an intolerably irreproachable person; and I asked Mrs. Nightingale if Lady Byron were warm-hearted. With some hesitation, or mental reservation, — at all events, not quite outspokenly, — she answered that she was.

I was too much engaged with these personal talks to attend much to what was going on elsewhere; but all through breakfast I had been more and more impressed by the aspect of one of the guests, sitting next to Milnes. He was a man of large presence, — a portly personage, gray-haired, but scarcely as yet aged; and his face had a remarkable intelligence, not vivid nor sparkling, but conjoined with great quietude, — and if it gleamed or brightened at one time more than another, it was like the sheen over a broad surface of sea. There was a somewhat careless self-possession, large and broad enough to be called dignity; and the more I looked at him, the more I knew that he was a distinguished person, and wondered who. He might have been a minister of state; only there is not one of them who has any right to such a face and presence. At last, — I do not know how the conviction came, — but I became aware that it was Macaulay, and began to see some slight resemblance to his portraits. But I have never seen any that is not wretchedly unworthy of the original. As soon as I knew him, I began to listen to his conversation, but he did not talk a great deal, — contrary to his usual custom; for I am told he is apt to engross all the talk to himself. Probably he may have been restrained by the presence of Ticknor, and Mr. Palfrey, who were among his auditors and interlocutors; and as the conversation seemed to turn much on American subjects, he could not well have assumed to talk them down. I am glad to have seen him, — a face fit for a scholar, a man of the world, a cultivated intelligence.

After we left the table, and went into the library, Mr. Browning introduced himself to me, — a younger man than I expected to see, handsome, with brown hair. He is very simple and agreeable in manner, gently impulsive, talking as if his heart were uppermost. He spoke of his pleasure in meeting me, and his appreciation of my books; and — which has not often happened to me — mentioned that The Blithedale Romance was the one he admired most. I wonder why. I hope I showed as much pleasure at his praise as he did at mine; for I was glad to see how pleasantly it moved him. After this, I talked with Ticknor and Milnes, and with Mr. Palfrey, to whom I had been introduced very long ago by George Hillard, and had never seen him since. We looked at some autographs, of which Mr. Milnes has two or three large volumes. I recollect a leaf from Swift's Journal to Stella; a letter from Addison; one from Chatterton, in a most neat and legible hand; and a characteristic sentence or two and signature of Oliver Cromwell, written in a religious book. There were many curious volumes in the library, but I had not time to look at them.

I liked greatly the manners of almost all, — yes, as far as I observed, — all the people at this breakfast, and it was doubtless owing to their being all people either of high rank or remarkable intellect, or both. An Englishman can hardly be a gentleman, unless he enjoy one or other of these advantages; and perhaps the surest way to give him good manners is to make a lord of him, or rather of his grandfather or great grandfather. In the third generation, scarcely sooner, he will be polished into simplicity and elegance, and his deportment will be all the better for the homely material out of which it is wrought and refined. The Marquis of Lansdowne, for instance, would have been a very commonplace man in the common ranks of life; but it has done him good to be a nobleman. Not that his tact is quite perfect. In going up to breakfast, he made me precede him; in returning to the library, he did the same, although I drew back, till he impelled me up the first stair, with gentle persistence. By insisting upon it, he showed his sense of condescension much more than if, when he saw me unwilling to take precedence, he had passed forward, as if the point were not worth either asserting or yielding. Heaven knows, it was in no humility that I would have trodden behind him. But he is a kind old man; and I am willing to believe of the English aristocracy generally that they are kind, and of beautiful deportment; for certainly there never can have been mortals in a position more advantageous for becoming so. I hope there will come a time when we shall be so; and I already know a few Americans, whose noble and delicate manners may compare well with any I have seen.

I left the house with Mr. Palfrey. He has come to England to make some researches in the State Paper Office, for the purposes of a work which he has in hand. He mentioned to me a letter which he had seen, written from New England in the time of Charles II. and referring to the order sent by the minister of that day for the appearance of Governor Bellingham and my ancestor on this side of the water. The signature of this letter is an anagram of my ancestor's name. The letter itself is a very bold and able one, controverting the propriety of the measure above indicated; and Mr. Palfrey feels certain that it was written by my aforesaid ancestor. I mentioned my wish to ascertain the place in England whence the family emigrated; and Mr. Palfrey took me to the Record Office, and introduced me to Mr. Joseph Hunter, — a venerable and courteous gentleman, of antiquarian pursuits. The office was odorous of musty parchments, hundreds of years old. Mr. Hunter received me with great kindness, and gave me various old records and rolls of parchment, in which to seek for my family name; but I was perplexed with the crabbed characters, and soon grew weary and gave up the quest. He says that it is very seldom that an American family, springing from the early settlers, can be satisfactorily traced back to their English ancestry.

July 16th. — Monday morning I took the rail from Blackheath to London. It is a very pleasant place, Blackheath, and far more rural than one would expect, within five or six miles of London, — a great many trees, making quite a mass of foliage in the distance; green enclosures; pretty villas, with their nicely kept lawns, and gardens, with grass plots and flower borders; and village streets, set along the sidewalks with ornamental trees; and the houses standing a little back, and separated one from another, — all this within what is called the Park, which has its gateways, and the sort of semi-privacy with which I first became acquainted at Rock Park.

. . . . .

From the London Bridge station I took a cab for Paddington, and then had to wait above two hours before a train started for Birkenhead. Meanwhile I walked a little about the neighborhood, which is very dull and uninteresting; made up of crescents and terraces, and rows of houses that have no individuality, and second-rate shops, — in short, the outskirts of the vast city, when it begins to have a kind of village character but no rurality or sylvan aspect, as at Blackheath. My journey, when at last we started, was quite unmarked by incident, and extremely tedious; it being a slow train, which plods on without haste and without rest. At about ten o'clock we reached Birkenhead, and there crossed the familiar and detestable Mersey, which, as usual, had a cloudy sky brooding over it. Mrs. Blodgett received me most hospitably, but was impelled, by an overflow of guests, to put me into a little back room, looking into the court, and formerly occupied by my predecessor, General Armstrong. . . . . She expressed a hope that I might not see his ghost, — nor have I, as yet. . . . .

Speaking of ghosts, Mr. H. A. B—— told me a singular story to-day of an apparition that haunts the Times Office, in Printing-House Square. A Mr. W—— is the engineer of the establishment, and has his residence in the edifice, which is built, I believe, on the site of Merchant Taylor's school, — an old house that was no longer occupied for its original purpose, and, being supposed haunted, was left untenanted. The father-in-law of Mr. W——, an old sea-captain, came on a visit to him and his wife, and was put into their guest-chamber, where he passed the night. The next morning, assigning no very satisfactory reason, he cut his visit short and went away. Shortly afterwards, a young lady came to visit the W——'s; but she too went away the next morning, — going first to make a call, as she said, to a friend, and sending thence for her trunks. Mrs. W—— wrote to this young lady, asking an explanation. The young lady replied, and gave a singular account of an apparition, — how she was awakened in the night by a bright light shining through the window, which was parallel to the bed; then, if I remember rightly, her curtains were withdrawn, and a shape looked in upon her, — a woman's shape, she called it; but it was a skeleton, with lambent flames playing about its bones, and in and out among the ribs. Other persons have since slept in this chamber, and some have seen the shape, others not. Mr. W—— has slept there himself without seeing anything. He has had investigations by scientific people, apparently under the idea that the phenomenon might have been caused by some of the Times's work-people, playing tricks on the magic-lantern principle; but nothing satisfactory has thus far been elucidated. Mr. B—— had this story from Mrs. Gaskell. . . . . Supposing it a ghost, nothing else is so remarkable as its choosing to haunt the precincts of the Times newspaper.

July 29th.—On Saturday, 26th, I took the rail from the Lime Street station for London, *via* the Trent Valley, and reached Blackheath in the evening. . . . .

Sunday morning my wife and I, with J——, railed into London, and drove to the Essex Street Chapel, where Mr. Channing was to preach. The Chapel is the same where Priestley and Belsham used to preach, — one of the plainest houses of worship I was ever in, as simple and undecorated as the faith there inculcated. They retain, however, all the form and ceremonial of the English Established Church, though so modified as to meet the doctrinal views of the Unitarians. There may be good sense in this, inasmuch as it greatly lessens the ministerial labor to have a stated form of prayer, instead of a necessity for extempore outpourings; but it must be, I should think, excessively tedious to the congregation, especially as, having made alterations in these prayers, they cannot attach much idea of sanctity to them.

[Here follows a long record of Mr. Hawthorne's visit to Miss Bacon, — condensed in Our Old Home, in the paper called "Recollections of a Gifted Woman."]

August 2d.—On Wednesday (30th July) we went to Marlborough House to see the Vernon gallery of pictures. They are the works, almost entirely, of English artists of the last and present century, and comprise many famous paintings; and I must acknowledge that I had more enjoyment of them than of those portions of the National Gallery which I had before seen, — including specimens of the grand old masters. My comprehension has not reached their height. I think nothing pleased me more than a picture by Sir David

Wilkie, — The Parish Beadle, with a vagrant boy and a monkey in custody; it is exceedingly good and true throughout, and especially the monkey's face is a wonderful production of genius, condensing within itself the whole moral and pathos of the picture.

Marlborough House was the residence of the Great Duke, and is to be that of the Prince of Wales, when another place is found for the pictures. It adjoins St. James's Palace. In its present state it is not a very splendid mansion, the rooms being small, though handsomely shaped, with vaulted ceilings, and carved white-marble fireplaces. I left S—— here after an hour or two, and walked forth into the hot and busy city with J——. . . . . I called at Routledge's bookshop, in hopes to make an arrangement with him about Miss Bacon's business. But Routledge himself is making a journey in the north, and neither of the partners was there, so that I shall have to go thither some other day. Then we stepped into St. Paul's Cathedral to cool ourselves, and it was delightful so to escape from the sunny, sultry turmoil of Fleet Street and Ludgate, and find ourselves at once in this remote, solemn, shadowy seclusion, marble-cool. O that we had cathedrals in America, were it only for the sensuous luxury! We strolled round the cathedral, and I delighted J—— much by pointing out the monuments of three British generals, who were slain in America in the last war, — the naughty and bloodthirsty little man! We then went to Guildhall, where I thought J—— would like to see Gog and Magog; but he had never heard of those illustrious personages, and took no interest in them. . . . . But truly I am grateful to the piety of former times for raising this vast, cool canopy of marble [St. Paul's] in the midst of the feverish city. I wandered quite round it, and saw, in a remote corner, a monument to the officers of the Coldstream Guards, slain in the Crimea. It was a mural tablet, with the names of the officers on an escutcheon; and two privates of the Guards, in marble bas-relief, were mourning over them. Over the tablet hung two silken banners, new and glossy, with the battles in which the regiment has been engaged inscribed on them, — not merely Crimean but Peninsular battles. These banners will hang there till they drop away in tatters.

After thus refreshing myself in the cathedral, I went again to Routledge's in Farrington Street, and saw one of the firm. He expressed great pleasure at seeing me, as indeed he might, having published and sold, without any profit on my part, uncounted thousands of my books. I introduced the subject of Miss Bacon's work; and he expressed the utmost willingness to do everything in his power towards bringing it before the world, but thought that his firm — it being their business to publish for the largest circle of readers — was not the most eligible for the publication of such a book. Very likely this may be so. At all events, however, I am to send him the manuscript, and he will at least give me his advice and assistance in finding a publisher. He was good enough to express great regret that I had no work of my own to give him for publication; and, truly, I regret it too, since, being a resident in England, I could now have all the publishing privileges of a native author. He presented me with a copy of an illustrated edition of Longfellow's Poems, and I took my leave.

Thence I went to the Picture Gallery at the British Institution, where there are three rooms full of paintings by the first masters, the property of private persons. Every one of them, no doubt, was worth studying for a long, long time; and I suppose I may have given, on an average, a minute to each. What an absurdity it would seem, to pretend to read two or three hundred poems, of all degrees between an epic and a ballad, in an hour or two! And a picture is a poem, only requiring the greater study to be felt and comprehended; because the spectator must necessarily do much for himself towards that end. I saw many beautiful things, — among them some landscapes by Claude, which to the eye were like the flavor of a rich, ripe melon to the palate.

. . . .

August 7th.— Yesterday we took the rail for London, it being a fine, sunny day, though not so very warm as many of the preceding days have been. . . . . We went along Piccadilly as far as the Egyptian Hall. It is quite remarkable how comparatively quiet the town has become, now that the season is over. One can see the difference in all the region west of Temple Bar; and, indeed, either the hot weather or some other cause seems to have operated in assuaging the turmoil in the city itself. I never saw London Bridge so little thronged as yesterday. At the Egyptian Hall, or in the same edifice, there is a gallery of pictures, the property of Lord Ward, who allows the public to see them, five days of the week, without any trouble or restriction, — a great kindness on his Lordship's part, it must be owned. It is a very valuable collection, I presume, containing specimens of many famous old masters; some of the early and hard pictures by Raphael and his master and fellow-pupils, — very curious, and nowise beautiful; a perfect, sunny glimpse of Venice, by Canaletto; and saints, and Scriptural, allegorical, and mythological people, by Titian, Guido, Correggio, and many more names than I can remember. There is likewise a dead Magdalen by Canova, and a Venus by the same, very pretty, and with a vivid light of joyous expression in her face; . . . . also Powers's Greek Slave, in which I see little beauty or merit; and two or three other statues.

. . . . .

We then drove to Ashley Place, to call on Mrs. S. C. Hall, whom we found at home. In fact, Wednesday is her reception-day; although, as now everybody is out of town, we were the only callers. She is an agreeable and kindly woman. She told us that her husband and herself propose going to America next year, and I heartily wish they may meet with a warm and friendly reception. I have been seldom more assured of the existence of a heart than in her; also a good deal of sentiment. She had been visiting Bessie, the widow of Moore, at Sloperton, and gave S—— a rose from his cottage. Such things are very true and unaffected in her. The only wonder is that she has not lost such girlish freshness of feeling as prompts them. We did not see Mr. Hall, he having gone to the Crystal Palace.

Taking our leave, we returned along Victoria Street — a new street, penetrating through what was recently one of the worst parts of the town, and now bordered with large blocks of buildings, in a dreary, half-finished state, and left so for want of funds — till we came to Westminster Abbey. We went in and spent an hour there, wandering all round the nave and aisles, admiring the grand old edifice itself, but finding more to smile at than to admire in the monuments. . . . . . The interior view of the Abbey is better than can be described; the heart aches, as one gazes at it, for lack of power and breadth enough to take its beauty and grandeur in. The effect was heightened by the sun shining through the painted window in the western end, and by the bright sunshine that came through the open portal, and lay on the pavement, — that space so bright, the rest of the vast floor so solemn and sombre. At the western end, in a corner from which spectators are barred out, there is a statue of Wordsworth, which I do not recollect seeing at any former visit. Its only companion in the same nook is Pope's friend, Secretary Craggs.

Downing Street, that famous official precinct, took its name from Sir George Downing, who was proprietor or lessee of property there. He was a native of my own old native town, and his descendants still reside there, — collateral descendants, I suppose, — and follow the dry-goods business (drapers).

August 10*th.* — I journeyed to Liverpool *via* Chester. . . . . One sees a variety of climate, temperature, and season in a ride of two hundred miles, north and south, through England. Near London, for instance, the grain was reaped, and stood in sheaves in the stubble-fields, over which girls and children might be seen gleaning; farther north, the golden, or greenish-golden, crops were waving in the wind. In one part of our way the atmosphere was hot and dry; at another point it had been cooled and refreshed by a heavy thunder-shower, the pools of which still lay along our track. It seems to me that local varieties of weather are more common in this island, and within narrower precincts, than in America. . . . . I never saw England of such a dusky and dusty green before,— almost sunbrowned, indeed. Sometimes the green hedges formed a marked framework to a broad sheet of golden grain-field. As we drew near Oxford, just before reaching the station I had a good view of its domes, towers, and spires,— better, I think, than when J—— and I rambled through the town a month or two ago.

Mr. Frank Scott Haydon, of the Record Office, London, writes me that he has found a "Henry Atte Hawthorne" on a roll which he is transcribing, of the first Edward III. He belonged to the Parish of Aldremeston, in the hundred of Blakenhurste, Worcester County.

August 21st. — Yesterday, at twelve o'clock, I took the steamer for Runcorn, from the pier-head. In the streets, I had noticed that it was a breezy day; but on the river there was a very stiff breeze from the north-east, right ahead, blowing directly in our face the whole way; and truly this river Mersey is never without a breeze, and generally in the direction of its course, — an evil-tempered, unkindly, blustering wind, that you cannot meet without being exasperated by it. As it came straight against us, it was impossible to find a shelter anywhere on deck, except it were behind the stove-pipe; and, besides, the day was overcast and threatening rain. I have undergone very miserable hours on the Mersey, where, in the space of two years, I voyaged thousands of miles, — and this trip to Runcorn reminded me of them, though it was less disagreeable after more than a twelvemonth's respite. We had a good many passengers on board, most of whom were of the second class, and congregated on the forward deck; more women than men, I think, and some of them with their husbands and children. Several produced lunch and bottles, and refreshed themselves very soon after we started. By and by the wind became so disagreeable that I went below, and sat in the cabin, only occasionally looking out, to get a peep at the shores of the river, which I had never before seen above Eastham. However, they are not worth looking at; level and monotonous, without trees or beauty of any kind, — here and there a village, and a modern church, on the low ridge behind; perhaps, a windmill, which the gusty day had set busily to work. The river continues very wide — no river indeed, but an estuary — during almost the whole distance to Runcorn; and nearly at the end of our voyage we approached some abrupt and prominent hills, which, many a time, I have seen on my passages to Rock Ferry, looking blue and dim, and serving for prophets of the weather; for when they can be distinctly seen adown the river, it is a token of coming rain. We met many vessels, and passed many which were beating up against the wind, and which keeled over, so that their decks must have dipped, — schooners and vessels that come from the Bridgewater Canal. We shipped a sea ourselves, which gave the fore-deck passengers a wetting.

Before reaching Runcorn, we stopped to land some passengers at another little port, where there was a pier and a lighthouse, and a church within a few yards of the river-side, — a good many of the river-craft, too, in dock, forming quite a crowd of masts. About ten minutes' further steaming brought us to Runcorn, where were two or three tall manufacturing chimneys, with a pennant of black smoke from each; two vessels of considerable size on the stocks; a church or two; and a meagre, uninteresting, shabby, brick-built town, rising from the edge of the river, with irregular streets, — not village-like, but paved, and looking like a dwarfed, stunted city. I wandered through it till I came to a tall, high, pedestaled windmill on the outer verge, the vans of which were going briskly round. Thence retracing my steps, I stopped at a poor hotel, and took lunch, and, finding that I was in time to take the steamer back, I hurried on board, and we set sail (or steam) before three. I have heard of an old castle at Runcorn, but could discover nothing of it. It was well that I returned so promptly, for we had hardly left the pier before it began to rain, and there was a heavy downfall throughout the voyage homeward. Runcorn is fourteen miles from Liverpool, and is the farthest point to which a steamer runs. I had intended to come home by rail, — a circuitous route, — but the advice of the landlady of the hotel, and the aspect of the weather, and a feeling of general discouragement prevented me.

An incident in S. C. Hall's Ireland, of a stone cross, buried in Cromwell's time, to prevent its destruction by his soldiers. It was forgotten, and became a mere doubtful tradition, but one old man had been told by his father, and he by his father, &c., that it was buried near a certain spot; and at last, two hundred years after the cross was buried, the vicar of the parish dug in that spot and found it. In my (English) romance, an American might bring the tradition from over the sea, and so discover the cross, which had been altogether forgotten.

August 24th. — Day before yesterday I took the rail for Southport, — a cool, generally overcast day, with glimmers of faint sunshine. The ride is through a most uninteresting tract of country, — at first, glimpses of the river, with the thousands of masts in the docks; the dismal outskirts of a great town, still spreading onward, with beginnings of streets, and insulated brick buildings and blocks; farther on, a wide monotony of level plain, and here and there a village and a church; almost always a windmill in sight, there being plenty of breeze to turn its vans on this windy coast. The railway skirts along the sea the whole distance, but is shut out from the sight of it by the low sand-hills, which seem to have been heaped up by the waves. There are one or two lighthouses on the shore. I have not seen a drearier landscape, even in Lancashire.

Reaching Southport at three, I rambled about, with a view to discover whether it be a suitable residence for my family during September. It is a large village, or rather more than a village, which seems to be almost entirely made up of lodging-houses, and, at any rate, has been built up by the influx of summer visitors, — a sandy soil, level, and laid out with well-paved streets, the principal of which are enlivened with bazaars, markets, shops, hotels of various degrees, and a showy vivacity of aspect. There are a great many donkey-carriages, — large vehicles, drawn by a pair of donkeys; bath-chairs, with invalid ladies; refreshment-rooms in great numbers, — a place where everybody seems to be a transitory guest, nobody at home. The main street leads directly down to the sea-shore, along which there is an elevated embankment, with a promenade on the top, and seats, and the toll of a penny. The shore itself, the tide being then low, stretched out interminably seaward, a wide waste of glistering sands; and on the dry border, people were riding on donkeys, with the drivers whipping behind; and children were digging with their little wooden spades; and there were donkey-carriages far out on the sands, — a pleasant and breezy drive. A whole city of bathing-machines was stationed near the shore, and I saw others in the seaward distance. The sea-air was refreshing and exhilarating, and if S—— needs a seaside residence, I should think this might do as well as any other.

I saw a large brick edifice, enclosed within a wall, and with somewhat the look of an almshouse or hospital; and it proved to be an Infirmary, charitably established for the reception of poor invalids, who need sea-air and cannot afford to pay for it. Two or three of such persons were sitting under its windows. I do not think that the visitors of Southport are generally of a very opulent class, but of the middle rank, from

Manchester and other parts of this northern region. The lodging-houses, however, are of sufficiently handsome style and arrangement.

OXFORD.

[Mr. Hawthorne extracted from his recorded Oxford experiences his excursion to Blenheim, but left his observations of the town itself untouched, — and these I now transcribe. — Ed.]

August 31st. — . . . . Yesterday we took the rail for London, and drove across the city to the Paddington station, where we met Bennoch, and set out with him for Oxford. I do not quite understand the matter, but it appears that we were expected guests of Mr. Spiers, a very hospitable gentleman, and Ex-Mayor of Oxford, and a friend of Bennoch and of the Halls. Mr. S. C. Hall met us at the Oxford station, and under his guidance we drove to a quiet, comfortable house in St. Giles Street, where rooms had been taken for us. Durham, the sculptor, is likewise of the party.

After establishing ourselves at these lodgings, we walked forth to take a preliminary glimpse of the city, and Mr. Hall, being familiar with the localities, served admirably as a guide. If I remember aright, I spoke very slightingly of the exterior aspect of Oxford, as I saw it with J—— during an hour or two's stay here, on my way to Southampton (to meet S—— on her return from Lisbon). I am bound to say that my impressions are now very different; and that I find Oxford exceedingly picturesque and rich in beauty and grandeur and in antique stateliness. I do not remember very particularly what we saw, — time-worn fronts of famous colleges and halls of learning everywhere about the streets, and arched entrances; passing through which, we saw bits of sculpture from monkish hands, — the most grotesque and ludicrous faces, as if the slightest whim of these old carvers took shape in stone, the material being so soft and manageable by them; an ancient stone pulpit in the quadrangle of Maudlin College (Magdalen), one of only three now extant in England; a splendid — no, not splendid, but dimly magnificent — chapel, belonging to the same College, with painted windows of rare beauty, not brilliant with diversified hues, but of a sombre tint. In this chapel there is an alabaster monument, — a recumbent figure of the founder's father, as large as life, — which, though several centuries old, is as well preserved as if fresh from the chisel.

In the High Street, which, I suppose, is the noblest old street in England, Mr. Hall pointed out the Crown Inn, where Shakespeare used to spend the night, and was most hospitably welcomed by the pretty hostess (the mother of Sir William Davenant) on his passage between Stratford and London. It is a three-story house, with other houses contiguous, — an old timber mansion, though now plastered and painted of a yellowish hue. The ground-floor is occupied as a shoe-shop; but the rest of the house is still kept as a tavern. . . . .

It is not now term time, and Oxford loses one of its most characteristic features by the absence of the gownsmen; but still there is a good deal of liveliness in the streets. We walked as far as a bridge beyond Maudlin College, and then drove homeward.

At six we went to dine with the hospitable Ex-Mayor, across the wide, tree-bordered street; for his house is nearly opposite our lodgings. He is an intelligent and gentlemanly person, and was Mayor two years ago, and has done a great deal to make peace between the University and the town, heretofore bitterly inimical. His house is adorned with pictures and drawings, and he has an especial taste for art. . . . . The dinner-table was decorated with pieces of plate, vases, and other things, which were presented to him as tokens of public or friendly regard, and approbation of his action in the Mayoralty. After dinner, too, he produced a large silver snuff-box, which had been given him on the same account; in fact, the inscription affirmed that it was one of five pieces of plate so presented. The vases are really splendid, — one of them two feet high, and richly ornamented. It will hold five or six bottles of wine, and he said that it had been filled, and, I believe, sent round as a loving cup at some of his entertainments. He cordially enjoys these things, and his genuine benevolence produces all this excellent hospitality. . . . . But Bennoch proposed a walk, and we set forth. We rambled pretty extensively about the streets, sometimes seeing the shapes of old edifices dimly and doubtfully, it being an overcast night; or catching a partial view of a gray wall, or a pillar, or a Gothic archway, by lamplight. . . . . The clock had some time ago struck eleven, when we were passing under a long extent of antique wall and towers, which were those of Baliol College. Mr. D—— led us into the middle of the street, and showed us a cross, which was paved into it, on a level with the rest of the road.

This was the spot where Latimer and Ridley and another Bishop were martyred in Bloody Mary's time. There is a memorial to them in another street; but this, where I set my foot at nearly midnight, was the very spot where their flesh burned to ashes, and their bones whitened. It has been a most beautiful morning, and I have seen few pleasanter scenes than this street in which we lodge, with its spacious breadth, its two rows of fine old trees, with sidewalks as wide as the whole width of some streets; and, on the opposite side, the row of houses, some of them ancient with picturesque gables, partially disclosed through the intervening foliage. . . . . . From our window we have a slantwise glimpse, to the right, of the walls of St. John's College, and the general aspect of St. Giles. It is of an antiquity not to shame those mediæval halls. Our own lodgings are in a house that seems to be very old, with panelled walls, and beams across the ceilings, lattice-windows in the chambers, and a musty odor such as old houses inevitably have. Nevertheless, everything is extremely neat, clean, and comfortable; and in term time our apartments are occupied by a Mr. Stebbing, whose father is known in literature by some critical writings, and who is a graduate and an admirable scholar. There is a bookcase of five shelves, containing his books, mostly standard works, and indicating a safe and solid taste.

After lunch to-day we (that is, Mrs. Hall, her adopted daughter, S——, and I, with the Ex-Mayor) set forth, in an open barouche, to see the remarkables of Oxford, while the rest of the guests went on foot. We first drew up at New College (a strange name for such an old place, but it was new some time since the Conquest), and went through its quiet and sunny quadrangles, and into its sunny and shadowy gardens. I am in despair about the architecture and old edifices of these Oxford colleges, it is so impossible to express them in words. They are themselves — as the architect left them, and as Time has modified and improved them — the expression of an idea which does not admit of being otherwise expressed, or translated into anything else. Those old battlemented walls around the quadrangles; many gables; the windows with stone pavilions, so very antique, yet some of them adorned with fresh flowers in pots, — a very sweet contrast; the ivy mantling the gray stone; and the infinite repose, both in sunshine and shadow, — it is as if half a dozen bygone centuries had set up their rest here, and as if nothing of the present time ever passed through the deeply recessed archway that shuts in the College from the street. Not but what people have very free admittance; and many parties of young men and girls and children came into the gardens while we were there.

These gardens of New College are indescribably beautiful, — not gardens in an American sense, but lawns of the richest green and softest velvet grass, shadowed over by ancient trees, that have lived a quiet life here for centuries, and have been nursed and tended with such care, and so sheltered from rude winds, that certainly they must have been the happiest of all trees. Such a sweet, quiet, sacred, stately seclusion — so agelong as this has been, and, I hope, will continue to be — cannot exist anywhere else. One side of the garden wall is formed by the ancient wall of the city, which Cromwell's artillery battered, and which still retains its pristine height and strength. At intervals, there are round towers that formed the bastions; that is to say, on the exterior they are round towers, but within, in the garden of the College, they are semicircular recesses, with iron garden-seats arranged round them. The loop-holes through which the archers and musketeers used to shoot still pierce through deep recesses in the wall, which is here about six feet thick. I wish I could put into one sentence the whole impression of this garden, but it could not be done in many pages.

We looked also at the outside of the wall, and Mr. Parker, deeply skilled in the antiquities of the spot, showed us a weed growing, — here in little sprigs, there in large and heavy festoons, — hanging plentifully downward from a shallow root. It is called the Oxford plant, being found only here, and not easily, if at all, introduced anywhere else. It bears a small and pretty blue flower, not altogether unlike the forget-me-not, and we took some of it away with us for a memorial. We went into the chapel of New College, which is in such fresh condition that I think it must be modern; and yet this cannot be, since there are old brasses inlaid into tombstones in the pavement, representing mediæval ecclesiastics and college dignitaries; and busts against the walls, in antique garb; and old painted windows, unmistakable in their antiquity. But there is likewise a window, lamentable to look at, which was painted by Sir Joshua Reynolds, and exhibits strikingly the difference between the work of a man who performed it merely as a matter of taste and business, and what was done religiously and with the whole heart; at least, it shows that the artists and public of the last age had no sympathy with Gothic art. In the chancel of this church there are more painted windows, which I take to be modern, too, though they are in much better taste, and have an infinitely better effect, than Sir Joshua's. At any rate, with the sunshine through them, they looked very beautiful, and tinted the high altar and the pavement with brilliant hues.

The sacristan opened a tall and narrow little recess in the wall of the chancel, and showed it entirely filled with the crosier of William of Wickham. It appears to be made of silver gilt, and is a most rich and elaborate relic, at least six feet high. Modern art cannot, or does not, equal the chasing and carving of this splendid crosier, which is enriched with figures of saints and apostles, and various Gothic devices, — very minute, but all executed as faithfully as if the artist's salvation had depended upon every notch he made in the silver. . . . .

Leaving New College, Bennoch and I, under Mr. Parker's guidance, walked round Christ Church meadows, part of our way lying along the banks of the Cherwell, which unites with the Isis to form the Thames, I believe. The Cherwell is a narrow and remarkably sluggish stream; but is deep in spots, and capriciously so, — so that a person may easily step from knee deep to fifteen feet in depth. A gentleman present used a queer expression in reference to the drowning of two college men; he said "it was an *awkward* affair." I think this is equal to Longfellow's story of the Frenchman who avowed himself very much "displeased" at the news of his father's death. At the confluence of the

Cherwell and Isis we saw a good many boats, belonging to the students of the various colleges; some of them being very large and handsome barges, capable of accommodating a numerous party, with room on board for dancing and merry-making. Some of them are calculated to be drawn by horses, in the manner of canal-boats; others are propellable by oars. It is practicable to perform the voyage between Oxford and London — a distance of about one hundred and thirty miles — in three days. The students of Oxford are famous boatmen; there is a constant rivalship, on this score, among the different colleges; and annually, I believe, there is a match between Oxford and Cambridge. The Cambridge men beat the Oxonians in this year's trial.

On our return into the city, we passed through Christ Church, which, as regards the number of students, is the most considerable college of the University. It has a stately dome; but my memory is confused with battlements, towers, and gables, and Gothic staircases and cloisters. If there had been nothing else in Oxford but this one establishment, my anticipations would not have been disappointed. The bell was tolling for worship in the chapel; and Mr. Parker told us that Dr. Pusey is a canon, or in some sort of dignity, in Christ Church, and would soon probably make his appearance in the quadrangle, on his way to chapel; so we walked to and fro, waiting an opportunity to see him. A gouty old dignitary, in a white surplice, came hobbling along from one extremity of the court; and by and by, from the opposite corner, appeared Dr. Pusey, also in a white surplice, and with a lady by his side. We met him, and

I stared pretty fixedly at him, as I well might; for he looked on the ground, as if conscious that he would be stared at. He is a man past middle life, of sufficient breadth and massiveness, with a pale, intellectual, manly face. He was talking with the lady, and smiled, but not jollily. Mr. Parker, who knows him, says that he is a man of kind and gentle affections. The lady was his niece.

Thence we went through High Street and Broad Street, and passing by Baliol College, — a most satisfactory pile and range of old towered and gabled edifices, — we came to the cross on the pavement, which is supposed to mark the spot where the bishops were martyred. But Mr. Parker told us the mortifying fact, that he had ascertained that this could not possibly have been the genuine spot of martyrdom, which must have taken place at a point within view, but considerably too far off to be moistened by any tears that may be shed here. It is too bad. We concluded the rambles of the day by visiting the gardens of St. John's College; and I desire, if possible, to say even more in admiration of them than of those of New College, — such beautiful lawns, with tall, ancient trees, and heavy clouds of foliage, and sunny glimpses through archways of leafy branches, where, to-day, we could see parties of girls, making cheerful contrast with the sombre walls and solemn shade. The world, surely, has not another place like Oxford; it is a despair to see such a place and ever to leave it, for it would take a lifetime and more than one, to comprehend and enjoy it satisfactorily.

At dinner, to-day, the golden vases were all ranged

on the table, the largest and central one containing a most magnificent bouquet of dahlias and other bright-hued flowers.

. . . . .

CHRIST CHURCH.

On Tuesday, our first visit was to Christ Church, where we saw the large and stately hall, above a hundred feet long by forty wide, and fifty to the top of its carved oaken roof, which is ornamented with festoons, as it were, and pendants of solid timber. The walls are panelled with oak, perhaps half-way upward, and above are the rows of arched windows on each side; but, near the upper end, two great windows come nearly to the floor. There is a dais, where the great men of the College and the distinguished guests sit at table, and the tables of the students are arranged along the length of the hall. All around, looking down upon those who sit at meat, are the portraits of a multitude of illustrious personages who were members of the learned fraternity in times past; not a portrait being admitted there (unless it be a king, and I remember only Henry VIII.) save those who were actually students on the foundation, receiving the eleemosynary aid of the College. Most of them were divines; but there are likewise many statesmen, eminent during the last three hundred years, and, among many earlier ones, the Marquis of Wellesley and Canning. It is an excellent idea, for their own glory, and as examples to the rising generations, to have this multitude of men, who have done good and great things, before the eyes of those who ought to do as well as they, in their own time. Archbishops, Prime Ministers, poets, deep scholars, — but, doubtless, an outward success has generally been their claim to this position, and Christ Church may have forgotten a better man than the best of them. It is not, I think, the tendency of English life, nor of the education of their colleges, to lead young men to high moral excellence, but to aim at illustrating themselves in the sight of mankind.

. . . . .

Thence we went into the kitchen, which is arranged very much as it was three centuries ago, with two immense fireplaces. There was likewise a gridiron, which, without any exaggeration, was large enough to have served for the martyrdom of St. Lawrence. The college dinners are good, but plain, and cost the students one shilling and eleven pence each, being rather cheaper than a similar one could be had at an inn. There is no provision for breakfast or supper in commons; but they can have these meals sent to their rooms from the buttery, at a charge proportioned to the dishes they order. There seems to be no necessity for a great expenditure on the part of Oxford students.

From the kitchen we went to the chapel, which is the cathedral of Oxford, and well worth seeing, if there had not been so many other things to see. It is now under repair, and there was a great heap of old woodwork and panelling lying in one of the aisles, which had been stripped away from some of the ancient pillars, leaving them as good as new. There is a shrine of a saint, with a wooden canopy over it; and some painted glass, old and new; and a statue of Cyril Jackson, with a face of shrewdness and insight; and busts, as mural monuments.

Our next visit was to

MERTON COLLEGE,

which, though not one of the great colleges, is as old as any of them, and looks exceedingly venerable. We were here received by a friend of Mr. Spiers, in his academic cap, but without his gown, which is not worn, except in term time. He is a very civil gentleman, and showed us some antique points of architecture, — such as a Norman archway, with a passage over it, through which the Queen of Charles I. used to go to chapel; and an edifice of the thirteenth century, with a stone roof, which is considered to be very curious.

How ancient is the aspect of these college quadrangles! so gnawed by time as they are, so crumbly, so blackened, and so gray where they are not black, — so quaintly shaped, too, with here a line of battlement and there a row of gables; and here a turret, with probably a winding stair inside; and lattice windows, with stone mullions, and little panes of glass set in lead; and the cloisters, with a long arcade, looking upon the green or pebbled enclosure. The quality of the stone has a great deal to do with the apparent antiquity. It is a stone found in the neighborhood of Oxford, and very soon begins to crumble and decay superficially, when exposed to the weather; so that twenty years do the work of a hundred, so far as appearances go. If you strike one of the old walls with a stick, a portion of it comes powdering down. The effect of this decay is very picturesque, and is especially striking, I think, on edifices of classic architecture, such as some of the Oxford colleges are, greatly enriching the Grecian columns, which look so cold when the outlines are hard and distinct. The Oxford people, however, are tired of this crumbly stone, and when repairs are necessary, they use a more durable material, which does not well assort with the antiquity into which it is intruded.

Mr. E—— showed us the library of Merton College. It occupies two sides of an old building, and has a very delightful fragrance of ancient books. The halls containing it are vaulted, and roofed with oak, not carved and ornamented, but laid flat, so that they look very like a grand and spacious old garret. All along, there is a row of alcoves on each side, with rude benches and reading-desks, in the simplest style, and nobody knows how old. The books look as old as the building. The more valuable were formerly chained to the bookcases; and a few of them have not yet broken their chains. It was a good emblem of the dark and monkish ages, when learning was imprisoned in their cloisters, and chained in their libraries, in the days when the schoolmaster had not yet gone abroad. Mr. E—— showed us a very old copy of the Bible; and a vellum manuscript, most beautifully written in black letter and illuminated, of the works of Duns Scotus, who was a scholar of Merton College.

He then showed us the chapel, a large part of which has been renewed and ornamented with pictured windows and other ecclesiastical splendor, and paved with encaustic tiles, according to the Puseyite taste of the day; for Merton has adopted the Puseyite doctrines, and is one of their chief strongholds in Oxford. If they do no other good, they at least do much for preservation and characteristic restoration of the old English churches; but perhaps, even here, there is as much antiquity spoiled as retained. In the portion of the chapel not yet restored, we saw the rude old pavement, inlaid with gravestones, in some of which were brasses, with the figures of the college dignitaries, whose dust slumbered beneath; and I think it was here that I saw the tombstone of Anthony-à-Wood, the gossiping biographer of the learned men of Oxford.

From the chapel we went into the college gardens, which are very pleasant, and possess the advantage of looking out on the broad verdure of Christ Church meadows and the river beyond. We loitered here awhile, and then went to Mr. E——'s rooms, to which the entrance is by a fine old staircase. They had a very comfortable aspect, — a wainscoted parlor and bedroom, as nice and cosey as a bachelor could desire, with a good collection of theological books; and on a peg hung his gown, with a red border about it, denoting him to be a proproctor. He was kind enough to order a lunch, consisting of bread and cheese, college ale, and a certain liquor called "Archdeacon." . . . . We ate and drank, ... and, bidding farewell to good Mr. E——, we pursued our way to the

RATCLIFFE LIBRARY.

This is a very handsome edifice, of a circular shape; the lower story consisting altogether of arches, open on all sides, as if to admit anybody to the learning here stored up. I always see great beauty and lightsomeness in these classic and Grecian edifices, though they seem cold and intellectual, and not to have had their mortar moistened with human life-blood, nor to have the mystery of human life in them, as Gothic structures do. The library is in a large and beautiful room, in the story above the basement, and, as far as I saw, consisted chiefly or altogether of scientific works. I saw Silliman's Journal on one of the desks, being the only trace of American science, or American learning or ability in any department, which I discovered in the University of Oxford. After seeing the library, we went to the top of the building, where we had an excellent view of Oxford and the surrounding country. Then we went to the Convocation Hall, and afterwards to the theatre, where S—— sat down in the Chancellor's chair, which is very broad, and ponderously wrought of oak. I remember little here, except the amphitheatre of benches, and the roof, which seems to be supported by golden ropes, and on the wall, opposite the door, some full-length portraits, among which one of that ridiculous coxcomb, George IV., was the most prominent. These kings thrust themselves impertinently forward by bust, statue, and picture, on all occasions, and it is not wise in them to show their shallow foreheads among men of mind.

THE BODLEIAN LIBRARY.

Mr. Spiers tried to get us admittance to the Bodleian Library; but this is just the moment when it is closed for the purpose of being cleaned; so we missed seeing the principal halls of this library, and were only admitted into what was called the Picture Gallery. This, however, satisfied all my desires, so far as the backs of books are concerned, for they extend through a gallery, running round three sides of a quadrangle, making an aggregate length of more than four hundred feet, — a solid array of bookcases, full of books, within a protection of open iron-work. Up and down the gallery there are models of classic temples; and about midway in its extent stands a brass statue of Earl Pembroke, who was Chancellor of the University in James I.'s time; not in scholarly garb, however, but in plate and mail, looking indeed like a thunderbolt of war. I rapped him with my knuckles, and he seemed to be solid metal, though, I should imagine, hollow at heart. A thing which interested me very much was the lantern of Guy Fawkes. It was once tinned, no doubt, but is now nothing but rusty iron, partly broken. As this is called the Picture Gallery, I must not forget the pictures, which are ranged in long succession over the bookcases, and include almost all Englishmen whom the world has ever heard of, whether in statesmanship or literature. I saw a canvas on which had once been a lovely and unique portrait of Mary of Scotland; but it was consigned to a picture-cleaner to be cleansed, and, discovering that it was painted over another picture, he had the curiosity to clean poor Mary quite away, thus revealing a wishy-washy woman's face, which now hangs in the gallery. I am so tired of seeing notable things that I almost wish that whatever else is remarkable in Oxford could be obliterated in some similar manner.

From the Bodleian we went to

THE TAYLOR INSTITUTE,

which was likewise closed; but the woman who had it in charge had formerly been a servant of Mr. Spiers, and he so overpersuaded her that she finally smiled and admitted us. It would truly have been a pity to miss it; for here, on the basement floor, are the original models of Chantrey's busts and statues, great and small; and in the rooms above are a far richer treasure, — a large collection of original drawings by Raphael and Michael Angelo. These are far better for my purpose than their finished pictures, — that is to say, they bring me much closer to the hands that drew them and the minds that imagined them. It is like looking into their brains, and seeing the first conception before it took shape outwardly (I have somewhere else said about the same thing of such sketches). I noticed one of Raphael's drawings, representing the effect of eloquence; it was a man speaking in the centre of a group, between whose ears and the orator's mouth connecting lines were drawn. Raphael's idea must have been to compose his picture in such a way that their auricular organs should not fail to be in a proper relation with the eloquent voice; and though this relation would not have been individually traceable in the finished picture, yet the general effect — that of deep and entranced attention — would have been produced.

In another room there are some copies of Raphael's cartoons, and some queer mediæval pictures, as stiff and ugly as can well be conceived, yet successful in telling their own story. We looked a little while at these, and then, thank Heaven! went home and dressed for dinner. I can write no more to-day. Indeed, what a mockery it is to write at all!

[Here follows the drive to Cumnor Place, Stanton Harcourt, Nuneham Courtney, Godstowe, &c., — already published in Our Old Home. — Ed.]

September 9th. — The morning after our excursion on the Thames was as bright and beautiful as many preceding ones had been. After breakfast S—— and I walked a little about the town, and bought Thomas à Kempis, in both French and English, for U——. . . . . Mr. De la Motte, the photographer, had breakfasted with us, and Mr. Spiers wished him to take a photograph of our whole party. So, in the first place, before the rest were assembled, he made an experimental group of such as were there; and I did not like my own aspect very much. Afterwards, when we were all come, he arranged us under a tree in the garden, — Mr. and Mrs. Spiers, with their eldest son, Mr. and Mrs. Hall and Fanny, Mr. Addison, my wife and me, — and stained the glass with our figures and faces in the twinkling of an eye; not S——'s face, however, for she turned it away, and left only a portion of her bonnet and dress, — and Mrs. Hall, too, refused to countenance the proceeding. But all the rest of us were caught to the life, and I was really a little startled at recognizing myself so apart from myself, and done so quickly too.

This was the last important incident of our visit to Oxford, except that Mr. Spiers was again most hospitable at lunch. Never did anybody attend more faithfully to the comfort of his friends than does this good gentleman. But he has shown himself most kind in every possible way, and I shall always feel truly grateful. No better way of showing our sense of his hospitality, and all the trouble he has taken for us (and our memory of him), has occurred to us, than to present him with a set of my Tales and Romances; so, by the next steamer, I shall write to Ticknor and Fields to send them, elegantly bound, and S—— will emblazon his coat of arms in each volume. He accompanied us and Mr. and Mrs. Hall to the railway station, and we left Oxford at two o'clock.

It had been a very pleasant visit, and all the persons whom we met were kind and agreeable, and disposed to look at one another in a sunny aspect. I saw a good deal of Mr. Hall. He is a thoroughly genuine man, of kind heart and true affections, a gentleman of taste and refinement, and full of honor.

On the Saturday after our return to Blackheath, we went to

HAMPTON COURT,

about which, as I have already recorded a visit to it, I need say little here. But I was again impressed with the stately grandeur of Wolsey's great Hall, with its great window at each end, and one side window, descending almost to the floor, and a row of windows on each side, high towards the roof, and throwing down their many-colored light on the stone pavement, and on the Gobelin tapestry, which must have been gorgeously rich when the walls were first clothed with it. I fancied, then, that no modern architect could produce so fine a room; but oddly enough, in the great entrance-hall of the Euston Station, yesterday, I could not see how this last fell very much short of Wolsey's Hall in grandeur. We were quite wearied in passing through the endless suites of rooms in Hampton Court, and gazing at the thousands of pictures; it is too much for one day, — almost enough for one life, in such measure as life can be bestowed on pictures. It would have refreshed us had we spent half the time in wandering about the grounds, which, as we glimpsed at them from the windows of the Palace, seemed very beautiful, though laid out with an antique formality of straight lines and broad gravelled paths. Before the central window there is a beautiful sheet of water, and a fountain upshooting itself and plashing into it, with a continuous and pleasant sound. How beautifully the royal robe of a monarchy is embroidered! Palaces, pictures, parks! They do enrich life; and kings and aristocracies cannot keep these things to themselves, they merely take care of them for others. Even a king, with all the glory that can be shed around him, is but the liveried and bedizened footman of his people, and the toy of their delight. I am very glad that I came to this country while the English are still playing with such a toy.

Yesterday J—— and I left Blackheath, and reached Liverpool last night. The rest of my family will follow in a few days; and so finishes our residence in Bennoch's house, where I, for my part, have spent some of the happiest hours that I have known since we left our American home. It is a strange, vagabond, gypsy sort of life, — this that we are leading; and I know not whether we shall finally be spoiled for any other, or shall enjoy our quiet Wayside, as we never did before, when once we reach it again.

. . . . .

The evening set in misty and obscure; and it was dark almost when J—— and I arrived at the landing stage on our return. I was struck with the picturesque effect of the high tower and tall spire of St.

Nicholas, rising upward, with dim outline, into the duskiness; while midway of its height the dial-plates of an illuminated clock blazed out, like two great eyes of a giant.

September 13th. — On Saturday my wife, with all her train, arrived at Mrs. B——'s; and on Tuesday — vagabonds as we are — we again struck our tent, and set out for

SOUTHPORT.

I do not know what sort of character it will form in the children, — this unsettled, shifting, vagrant life, with no central home to turn to, except what we carry in ourselves. It was a windy day, and, judging by the look of the trees, on the way to Southport, it must be almost always windy, and with the blast in one prevailing direction; for invariably their branches, and the whole contour and attitude of the tree, turn from seaward, with a strangely forlorn aspect. Reaching Southport, we took an omnibus, and under the driver's guidance came to our tall stone house, fronting on the sands, and styled "Brunswick Terrace." . . . .

The English system of lodging-houses has its good points; but it is, nevertheless, a contrivance for bearing the domestic cares of home about with you whithersoever you go; and immediately you have to set about producing your own bread and cheese. However, Fanny took most of this trouble off our hands, though there was inevitably the stiffness and discomfort of a new housekeeping on the first day of our arrival; besides that, it was cool, and the wind whistled and grumbled and eddied into the chinks of the house.

Meanwhile, in all my experience of Southport, I have never yet seen the sea, but only an interminable breadth of sands, looking pooly or plashy in some places, and barred across with drier reaches of sand, but no expanse of water. It must be miles and miles, at low water, to the veritable seashore. We are about twenty miles north of Liverpool, on the border of the Irish Sea; and Ireland and, I suppose, the Isle of Man intervene betwixt us and the ocean, not much to our benefit; for the air of the English coast, under ocean influences, is said to be milder than when it comes across the land, — milder, therefore, above or below Ireland, because then the Gulf Stream ameliorates it.

Betimes, the forenoon after our arrival, I had to take the rail to Liverpool, but returned, a little after five, in the midst of a rain, — still low water and interminable sands; still a dreary, howling blast. We had a cheerful fireside, however, and should have had a pleasant evening, only that the wind on the sea made us excessively drowsy. This morning we awoke to hear the wind still blustering, and blowing up clouds, with fitful little showers, and soon blowing them away again, and letting the brightest of sunshine fall over the plashy waste of sand. We have already walked forth on the shore with J—— and R——, who pick up shells, and dig wells in the sand with their little wooden spades; but soon we saw a rainbow on the western sky, and then a shower came spattering down upon us in good earnest. We first took refuge under the bridge that stretches between the two portions of the promenade; but as there was a chill draught there, we made the best of our way home. The sun has now again come out brightly, though the wind is still tumbling a great many clouds about the sky.

. . . . . .

Evening. — Later, I walked out with U——, and, looking seaward, we saw the foam and spray of the advancing tide, tossed about on the verge of the horizon, — a long line, like the crests and gleaming helmets of an army. In about half an hour we found almost the whole waste of sand covered with water, and white waves breaking out all over it; but, the bottom being so nearly level, and the water so shallow, there was little of the spirit and exultation of the sea in a strong breeze. Of the long line of bathing-machines, one after another was hitched to a horse, and trundled forth into the water, where, at a long distance from shore, the bathers found themselves hardly middle deep.

September 19*th.* — The wind grumbled and made itself miserable all last night, and this morning it is still howling as ill-naturedly as ever, and roaring and rumbling in the chimneys. The tide is far out, but, from an upper window, I fancied, at intervals, that I could see the plash of the surf-wave on the distant limit of the sand; perhaps, however, it was only a gleam on the sky. Constantly there have been sharp spatters of rain, hissing and rattling against the windows, while a little before or after, or perhaps simultaneously, a rainbow, somewhat watery of texture, paints itself on the western clouds. Gray, sullen clouds hang about the sky, or sometimes cover it with a uniform dulness; at other times, the portions towards the sun gleam almost lightsomely; now, there may be an airy glimpse of clear blue sky in a fissure of the clouds; now, the very brightest of sunshine comes out all of a sudden, and gladdens everything. The breadth of sands has a various aspect, according as there are pools, or moisture enough to glisten, or a drier tract; and where the light gleams along a yellow ridge or bar, it is like sunshine itself. Certainly the temper of the day shifts; but the smiles come far the seldomest, and its frowns and angry tears are most reliable. By seven o'clock pedestrians began to walk along the promenade, close buttoned against the blast; later, a single bathing-machine got under way, by means of a horse, and travelled forth seaward; but within what distance it finds the invisible margin I cannot say, — at all events, it looks like a dreary journey. Just now I saw a sea-gull, wheeling on the blast, close in towards the promenade.

September 21*st.* — Yesterday morning was bright, sunny and windy, and cool and exhilarating. I went to Liverpool at eleven, and, returning at five, found the weather still bright and cool. The temperature, methinks, must soon diminish the population of Southport, which, judging from appearances, must be mainly made up of temporary visitors. There is a newspaper, The Southport Visitor, published weekly, and containing a register of all the visitants in the various hotels and lodging-houses. It covers more than two sides of the paper, to the amount of some hundreds. The guests come chiefly from Liverpool, Manchester, and the neighboring country-towns, and belong to the middle classes. It is not a fashionable watering-place. Only one nobleman's name, and those of two or three baronets, now adorn the list. The people whom we see loitering along the beach and the promenade have, at best, a well-to-do, tradesmanlike air. I do not find that there are any public amusements; nothing but strolling on the sands, donkey-riding, or drives in donkey-carts; and solitary visitors must find it a dreary place. Yet one or two of the streets are brisk and lively, and, being well thronged, have a holiday aspect. There are no carriages in town save donkey-carts; some of which are drawn by three donkeys abreast, and are large enough to hold a whole family. These conveyances will take you far out on the sands through wet and dry. The beach is haunted by The Flying Dutchman, — a sort of boat on wheels, schooner-rigged with sails, and which sometimes makes pretty good speed, with a fair wind.

This morning we have been walking with J—— and R—— out over the "ribbed sea sands," a good distance from shore. Throughout the week, the tides will be so low as not to cover the shallow basin of this bay, if a bay it be. The weather was sullen, with now and then a faint gleam of sunshine, lazily tracing our shadows on the sand; the wind rather quieter than on preceding days. . . . . In the sunshine the sands seem to be frequented by great numbers of gulls, who begin to find the northern climate too wintry. You see their white wings in the sunlight, but they become almost or quite invisible in the shade. We shall soon have an opportunity of seeing how a watering-place looks when the season is quite over; for we have concluded to remain here till December, and everybody else will take flight in a week or two.

A short time ago, in the evening, in a street of Liverpool, I saw a decent man, of the lower orders, taken much aback by being roughly brushed against by a rowdy fellow. He looked after him, and exclaimed indignantly, "Is that a Yankee?" It shows the kind of character we have here.

October 7th.—On Saturday evening I gave a dinner to Bennoch, at the Adelphi Hotel. The chief point or characteristic of English customs was, that Mr. Radley, our landlord, himself attended at table, and officiated as chief waiter. He has a fortune of £100,000,—half a million of dollars,—and is an elderly man of good address and appearance. In America, such a man would very probably be in Congress; at any rate, he would never conceive the possibility of changing plates, or passing round the table with hock and champagne. Some of his hock was a most rich and imperial wine, such as can hardly be had on the Rhine itself. There were eight gentlemen besides Bennoch.

A donkey, the other day, stubbornly refusing to come out of a boat which had brought him across the Mersey; at last, after many kicks had been applied, and other persecutions of that kind, a man stepped forward, addressing him affectionately, "Come along, brother,"—and the donkey obeyed at once.

October 26th.—On Thursday, instead of taking the rail for Liverpool, I set out, about eleven, for a long walk. It was an overcast morning, such as in New England would have boded rain; but English clouds are not nearly so portentous as American in that respect. Accordingly, the sun soon began to peep through crevices, and I had not gone more than a mile or two when it shone a little too warmly for comfort, yet not more than I liked. It was very much like our pleasant October days at home; indeed, the climates of the two countries more nearly coincide during the present month than at any other season of the year. The air was almost perfectly still; but once in a while it stirred, and breathed coolly in my face; it is very delightful, this latent freshness, in a warm atmosphere.

The country about Southport has as few charms as it is possible for any region to have. In the close neighborhood of the shore, it is nothing but sand-hillocks, covered with coarse grass; and this is the original nature of the whole site on which the town stands, although it is now paved, and has been covered with soil enough to make gardens, and to nourish here and there a few trees. A little farther inland the surface seems to have been marshy, but has been drained by ditches across the fields and along the roadside; and the fields are embanked on all sides with parapets of earth which appear as if intended to keep out inundations. In fact, Holland itself cannot be more completely on a level with the sea. The only dwellings are the old, whitewashed stone cottages, with thatched roofs, on the brown straw of which grow various weeds and mosses, brightening it with green patches, and sprouting along the ridgepole, — the homeliest hovels that ever mortals lived in, and which they share with pigs and cows at one end. Hens, too, run in and out of the door. One or two of these hovels bore signs, "Licensed to sell beer, ale, and tobacco," and generally there were an old woman and some children visible. In all cases there was a ditch, full of water, close at hand, stagnant, and often quite covered with a growth of water-weeds, — very unwholesome, one would think, in the neighborhood of a dwelling; and, in truth, the children and grown people did look pale.

In the fields, along the roadside, men and women were harvesting their carrots and other root-crops, especially digging potatoes, — the pleasantest of all farm labor, in my opinion, there being such a continual interest in opening the treasures of each hill. As I went on, the country began to get almost imperceptibly less flat, and there was some little appearance of trees. I had determined to go to Omskirk, but soon got out of the way, and came to a little hamlet that looked antique and picturesque, with its small houses of stone and brick, built with the one material and repaired with the other perhaps ages afterward. Here I inquired my way of a woman, who told me, in broad Lancashire dialect, "that I maun go back, and turn to my left, till I came to a finger-post"; and so I did, and found another little hamlet, the principal object in which was a public house, with a large sign, representing a dance round a May-pole. It was now about one o'clock; so I entered, and, being ushered into what, I suppose, they called the coffee-room, I asked for some cold meat and ale. There was a jolly, round, rather comely woman for a hostess, with a free, hospitable, yet rather careless manner.

The coffee-room smelt rather disagreeably of bad tobacco-smoke, and was shabbily furnished with an old sofa and flag-bottomed chairs, and adorned with a print of "Old Billy," a horse famous for a longevity of about sixty years; and also with colored engravings of old-fashioned hunting-scenes, conspicuous with scarlet coats. There was a very small bust of Milton on the mantel-piece. By and by the remains of an immense round of beef, three quarters cut away, were put on the table; then some smoking-hot potatoes; and finally the hostess told me that their own dinner was just ready, and so she had brought me in some hot chops, thinking I might prefer them to the cold meat. I did prefer them; and they were stewed or fried chops, instead of broiled, and were very savory. There was household bread too, and rich cheese, and a pint of ale, home brewed, not very mighty, but good to quench thirst, and, by way of condiment, some pickled cabbage; so, instead of a lunch, I made quite a comfortable dinner. Moreover, there was a cold pudding on the table, and I called for a clean plate, and helped myself to some of it. It was of rice, and was strewn over, rather than intermixed, with some kinds of berries, the nature of which I could not exactly make out.

I then set forth again. It was still sunny and warm, and I walked more slowly than before dinner; in fact, I did little more than lounge along, sitting down, at last, on the stone parapet of a bridge.

The country grew more pleasant, more sylvan, and, though still of a level character, not so drearily flat. Soon appeared the first symptom that I had seen of a gentleman's residence, — a lodge at a park gate, then a long stretch of wall, with a green lawn, and afterwards an extent of wooded land; then another gateway, with a neat lodge on each side of it, and, lastly, another extent of wood. The Hall or Mansion-house, however, was nowhere apparent, being, doubtless, secluded deep and far within its grounds. I inquired of a boy who was the owner of the estate, and he answered, "Mr. Scarybrick"; and no doubt it is a family of local eminence.

Along the road, — an old inn; some aged stone houses, built for merely respectable occupants; a canal, with two canal-boats, heaped up with a cargo of potatoes; two little girls, who were watching lest some cows should go astray, and had their two little chairs by the roadside, and their dolls and other playthings, and so followed the footsteps of the cows all day long. I met two boys, coming from Omskirk, mounted on donkeys, with empty panniers, on which they had carried vegetables to market. Finally, between two and three o'clock, I saw the great tower of Omskirk Church, with its spire, not rising out of the tower, but sprouting up close beside it; and, entering the town, I directed my steps first to this old church.

OMSKIRK CHURCH.

It stands on a gentle eminence, sufficient to give it a good site, and has a pavement of flat gravestones in front. It is doubtless, as regards its foundation, a very ancient church, but has not exactly a venerable aspect, being in too good repair, and much restored in various parts; not ivy-grown, either, though green with moss here and there. The tower is square and immensely massive, and might have supported a very lofty spire; so that it is the more strange that what spire it has should be so oddly stuck beside it, springing out of the church wall. I should have liked well enough to enter the church, as it is the burial-place of the Earls of Derby, and perhaps may contain some interesting monuments; but as it was all shut up, and even the iron gates of the churchyard closed and locked, I merely looked at the outside.

From the church, a street leads to the market-place, in which I found a throng of men and women, it being market-day; wares of various kinds, tin, earthen, and cloth, set out on the pavements; droves of pigs; ducks and fowls; baskets of eggs; and a man selling quack medicines, recommending his nostrums as well as he could. The aspect of the crowd was very English,—portly and ruddy women; yeomen with small-clothes and broad-brimmed hats, all very quiet and heavy and good-humored. Their dialect was so provincial that I could not readily understand more than here and there a word.

But, after all, there were few traits that could be made a note of. I soon grew weary of the scene, and so I went to the railway station, and waited there nearly an hour for the train to take me to Southport. Omskirk is famous for its gingerbread, which women sell to the railway passengers at a sixpence for a rouleau of a dozen little cakes.

November 30th.—A week ago last Monday, Herman Melville came to see me at the Consulate, looking much as he used to do, and with his characteristic gravity and reserve of manner. . . . . We soon found ourselves on pretty much our former terms of sociability and confidence. . . . . He is thus far on his way to Constantinople. I do not wonder that he found it necessary to take an airing through the world, after so many years of toilsome pen-labor, following upon so wild and adventurous a youth as his was. I invited him to come and stay with us at Southport, as long as he might remain in this vicinity, and accordingly he did come the next day. . . . . On Wednesday we took a pretty long walk together, and sat down in a hollow among the sand-hills, sheltering ourselves from the high cool wind. Melville, as he always does, began to reason of Providence and futurity, and of everything else that lies beyond human ken. . . . . He has a very high and noble nature, and is better worth immortality than the most of us. . . . . On Saturday we went to Chester together. I love to take every opportunity of going to Chester; it being the one only place, within easy reach of Liverpool, which possesses any old English interest.

. . . .

We went to

THE CATHEDRAL.

Its gray nave impressed me more than at any former visit. Passing into the cloisters, an attendant took possession of us, and showed us about.

Within the choir there is a profusion of very rich oaken carving, both on the screen that separates it from the nave, and on the seats and walls; very curious and most elaborate, and lavished (one would say) most wastefully, where nobody would think of looking for it, — where, indeed, amid the dimness of the cathedral, the exquisite detail of the elaboration could not possibly be seen. Our guide lighted some of the gas-burners, of which there are many hundreds, to help us see them; but it required close scrutiny, even then. It must have been out of the question, when the whole means of illumination were only a few smoky torches or candles. There was a row of niches, where the monks used to stand, for four hours together, in the performance of some of their services; and to relieve them a little, they were allowed partially to sit on a projection of the seats, which were turned up in the niche for that purpose; but if they grew drowsy, so as to fail to balance themselves, the seat was so contrived as to slip down, thus bringing the monk to the floor. These projections on the seats are each and all of them carved with curious devices, no two alike. The guide showed us one, representing, apparently, the first quarrel of a new-married couple, wrought with wonderful expression. Indeed, the artist never failed to bring out his idea in the most striking manner, — as, for instance, Satan, under the guise of a lion, devouring a sinner bodily; and again in the figure of a dragon, with a man half-way down his gullet, the legs hanging out. The carver may not have seen anything grotesque in this, nor intended it at all by way of joke; but certainly there would appear to be a grim mirthfulness in some of the designs. One does not see why such fantasies should be strewn about the holy interior of a cathedral, unless it were intended to contain everything that belongs to the heart of man, both upward and downward.

In a side aisle of the choir, we saw a tomb, said to be that of the Emperor Henry IV. of Germany, though on very indistinct authority. This is an oblong tomb, carved, and, on one side, painted with bright colors and gilded. During a very long period it was built and plastered into the wall, and the exterior side was white-washed; but, on being removed, the inner side was found to have been ornamented with gold and color, in the manner in which we now see it. If this were customary with tombs, it must have added vastly to the gorgeous magnificence, to which the painted windows and polished pillars and ornamented ceilings contributed so much. In fact, a cathedral in its fresh estate seems to have been like a pavilion of the sunset, all purple and gold; whereas now it more resembles deepest and grayest twilight.

Afterwards, we were shown into the ancient refectory, now used as the city grammar school, and furnished with the usual desks and seats for the boys. In one corner of this large room was the sort of pulpit or elevated seat, with a broken staircase of stone ascending to it, where one of the monks used to read to his brethren, while sitting at their meals. The desks were cut and carved with the scholars' knives, just as they used to be in the school-rooms where I was a scholar. Thence we passed into the chapter-house, but, before that, we went through a small room, in which Melville opened a cupboard, and discovered a dozen or two of wine-bottles; but our guide told us that they were now empty, and never were meant for jollity, having held only sacramental wine. In the chapter-house, we saw the library, some of the volumes of which were antique folios. There were two dusty and tattered banners hanging on the wall, and the attendant promised to make us laugh by something that he would tell us about them. The joke was that these two banners had been in the battle of Bunker Hill; and our countrymen, he said, always smiled on hearing this. He had discovered us to be Americans by the notice we took of a mural tablet in the choir, to the memory of a Lieutenant-Governor Clarke, of New York, who died in Chester before the Revolution. From the chapter-house he ushered us back into the nave, ever and anon pointing out some portion of the edifice more ancient than the rest, and when I asked him how he knew this, he said that he had learnt it from the archæologists, who could read off such things like a book. This guide was a lively, quick-witted man, who did his business less by rote, and more with a vivacious interest, than any guide I ever met.

After leaving the cathedral we sought out the Yacht Inn, near the water-gate. This was, for a long period of time, the principal inn of Chester, and was the house at which Swift once put up, on his way to Holyhead, and where he invited the clergy to come and sup with him. We sat down in a small snuggery, conversing with the landlord. The Chester people, according to my experience, are very affable, and fond of talking with strangers about the antiquities and picturesque characteristics of their town. It partly lives, the landlord told us, by its visitors, and many people spend the summer here on account of the antiquities and the good air. He showed us a broad, balustraded staircase, leading into a large, comfortable, old-fashioned parlor, with windows looking on the street and on the Custom-House that stood opposite. This was the room where Swift expected to receive the clergy of Chester; and on one of the window-panes were two acrid lines, written with the diamond of his ring, satirizing those venerable gentlemen, in revenge for their refusing his invitation. The first line begins rather indistinctly; but the writing grows fully legible, as it proceeds.

The Yacht Tavern is a very old house, in the gabled style. The timbers and framework are still perfectly sound. In the same street is the Bishop's house (so called as having been the residence of a prelate long ago), which is covered with curious sculpture, representing Scriptural scenes. And in the same neighborhood is the county court, accessible by an archway, through which we penetrated, and found ourselves in a passage, very ancient and dusky, overlooked from the upper story by a gallery, to which an antique staircase ascended, with balustrades and square landing-places. A printer saw us here, and asked us into his printing-office, and talked very affably; indeed, he could have hardly been more civil, if he had known that both Melville and I have given a good deal of employment to the brethren of his craft.

December 15th. — An old gentleman has recently paid me a good many visits, — a Kentucky man, who has been a good deal in England and Europe generally without losing the freshness and unconventionality of his earlier life. He was a boatman, and afterwards captain of a steamer on the Ohio and Mississippi; but has gained property, and is now the owner of mines of coal and iron, which he is endeavoring to dispose of here in England. A plain, respectable, well-to-do-looking personage, of more than seventy years; very free of conversation, and beginning to talk with everybody as a matter of course; tall, stalwart, a dark face, with white curly hair and keen eyes; and an expression shrewd, yet kindly and benign. He fought through the whole war of 1812, beginning with General Harrison at the battle of Tippecanoe, which he described to me. He says that at the beginning of the battle, and for a considerable time, he heard Tecumseh's voice, loudly giving orders. There was a man named Wheatley in the American camp, a strange, incommunicative person, — a volunteer, making war entirely on his own hook, and seeking revenge for some relatives of his, who had been killed by the Indians. In the midst of the battle this Wheatley ran at a slow trot past R—— (my informant), trailing his rifle, and making towards the point where Tecumseh's voice was heard. The fight drifted around, and R—— along with it; and by and by he reached a spot where Wheatley lay dead, with his head on Tecumseh's breast. Tecumseh had been shot with a rifle, but, before expiring, appeared to have shot Wheatley with a pistol, which he still held in his hand. R—— affirms that Tecumseh was flayed by the Kentucky men on the spot, and his skin converted into razor-strops. I have left out the most striking point of the narrative, after all, as R—— told it, viz. that soon after Wheatley passed him, he suddenly ceased to hear Tecumseh's voice ringing through the forest, as he gave his orders. He was at the battle of New Orleans, and gave me the story of it from beginning to end; but I remember only a few particulars in which he was personally concerned. He confesses that his hair bristled upright — every hair in his head — when he heard the shouts of the British soldiers before advancing to the attack. His uncomfortable sensations lasted till he began to fire, after which he felt no more of them. It was in the dusk of the morning, or a little before sunrise, when the assault was made; and the fight lasted about two hours and a half, during which R—— fired twenty-four times; and said he, "I saw my object distinctly each time, and I was a good rifle-shot." He was raising his rifle to fire the twenty-fifth time, when an American officer, General Carroll, pressed it down, and bade him fire no more. "Enough is enough," quoth the General. For there needed no more slaughter, the British being in utter rout and confusion. In this retreat many of the enemy would drop down among the dead, then rise, run a considerable distance, and drop again, thus confusing the riflemen's aim. One fellow had thus got about four hundred and fifty yards from the American line, and, thinking himself secure, he made a derisive gesture. "I'll have a shot at him anyhow," cried a rifleman; so he fired, and the poor devil dropped.

R—— himself, with one of his twenty-four shots, hit a British officer, who fell forward on his face, about thirty paces from our line, and as the enemy were then retreating (they advanced and were repelled two or three times) R—— ran out, and turned him over on his back. The officer was a man about thirty-eight, tall and fine-looking; his eyes were wide open, clear and bright, and were fixed full on R—— with a somewhat stern glance, but there was the sweetest and happiest smile over his face that could be conceived. He seemed to be dead; — at least, R—— thinks that he did not really see him, fixedly as he appeared to gaze. The officer held his sword in his hand, and R—— tried in vain to wrest it from him, until suddenly the clutch relaxed. R—— still keeps the sword hung up over his mantel-piece. I asked him how the dead man's aspect affected him. He replied that he felt nothing at the time; but that ever since, in all trouble, in uneasy sleep, and whenever he is out of tune, or waking early, or lying awake at night, he sees this officer's face, with the clear bright eyes and the pleasant smile, just as distinctly as if he were bending over him. His wound was in the breast, exactly on the spot that R—— had aimed at, and bled profusely. The enemy advanced in such masses, he says, that it was impossible not to hit them unless by purposely firing over their heads.

After the battle, R—— leaped over the rampart, and took a prisoner who was standing unarmed in the midst of the slain, having probably dropped down during the heat of the action, to avoid the hail-storm of rifle-shots. As he led him in, the prisoner paused, and pointed to an officer who was lying dead beside his dead horse, with his foot still in the stirrup. "There lies our General," said he. The horse had been killed by a grape-shot, and Pakenham himself, apparently, by a six-pounder ball, which had first struck the earth, covering him from head to foot with mud and clay, and had then entered his side, and gone upward through his breast. His face was all besmirched with the moist earth. R—— took the slain General's foot out of the stirrup, and then went to report his death.

Much more he told me, being an exceedingly talkative old man, and seldom, I suppose, finding so good a listener as myself. I like the man, — a good-tempered, upright, bold and free old fellow; of a rough breeding. but sufficiently smoothed by society to be of pleasant intercourse. He is as dogmatic as possible, having formed his own opinions, often on very disputable grounds, and hardened in them; taking queer views of matters and things, and giving shrewd and not ridiculous reasons for them; but with a keen, strong sense at the bottom of his character.

. . . . .

A little while ago I met an Englishman in a railway carriage, who suggests himself as a kind of contrast to this warlike and vicissitudinous backwoodsman. He was about the same age as R——, but had spent, apparently, his whole life in Liverpool, and has long occupied the post of Inspector of Nuisances, — a rather puffy and consequential man; gracious, however, and affable, even to casual strangers like myself. The great contrast betwixt him and the American lies in the narrower circuit of his ideas; the latter talking about matters of history of his own country and the world, — glancing over the whole field of politics, propounding opinions and theories of his own, and showing evidence that his mind had operated for better or worse on almost all conceivable matters; while the Englishman was odorous of his office, strongly flavored with that, and otherwise most insipid. He began his talk by telling me of a dead body which he had lately discovered in a house in Liverpool, where it had been kept about a fortnight by the relatives, partly from want of funds for the burial, and partly in expectation of the arrival of some friends from Glasgow. There was a plate of glass in the coffin lid, through which the Inspector of Nuisances, as he told me, had looked and seen the dead man's face in an ugly state of decay, which he minutely described. However, his conversation was not altogether of this quality; for he spoke about larks, and how abundant they are just now, and what a good pie they make, only they must be skinned, else they will have a bitter taste. We have since had a lark-pie ourselves, and I believe it was very good in itself; only the recollection of the Nuisance-man's talk was not a very agreeable flavor. A very racy and peculiarly English character might be made out of a man like this, having his life-concern wholly with the disagreeables of a great city. He seemed to be a good and kindly person, too, but earthy, — even as if his frame had been moulded of clay impregnated with the draining of slaughter-houses.

. . . . .

December 21st. — On Thursday evening I dined for the first time with the new Mayor at the Town Hall. I wish to preserve all the characteristic traits of such banquets, because, being peculiar to England, these municipal feasts may do well to picture in a novel. There was a big old silver tobacco-box, nearly or quite as large round as an ordinary plate, out of which the dignitaries of Liverpool used to fill their pipes, while sitting in council or after their dinners. The date "1690" was on the lid. It is now used as a snuff-box, and wends its way, from guest to guest, round the table. We had turtle, and, among other good things, American canvas-back ducks. . . . . These dinners are certainly a good institution, and likely to be promotive of good feeling; the Mayor giving them often, and inviting, in their turn, all the respectable and eminent citizens of whatever political bias. About fifty gentlemen were present that evening. I had the post of honor at the Mayor's right hand; and France, Turkey, and Austria were toasted before the Republic, for, as the Mayor whispered me, he must first get his allies out of the way. The Turkish Consul and the Austrian both made better English speeches than any Englishman, during the evening; for it is inconceivable what shapeless and ragged utterances Englishmen are content to put forth, without attempting anything like a wholeness; but inserting a patch here and a patch there, and finally getting out what they wish to say, indeed, but in most disorganized guise. . . . . I can conceive of very high enjoyment in making a speech; one is in such a curious sympathy with his audience, feeling instantly how every sentence affects them, and wonderfully excited and encouraged by the sense that it has gone to the right spot. Then, too, the imminent emergency, when a man is overboard, and must sink or swim, sharpens, concentrates, and invigorates the mind, and causes matters of thought and sentiment to assume shape and expression, though, perhaps, it seemed hopeless to express them, just before you rose to speak. Yet I question much whether public speaking tends to elevate the orator, intellectually or morally; the effort, of course, being to say what is immediately received by the audience, and to produce an effect on the instant. I don't quite see how an honest man can be a good and successful orator; but I shall hardly undertake to decide the question on my merely post-prandial experience.

The Mayor toasted his guests by their professions, — the merchants, for instance, the bankers, the solicitors, — and while one of the number responded, his brethren also stood up, each in his place, thus giving their assent to what he said. I think the very worst orator was a major of Artillery, who spoke in a meek, little, nervous voice, and seemed a good deal more discomposed than probably he would have been in the face of the enemy. The first toast was "The Ladies," to which an old bachelor responded.

December 31*st*. — Thus far we have come through the winter, on this bleak and blasty shore of the Irish Sea, where, perhaps, the drowned body of Milton's friend Lycidas might have been washed ashore more than two centuries ago. This would not be very likely, however; so wide a tract of sands, never deeply covered by the tide, intervening betwixt us and the sea. But it is an excessively windy place, especially here on the Promenade; always a whistle and a howl, — always an eddying gust through the corridors and chambers, — often a patter of hail or rain or snow against the windows; and in the long evenings the sounds outside are very much as if we were on shipboard in mid-ocean, with the waves dashing against the vessel's sides. I go to town almost daily, starting at about eleven, and reaching Southport again at a little past five; by which time it is quite dark, and continues so till nearly eight in the morning.

Christmas time has been marked by few characteristics. For a week or two previous to Christmas day, the newspapers contained rich details respecting market-stalls and butchers' shops, — what magnificent carcasses of prize oxen and sheep they displayed. . . . .

The Christmas Waits came to us on Christmas eve,

and on the day itself, in the shape of little parties of boys or girls, singing wretched doggerel rhymes, and going away well pleased with the guerdon of a penny or two. Last evening came two or three older choristers at pretty near bedtime, and sang some carols at our door. They were psalm tunes, however. Everybody with whom we have had to do, in any manner of service, expects a Christmas-box; but, in most cases, a shilling is quite a satisfactory amount. We have had holly and mistletoe stuck up on the gas-fixtures and elsewhere about the house.

On the mantel-piece in the coroner's court the other day, I saw corked and labelled phials, which it may be presumed contained samples of poisons that have brought some poor wretches to their deaths, either by murder or suicide. This court might be wrought into a very good and pregnant description, with its grimy gloom illuminated by a conical skylight, constructed to throw daylight down on corpses; its greasy Testament covered over with millions of perjured kisses; the coroner himself, whose life is fed on all kinds of unnatural death; its subordinate officials, who go about scenting murder, and might be supposed to have caught the scent in their own garments; its stupid, brutish juries, settling round corpses like flies; its criminals, whose guilt is brought face to face with them here, in closer contact than at the subsequent trial.

O—— P——, the famous Mormonite, called on me a little while ago, — a short, black-haired, dark-complexioned man; a shrewd, intelligent, but unrefined countenance, excessively unprepossessing; an uncouth gait and deportment; the aspect of a person in comfortable circumstances, and decently behaved, but of a vulgar nature and destitute of early culture. I think I should have taken him for a shoemaker, accustomed to reflect in a rude, strong, evil-disposed way on matters of this world and the next, as he sat on his bench. He said he had been residing in Liverpool about six months; and his business with me was to ask for a letter of introduction that should gain him admittance to the British Museum, he intending a visit to London. He offered to refer me to respectable people for his character; but I advised him to apply to Mr. Dallas, as the proper person for his purpose.

March 1st, 1857. — On the night of last Wednesday week, our house was broken into by robbers. They entered by the back window of the breakfast-room, which is the children's school-room, breaking or cutting a pane of glass, so as to undo the fastening. I have a dim idea of having heard a noise through my sleep; but if so, it did not more than slightly disturb me. U—— heard it, she being at watch with R——; and J——, having a cold, was also wakeful, and thought the noise was of servants moving about below. Neither did the idea of robbers occur to U——. J——, however, hearing U—— at her mother's door, asking for medicine for R——, called out for medicine for his cold, and the thieves probably thought we were bestirring ourselves, and so took flight. In the morning the servants found the hall door and the breakfast-room window open; some silver cups and some other trifles of plate were gone from the sideboard, and there were tokens that the whole lower part of the house had been ransacked; but the thieves had evidently gone off in a hurry, leaving some articles which they would have taken, had they been more at leisure.

We gave information to the police, and an inspector and constable soon came to make investigations, taking a list of the missing articles, and informing themselves as to all particulars that could be known. I did not much expect ever to hear any more of the stolen property; but on Sunday a constable came to request my presence at the police-office to identify the lost things. The thieves had been caught in Liverpool, and some of the property found upon them, and some of it at a pawnbroker's, where they had pledged it. The police-office is a small dark room, in the basement story of the Town Hall of Southport; and over the mantel-piece, hanging one upon another, there are innumerable advertisements of robberies in houses, and on the highway, — murders, too, and garrotings; and offences of all sorts, not only in this district, but wide away, and forwarded from other police-stations. Being thus aggregated together, one realizes that there are a great many more offences than the public generally takes note of. Most of these advertisements were in pen and ink, with minute lists of the articles stolen; but the more important were in print; and there, too, I saw the printed advertisement of our own robbery, not for public circulation, but to be handed about privately, among police-officers and pawnbrokers. A rogue has a very poor chance in England, the police being so numerous, and their system so well organized.

In a corner of the police-office stood a contrivance

for precisely measuring the heights of prisoners; and I took occasion to measure J——, and found him four feet seven inches and a half high. A set of rules for the self-government of police-officers was nailed on the door, between twenty and thirty in number, and composing a system of constabulary ethics. The rules would be good for men in almost any walk of life; and I rather think the police-officers conform to them with tolerable strictness. They appear to be subordinated to one another on the military plan. The ordinary constable does not sit down in the presence of his inspector, and this latter seems to be half a gentleman; at least, such is the bearing of our Southport inspector, who wears a handsome uniform of green and silver, and salutes the principal inhabitants, when meeting them in the street, with an air of something like equality. Then again there is a superintendent who certainly claims the rank of a gentleman, and has perhaps been an officer in the army. The superintendent of this district was present on this occasion.

The thieves were brought down from Liverpool on Tuesday, and examined in the Town Hall. I had been notified to be present, but, as a matter of courtesy, the police-officers refrained from calling me as a witness, the evidence of the servants being sufficient to identify the property. The thieves were two young men, not much over twenty, — James and John Macdonald, terribly shabby, dirty, jail-bird like, yet intelligent of aspect, and one of them handsome. The police knew them already, and they seemed not much abashed by their position. There were half a dozen magistrates on the bench, — idle old gentlemen of Southport and the vicinity, who lounged into the court, more as a matter of amusement than anything else, and lounged out again at their own pleasure; for these magisterial duties are a part of the pastime of the country gentlemen of England. They wore their hats on the bench. There were one or two of them more active than their fellows; but the real duty was done by the Clerk of the Court. The seats within the bar were occupied by the witnesses, and around the great table sat some of the more respectable people of Southport; and without the bar were the commonalty in great numbers; for this is said to be the first burglary that has occurred here within the memory of man, and so it has caused a great stir.

There seems to be a strong case against the prisoners. A boy attached to the railway testified to having seen them at Birchdale on Wednesday afternoon, and directed them on their way to Southport; Peter Pickup recognized them as having applied to him for lodgings in the course of that evening; a pawnbroker swore to one of them as having offered my top-coat for sale or pledge in Liverpool; and my boots were found on the feet of one of them, — all this in addition to other circumstances of pregnant suspicion. So they were committed for trial at the Liverpool assizes, to be holden some time in the present month. I rather wished them to escape.

February 27th. — Coming along the promenade, a little before sunset, I saw the mountains of the Welsh coast shadowed very distinctly against the horizon. Mr. Channing told me that he had seen these mountains once or twice during his stay at Southport; but, though constantly looking for them they have never before greeted my eyes in all the months that we have spent here. It is said that the Isle of Man is likewise discernible occasionally; but as the distance must be between sixty and seventy miles, I should doubt it. How misty is England! I have spent four years in a gray gloom. And yet it suits me pretty well.

TO YORK.

April 10*th*. — At Skipton. My wife, J——, and I left Southport to-day for a short tour to York and its neighborhood. The weather has been exceedingly disagreeable for weeks past, but yesterday and to-day have been pleasant, and we take advantage of the first glimpses of spring-like weather. We came by Preston, along a road that grew rather more interesting as we proceeded to this place, which is about sixty miles from Southport, and where we arrived between five and six o'clock. First of all, we got some tea; and then, as it was a pleasant sunset, we set forth from our old-fashioned inn to take a walk.

Skipton is an ancient town, and has an ancient though well-repaired aspect, the houses being built of gray stone, but in no picturesque shapes; the streets well paved; the site irregular and rising gradually towards Skipton Castle, which overlooks the town, as an old lordly castle ought to overlook the feudal village which it protects. The castle was built shortly after the Conquest by Robert de Romeli, and was afterwards the property and residence of the famous Cliffords. We met an honest man, as we approached the gateway, who kindly encouraged us to apply for admittance, notwithstanding it was Good Friday; telling us how to find the housekeeper, who would probably show us over the castle. So we passed through the gate, between two embattled towers; and in the castle court we met a flock of young damsels, who had been rambling about the precincts. They likewise directed us in our search for the housekeeper, and S——, being bolder than I in such assaults on feudal castles, led the way down a dark archway, and up an exterior stairway, and, knocking at a door, immediately brought the housekeeper to a parley.

She proved to be a nowise awful personage, but a homely, neat, kindly, intelligent, and middle-aged body. She seemed to be all alone in this great old castle, and at once consented to show us about, — being, no doubt, glad to see any Christian visitors. The castle is now the property of Sir R. Tufton; but the present family do not make it their permanent residence, and have only occasionally visited it. Indeed, it could not well be made an eligible or comfortable residence, according to modern ideas; the rooms occupying the several stories of large round towers, and looking gloomy and sombre, if not dreary, — not the less so for what has been done to modernize them; for instance, modern paper-hangings, and, in some of the rooms, marble fireplaces. They need a great deal more light and higher ceilings; and I rather imagine that the warm, rich effect of glowing tapestry is essential to keep one's spirit cheerful in these ancient rooms. Modern paper-hangings are too superficial and wishy-washy for the purpose. Tapestry, it is true, there is now, completely covering the walls of several of the rooms, but all faded into ghastliness; nor could some of it have been otherwise than ghastly, even in its newness, for it represented persons suffering various kinds of torture, with crowds of monks and nuns looking on. In another room there was the story of Solomon and the Queen of Sheba, and other subjects not to be readily distinguished in the twilight that was gathering in these antique chambers. We saw, too, some very old portraits of the Cliffords and the Thanets, in black frames, and the pictures themselves sadly faded and neglected. The famous Countess Anne of Pembroke, Dorset, and Montgomery was represented on one of the leaves of a pair of folding doors, and one of her husbands, I believe, on the other leaf. There was the picture of a little idiot lordling, who had choked himself to death; and a portrait of Oliver Cromwell, who battered this old castle, together with almost every other English or Welsh castle that I ever saw or heard of. The housekeeper pointed out the grove of trees where his cannon were planted during the siege. There was but little furniture in the rooms; amongst other articles, an antique chair, in which Mary, Queen of Scots, is said to have rested.

The housekeeper next took us into the part of the castle which has never been modernized since it was repaired, after the siege of Cromwell. This is a dismal series of cellars above ground, with immensely thick walls, letting in but scanty light, and dim staircases of stone; and a large hall, with a vast fireplace, where every particle of heat must needs have gone up chimney, — a chill and heart-breaking place enough. Quite in the midst of this part of the castle is the court-yard, — a space of some thirty or forty feet in length and breadth, open to the sky, but shut completely in on every side by the buildings of the castle, and paved over with flat stones. Out of this pavement, however, grows a yew-tree, ascending to the tops of the towers, and completely filling, with its branches and foliage, the whole open space between them. Some small birds — quite a flock of them — were twittering and fluttering among the upper branches. We went upward, through two or three stories of dismal rooms, — among others, through the ancient guard-room, — till we came out on the roof of one of the towers, and had a very fine view of an amphitheatre of ridgy hills which shut in and seclude the castle and the town. The upper foliage was within our reach, close to the parapet of the tower; so we gathered a few twigs as memorials. The house-keeper told us that the yew-tree is supposed to be eight hundred years old, and, comparing it with other yews that I have seen, I should judge that it must measure its antiquity by centuries, at all events. It still seems to be in its prime.

Along the base of the castle, on the opposite side to the entrance, flows a stream, sending up a pleasant murmur from among the trees. The housekeeper said it was not a stream, but only a "wash," whatever that may be; and I conjecture that it creates the motive power of some factory-looking edifices, which we saw on our first arrival at Skipton.

We now took our leave of the housekeeper, and came homeward to our inn, where I have written the foregoing pages by a bright fire; but I think I write better descriptions after letting the subject lie in my mind a day or two. It is too new to be properly dealt with immediately after coming from the scene.

The castle is not at all crumbly, but in excellent repair, though so venerable. There are rooks cawing about the shapeless patches of their nests, in the tops of the trees. In the castle wall, as well as in the round towers of the gateway, there seem to be little tenements, perhaps inhabited by the servants and dependants of the family. They looked in very good order, with tokens of present domesticity about them. The whole of this old castle, indeed, was as neat as a new, small dwelling, in spite of an inevitable musty odor of antiquity.

April 11*th.* — This morning we took a carriage and two horses, and set out for

BOLTON PRIORY,

a distance of about six miles. The morning was cool, with breezy clouds, intermingled with sunshine, and, on the whole, as good as are nine tenths of English mornings. J—— sat beside the driver, and S—— and I in the carriage, all closed but one window. As we drove through Skipton, the little town had a livelier aspect than yesterday when it wore its Good Friday's solemnity; but now its market-place was thronged, principally with butchers, displaying their meat under little movable pent-houses, and their customers. The English people really like to think and talk of butcher's meat, and gaze at it with delight; and they crowd through the avenues of the market-houses and stand enraptured round a dead ox.

We passed along by the castle wall, and noticed the escutcheon of the Cliffords or the Thanets carved in stone over the portal, with the motto *Desormais*, the application of which I do not well see; these ancestral devices usually referring more to the past than to the future. There is a large old church, just at the extremity of the village, and just below the castle, on the slope of the hill. The gray wall of the castle extends along the road a considerable distance, in good repair, with here and there a buttress, and the semicircular bulge of a tower.

The scenery along the road was not particularly striking, — long slopes, descending from ridges; a generally hard outline of country, with not many trees, and those, as yet, destitute of foliage. It needs to be softened with a good deal of wood. There were stone farm-houses, looking ancient, and able to last till twice as old. Instead of the hedges, so universal in other parts of England, there were stone fences of good height and painful construction, made of small stones, which I suppose have been picked up out of the fields through hundreds of years. They reminded me of old Massachusetts, though very unlike our rude stone walls, which, nevertheless, last longer than anything else we build. Another New England feature was the little brooks, which here and there flowed across our road, rippling over the pebbles, clear and bright. I fancied, too, an intelligence and keenness in some of the Yorkshire physiognomies, akin to those characteristics in my countrymen's faces.

We passed an ancient, many-gabled inn, large, low, and comfortable, bearing the name of the Devonshire House, as does our own hotel, for the Duke of Devonshire is a great proprietor in these parts. A mile or so beyond, we came to a gateway, broken through what, I believe, was an old wall of the Priory grounds; and here we alighted, leaving our driver to take the carriage to the inn. Passing through this hole in the wall, we saw the ruins of the Priory at the bottom of the beautiful valley about a quarter of a mile off; and, well as the monks knew how to choose the sites of their establishments, I think they never chose a better site than this, — in the green lap of protecting hills, beside a stream, and with peace and fertility looking down upon it on every side. The view down the valley is very fine, and, for my part, I am glad that some peaceable and comfort-loving people possessed these precincts for many hundred years, when nobody else knew how to appreciate peace and comfort.

The old gateway tower, beneath which was formerly the arched entrance into the domain of the Priory, is now the central part of a hunting-seat of the Duke of Devonshire, and the edifice is completed by a wing of recent date on each side. A few hundred yards from this hunting-box are the remains of the Priory, consisting of the nave of the old church, which is still in good repair, and used as the worshipping-place of the neighborhood (being a perpetual curacy of the parish of Skipton), and the old ruined choir, roofless, with broken arches, ivy-grown, but not so rich and rare a ruin as either Melrose, Netley, or Furness. Its situation makes its charm. It stands near the river Wharfe, — a broad and rapid stream, which hurries along between high banks, with a sound which the monks must have found congenial to their slumberous moods. It is a good river for trout, too; and I saw two or three anglers, with their rods and baskets, passing through the ruins towards its shore. It was in this river Wharfe that the boy of Egremont was drowned, at the Strid, a mile or two higher up the stream.

In the first place, we rambled round the exterior of the ruins; but, as I have said, they are rather bare and meagre in comparison with other abbeys, and I am not sure that the especial care and neatness with which they are preserved does not lessen their effect on the beholder. Neglect, wildness, crumbling walls, the climbing and conquering ivy; masses of stone lying where they fell; trees of old date, growing where the pillars of the aisles used to stand, — these are the best points of ruined abbeys. But everything here is kept with such trimness that it gives you the idea of a petrifaction. Decay is no longer triumphant; the Duke of Devonshire has got the better of it. The grounds around the church and the ruins are still used for burial, and there are several flat tombstones and altar tombs, with crosiers engraved or carved upon them, which at first I took to be the memorials of bishops or abbots, and wondered that the sculpture should still be so distinct. On one, however, I read the date 1850 and the name of a layman; for the tombstones were all modern, the humid English atmosphere giving them their mossy look of antiquity, and the crosier had been assumed only as a pretty device.

Close beside the ruins there is a large, old stone farm-house, which must have been built on the site of a part of the Priory, — the cells, dormitories, refectory, and other portions pertaining to the monks' daily life, I suppose, and built, no doubt, with the sacred stones. I should imagine it would be a haunted house, swarming with cowled spectres. We wished to see the interior of the church, and procured a guide from this farm-house, — the sexton, probably, — a gray-haired, ruddy, cheery, and intelligent man, of familiar though respectful address. The entrance of the church was undergoing improvement, under the last of the abbots, when the Reformation occurred; and it has ever remained in an unfinished state, till now it is mossy with age, and has a beautiful tuft of wall-flowers growing on a ledge over the Gothic arch of the doorway. The body of the church is of much anterior date, though the oaken roof is supposed to have been renewed in Henry VIII.'s time. This, as I said before, was the nave of the old Abbey church, and has a one-sided and unbalanced aspect, there being only a single aisle, with its row of sturdy pillars. The pavement is covered with pews of old oak, very homely and unornamental; on the side opposite the aisle there are two or three windows of modern stained glass, somewhat gaudy and impertinent; there are likewise some hatchments and escutcheons over the altar and elsewhere. On the whole, it is not an impressive interior; but, at any rate, it had the true musty odor which I never conceived of till I came to England, — the odor of dead men's decay, garnered up and shut in, and kept from generation to generation; not disgusting nor sickening, because it is so old, and of the past.

On one side of the altar there was a small square chapel, — or what had once been a chapel, — separated from the chancel by a partition about a man's height, if I remember aright. Our guide led us into it, and observed that some years ago the pavement had been taken up in this spot, for burial purposes; but it was found that it had already been used in that way, and that the corpses had been buried upright. Inquiring further, I found that it was the Clapham family, and another that was called Morley, that were so buried; and then it occurred to me that this was the vault Wordsworth refers to in one of his poems, — the burial-place of the Claphams and Mauleverers, whose skeletons, for aught I know, were even then standing upright under our feet. It is but a narrow place, perhaps a square of ten feet. We saw little or nothing else that was memorable, unless it were the signature of Queen Adelaide in a visitors' book.

On our way back to Skipton it rained and hailed, but the sun again shone out before we arrived. We took the train for Leeds at half past ten, and arrived there in the afternoon, passing the ruined Abbey of Kirkstall on our way. The ruins looked more interesting than those of Bolton, though not so delightfully situated, and now in the close vicinity of manufactories, and only two or three miles from Leeds. We took a dish of soup, and spent a miserable hour in and about the railway station of Leeds; whence we departed at four, and reached

YORK

in an hour or two. We put up at the Black Swan, and before tea went out, on the cool bright edge of evening, to get a glimpse of the Cathedral, which impressed me more grandly than when I first saw it, nearly a year ago. Indeed, almost any object gains upon me at the second sight. I have spent the evening in writing up my journal, — an act of real virtue.

After walking round the cathedral, we went up a narrow and crooked street, very old and shabby, but with an antique house projecting as much as a yard over the pavement on one side, — a timber house it seemed to be, plastered over and stained yellow or buff. There was no external door, affording entrance into this edifice; but about midway of its front we came to a low, Gothic, stone archway, passing right through the house; and as it looked much time-worn, and was sculptured with untraceable devices, we went through. There was an exceedingly antique, battered, and shattered pair of oaken leaves, which used doubtless to shut up the passage in former times, and keep it secure; but for the last centuries, probably, there has been free ingress and egress. Indeed, the portal arch may never have been closed since the Reformation. Within, we found a quadrangle, of which the house upon the street formed one side, the others being composed of ancient houses, with gables in a row, all looking upon the paved quadrangle, through quaint windows of various fashion. An elderly, neat, pleasant-looking woman now came in beneath the arch, and as she had a look of being acquainted here, we asked her what the place was; and she told us, that in the old Popish times the prebends of the cathedral used to live here, to keep them from doing mischief in the town. The establishment, she said, was now called "The College," and was let in rooms and small tenements to poor people. On consulting the York Guide, I find that her account was pretty correct; the house having been founded in Henry VI.'s time, and called St. William's College, the statue of the patron saint being sculptured over the arch. It was intended for the residence of the parsons and priests of the cathedral, who had formerly caused troubles and scandals by living in the town.

We returned to the front of the cathedral on our way homeward, and an old man stopped us, to inquire if we had ever seen the Fiddler of York. We answered in the negative, and said that we had not time to see him now; but the old gentleman pointed up to the highest pinnacle of the southern front, where stood the Fiddler of York, one of those Gothic quaintnesses which blotch the grandeur and solemnity of this and other cathedrals.

April 12th. — This morning was bleak and most ungenial; a chilly sunshine, a piercing wind, a prevalence of watery cloud, — April weather, without the tenderness that ought to be half revealed in it. This is

EASTER SUNDAY,

and service at the cathedral commenced at half past ten; so we set out betimes, and found admittance into the vast nave, and thence into the choir. An attendant ushered S—— and J—— to a seat at a distance from me, and then gave me a place in one of the stalls where the monks used to sit or kneel while chanting the services. I think these stalls are now appropriated to the prebends. They are of carved oaken wood, much less elaborate and wonderfully wrought than those of Chester Cathedral, where all was done with head and heart, each a separate device, instead of cut by machinery like this. The whole effect of this carved work, however, lining the choir with its light tracery and pinnacles, is very fine. The whole choir, from the roof downward, except the old stones of the outer walls, is of modern renovation, it being but a few years since this part of the cathedral was destroyed by fire. The arches and pillars and lofty roof, however, have been well restored; and there was a vast east window, full of painted glass, which, if it be modern, is wonderfully chaste and Gothic-like. All the other windows have painted glass, which does not flare and glare as if newly painted. But the light, whitewashed aspect of the general interior of the choir has a cold and dreary effect. There is an enormous organ, all clad in rich oaken carving, of similar pattern to that of the stalls. It was communion day, and near the high altar, within a screen, I saw the glistening of the gold vessels wherewith the services were to be performed.

The choir was respectably filled with a pretty numerous congregation, among whom I saw some officers in full dress, with their swords by their sides, and one old white-bearded warrior, who sat near me, seemed very devout at his religious exercises. In front of me and on the corresponding benches, on the other side of the choir, sat two rows of white-robed choristers, twenty in all, and these, with some women, performed the vocal part of the music. It is not good to see musicians, for they are sometimes coarse and vulgar people, and so the auditor loses faith in any fine and spiritual tones that they may breathe forth.

The services of Easter Sunday comprehend more than the ordinary quantity of singing and chanting; at all events, nearly an hour and a half were thus employed, with some intermixture of prayers and reading of Scriptures; and, being almost congealed with cold, I thought it would never come to an end. The spirit of my Puritan ancestors was mighty within me, and I did not wonder at their being out of patience with all this mummery, which seemed to me worse than papistry because it was a corruption of it. At last a canon gave out the text, and preached a sermon of about twenty minutes long, — the coldest, driest, most superficial rubbish; for this gorgeous setting of the magnificent cathedral, the elaborate music, and the rich ceremonies, seem inevitably to take the life out of the sermon, which, to be anything, must be all. The Puritans showed their strength of mind and heart by preferring a sermon an hour and a half long, into which the preacher put his whole soul, and lopping away all these externals, into which religious life had first leafed and flowered, and then petrified.

After the service, while waiting for my wife in the nave, I was accosted by a young gentleman who seemed to be an American, and whom I have certainly seen before, but whose name I could not recollect. This, he said, was his first visit to York, and he was evidently inclined to join me in viewing the curiosities of the place, but, not knowing his name, I could not introduce him to my wife, and so made a parting salute.

After dinner, we set forth and took a promenade along the wall, and a ramble through some of the crooked streets, noting the old, jutting storied houses, story above story, and the old churches, gnawed like a bone by the teeth of Time, till we came suddenly to the Black

Swan before we expected it. . . . . I rather fancy that I must have observed most of the external peculiarities at my former visit, and therefore need not make another record of them in this journal.

In the course of our walk we saw a procession of about fifty charity-school-boys, in flat caps, each with bands under his chin, and a green collar to his coat; all looking unjoyous, and as if they had no home nor parents' love. They turned into a gateway, which closed behind them; and as the adjoining edifice seemed to be a public institution, — at least, not private, — we asked what it was, and found it to be a hospital or residence for Old Maiden ladies, founded by a gentlewoman of York; I know not whether she herself is of the sisterhood. It must be a very singular institution, and worthy of intimate study, if it were possible to make one's way within the portal.

After writing the above, J—— and I went out for another ramble before tea; and, taking a new course, we came to a grated iron fence and gateway, through which we could see the ruins of St. Mary's Abbey. They are very extensive, and situated quite in the midst of the city, and the wall and then a tower of the Abbey seem to border more than one of the streets. Our walk was interesting, as it brought us unexpectedly upon several relics of antiquity, — a loop-holed and battlemented gateway; and at various points fragments of the old Gothic stone-work, built in among more recent edifices, which themselves were old; grimness intermixed with quaintness and grotesqueness; old fragments of religious or warlike architecture mingled with queer domestic structures, — the general effect sombre, sordid, and grimy; but yet with a fascination that makes us fain to linger about such scenes, and come to them again.

We passed round the cathedral, and saw jackdaws fluttering round the pinnacles, while the bells chimed the quarters, and little children played on the steps under the grand arch of the entrance. It is very stately, very beautiful, this minster; and doubtless would be very satisfactory, could I only know it long and well enough, — so rich as its front is, even with almost all the niches empty of their statues; not stern in its effect, which I suppose must be owing to the elaborate detail with which its great surface is wrought all over, like the chasing of a lady's jewel-box, and yet so grand! There is a dwelling-house on one side, gray with antiquity, which has apparently grown out of it like an excrescence; and though a good-sized edifice, yet the cathedral is so large that its vastness is not in the least deformed by it. If it be a dwelling-house, I suppose it is inhabited by the person who takes care of the cathedral. This morning, while listening to the tedious chanting and lukewarm sermon, I depreciated the whole affair, cathedral and all; but now I do more justice, at least to the latter, and am only sorry that its noble echoes must follow at every syllable, and re-reverberate at the commas and semicolons, such poor discourses as the canon's. But, after all, it was the Puritans who made the sermon of such importance in religious worship as we New-Englanders now consider it; and we are absurd in considering this magnificent church and all those embroidered ceremonies only in reference to it.

Before going back to the hotel, I went again up the

narrow and twisted passage of College Street, to take another glance at St. William's College. I underestimated the projection of the front over the street; it is considerably more than three feet, and is about eight or nine feet above the pavement. The little statue of St. William is an alto-relievo over the arched entrance, and has an escutcheon of arms on each side, all much defaced. In the interior of the quadrangle, the houses have not gables nor peaked fronts, but have peaked windows on the red-tiled roofs. The doorway, opposite the entrance-arch, is rather stately; and on one side is a large, projecting window, which is said to belong to the room where the printing-press of Charles I. was established in the days of the Parliament.

THE MINSTER.

Monday, April 13*th.* — This morning was chill, and, worse, it was showery, so that our purposes to see York were much thwarted. At about ten o'clock, however, we took a cab, and drove to the cathedral, where we arrived while service was going on in the choir, and ropes were put up as barriers between us and the nave; so that we were limited to the south transept, and a part of one of the aisles of the choir. It was dismally cold. We crept cheerlessly about within our narrow precincts (narrow, that is to say, in proportion to the vast length and breadth of the cathedral), gazing up into the hollow height of the central tower, and looking at a monumental brass, fastened against one of the pillars, representing a beruffled lady of the Tudor times, and at the canopied tomb of Archbishop de Grey, who ruled over the diocese in the thirteenth century. Then we went into the side aisle of the choir, where there were one or two modern monuments; and I was appalled to find that a sermon was being preached by the ecclesiastic of the day, nor were there any signs of an imminent termination. I am not aware that there was much pith in the discourse, but there was certainly a good deal of labor and earnestness in the preacher's mode of delivery; although, when he came to a close, it appeared that the audience was not more than half a dozen people.

The barriers being now withdrawn, we walked adown the length of the nave, which did not seem to me so dim and vast as the recollection which I have had of it since my visit of a year ago. But my pre-imaginations and my memories are both apt to play me false with all admirable things, and so create disappointments for me, while perhaps the thing itself is really far better than I imagine or remember it. We engaged an old man, one of the attendants pertaining to the cathedral, to be our guide, and he showed us first the stone screen in front of the choir, with its sculptured kings of England; and then the tombs in the north transept, — one of a modern archbishop, and one of an ancient one, behind which the insane person who set fire to the church a few years ago hid himself at nightfall. Then our guide unlocked a side door, and led us into the chapter-house, — an octagonal hall, with a vaulted roof, a tessellated floor, and seven arched windows of old painted glass, the richest that I ever saw or imagined, each looking like an inestimable treasury of precious stones, with a gleam and glow even in the sullen light of this gray morning. What would they be with the sun shining through them! With all their brilliancy, moreover, they were as soft as rose-leaves. I never saw any piece of human architecture so beautiful as this chapter-house; at least, I thought so while I was looking at it, and think so still; and it owed its beauty in very great measure to the painted windows: I remember looking at these windows from the outside yesterday, and seeing nothing but an opaque old crust of conglomerated panes of glass; but now that gloomy mystery was radiantly solved.

Returning into the body of the cathedral, we next entered the choir, where, instead of the crimson cushions and draperies which we had seen yesterday, we found everything folded in black. It was a token of mourning for one of the canons, who died on Saturday night. The great east window, seventy-five feet high, and full of old painted glass in many exquisitely wrought and imagined Scriptural designs, is considered the most splendid object in the Minster. It is a pity that it is partially hidden from view, even in the choir, by a screen before the high altar; but indeed, the Gothic architects seem first to imagine beautiful and noble things, and then to consider how they may best be partially screened from sight. A certain secrecy and twilight effect belong to their plan.

We next went round the side aisles of the choir, which contain many interesting monuments of prelates, and a specimen of the very common Elizabethan design of an old gentleman in a double ruff and trunk breeches, with one of his two wives on either side of him, all kneeling in prayer; and their conjoint children, in two rows, kneeling in the lower compartments of the tomb. We saw, too, a rich marble monument of one of the Strafford family, and the tombstone of the famous Earl himself, — a flat tombstone in the pavement of the aisle, covering the vault where he was buried, and with four iron rings fastened into the four corners of the stone, whereby to lift it.

And now the guide led us into the vestry, where there was a good fire burning in the grate, and it really thawed my heart, which was congealed with the dismal chill of the cathedral. Here we saw a good many curious things, — for instance, two wooden figures in knightly armor, which had stood sentinels beside the ancient clock before it was replaced by a modern one; and, opening a closet, the guide produced an old iron helmet, which had been found in a tomb where a knight had been buried in his armor; and three gold rings and one brass one, taken out of the graves, and off the finger-bones of mediæval archbishops, — one of them with a ruby set in it; and two silver-gilt chalices, also treasures of the tombs; and a wooden head, carved in human likeness, and painted to the life, likewise taken from a grave where an archbishop was supposed to have been buried. They found no veritable skull nor bones, but only this block-head, as if Death had betrayed the secret of what the poor prelate really was. We saw, too, a canopy of cloth, wrought with gold threads, which had been borne over the head of King James I., when he came to York, on his way to receive the English Crown. There were also some old brass dishes, in which pence used to be collected in monkish times. Over the door of this vestry were hung two banners of a Yorkshire regiment, tattered in the Peninsular wars, and inscribed with the names of the battles through which they had been borne triumphantly; and Waterloo was among them. The vestry, I think, occupies that excrescential edifice which I noticed yesterday as having grown out of the cathedral.

After looking at these things, we went down into the crypts, under the choir. These were very interesting, as far as we could see them; being more antique than anything aboveground, but as dark as any cellar. There is here, in the midst of these sepulchral crypts, a spring of water, said to be very pure and delicious, owing to the limestone through which the rain that feeds its source is filtered. Near it is a stone trough, in which the monks used to wash their hands.

I do not remember anything more that we saw at the cathedral, and at noon we returned to the Black Swan. The rain still continued so that S—— could not share in any more of my rambles, but J—— and I went out again, and discovered the Guildhall. It is a very ancient edifice of Richard II.'s time, and has a statue over the entrance which looks time-gnawed enough to be of coeval antiquity, although in reality it is only a representation of George II. in his royal robes. We went in, and found ourselves in a large and lofty hall, with an oaken roof and a stone pavement, and the farther end was partitioned off as a court of justice. In that portion of the hall the Judge was on the bench, and a trial was going forward; but in the hither portion a mob of people, with their hats on, were lounging and talking, and enjoying the warmth of the stoves. The window over the judgment-seat had painted glass in it, and so, I think, had some of the hall windows. At the end of the hall hung a great picture of Paul defending himself before Agrippa, where the Apostle looked like an athlete, and had a remarkably bushy black beard. Between two of the windows, huug an Indian bell from Burmah, ponderously thick and massive. Both the picture and the bell had been presented to the city as tokens of affectionate remembrance by its children; and it is pleasant to think that such feelings exist in these old stable communities, and that there are permanent localities where such gifts can be kept from generation to generation.

At four o'clock we left the city of York, still in a pouring rain. The Black Swan, where we had been staying, is a good specimen of the old English inn, sombre, quiet, with dark staircases, dingy rooms, curtained beds, — all the possibilities of a comfortable life and good English fare, in a fashion which cannot have been much altered for half a century. It is very homelike when one has one's family about him, but must be prodigiously stupid for a solitary man.

We took the train for

MANCHESTER,

over pretty much the same route that I travelled last year. Many of the higher hills in Yorkshire were white with snow, which, in our lower region, softened into rain; but as we approached Manchester, the western sky reddened, and gave promise of better weather. We arrived at nearly eight o'clock, and put up at the Palatine Hotel. In the evening I scrawled away at my journal till past ten o'clock; for I have really made it a matter of conscience to keep a tolerably full record of my travels, though conscious that everything good escapes in the process. In the morning we went out and visited the

MANCHESTER CATHEDRAL,

a particularly black and grimy edifice, containing some genuine old wood carvings within the choir. We stayed a good while, in order to see some people married. One couple, with their groomsman and bride's-maid, were sitting within the choir; but when the clergyman was robed and ready, there entered five other couples, each attended by groomsman and bride's-maid. They all were of the lower orders; one or two respectably dressed, but most of them poverty-stricken, — the men in their ordinary loafer's or laborer's attire, the women with their poor, shabby shawls drawn closely about them; faded untimely, wrinkled with penury and care; nothing fresh, virgin-like, or hopeful about them; joining themselves to their mates with the idea of making their own misery less intolerable by adding another's to it. All the six couple stood up in a row before the altar, with the groomsmen and bride's-maids in a row behind them; and the clergyman proceeded to marry them in such a way that it almost seemed to make every man and woman the husband and wife of every other. However, there were some small portions of the service directed towards each separate couple; and they appeared to assort themselves in their own fashion afterwards, each one saluting his bride with a kiss. The clergyman, the sexton, and the clerk all seemed to find something funny in this affair; and the woman who admitted us into the church smiled too, when she told us that a wedding-party was waiting to be married. But I think it was the saddest thing we have seen since leaving home; though funny enough if one likes to look at it from a ludicrous point of view. This mob of poor marriages was caused by the fact that no marriage fee is paid during Easter.

This ended the memorable things of our tour; for my wife and J—— left Manchester for Southport, and I for Liverpool, before noon.

April 19*th.* — On the 15th, having been invited to attend at the laying of the corner-stone of

MR. BROWNE'S FREE LIBRARY,

I went to the Town Hall, according to the programme, at eleven o'clock. There was already a large number of people (invited guests, members of the Historical Society, and other local associations) assembled in the great ball-room, and one of these was delivering an address to Mr. Browne as I entered. Approaching the outer edge of the circle, I was met and cordially greeted by Monckton Milnes, whom I like, and who always reminds me of Longfellow, though his physical man is more massive. While we were talking together, a young man approached him with a pretty little expression of surprise and pleasure at seeing him there. He had a slightly affected or made-up manner, and was rather a comely person. Mr. Milnes introduced him to me as Lord ——. Hereupon, of course, I observed him more closely; and I must say that I was not long in discovering a gentle dignity and half-imperceptible reserve in his manner; but still my first impression was quite as real as my second one. He occupies, I suppose, the foremost position among the young men of England, and has the fairest prospects of a high course before him; nevertheless, he did not impress me as possessing the native qualities that could entitle him to a high public career. He has adopted public life as his hereditary profession, and makes the very utmost of all his abilities, cultivating himself to a determined end, knowing that he shall have every advantage towards attaining his object. His natural disadvantages must have been, in some respects, unusually great; his voice, for instance, is not strong, and appeared to me to have a more positive defect than mere weakness. Doubtless he has struggled manfully against this defect; and it made me feel a certain sympathy, and, indeed, a friendliness, for which he would not at all have thanked me, had he known it. I felt, in his person, what a burden it is upon human shoulders, the necessity of keeping up the fame and historical importance of an illustrious house; at least, when the heir to its honors has sufficient intellect and sensibility to feel the claim that his country and his ancestors and his posterity all have upon him. Lord —— is fully capable of feeling these claims; but I would not care, methinks, to take his position, unless I could have considerably more than his strength.

In a little while we formed ourselves into a procession, four in a row, and set forth from the Town Hall, through James Street, Lord Street, Lime Street, all the way through a line of policemen and a throng of people; and the windows were alive with heads, and I never before was so conscious of a great mass of humanity, though perhaps I may often have seen as great a crowd. But a procession is the best point of view from which to see the crowd that collects together. The day, too, was very fine, even sunshiny, and the streets dry, — a blessing which cannot be overestimated; for we should have been in a strange trim for the banquet, had we been compelled to wade through the ordinary mud of Liverpool. The procession itself could not have been a very striking object. In America, it would have had a hundred picturesque and perhaps ludicrous features, — the symbols of the different trades, banners with strange devices, flower shows, children, volunteer soldiers, cavalcades, and every suitable and unsuitable contrivance; but we were merely a trail of ordinary-looking individuals, in great-coats, and with precautionary umbrellas. The only characteristic or professional costume, as far as I noticed, was that of the Bishop of Chester, in his flat cap and black silk gown; and that of Sir Henry Smith, the General of the District, in full uniform, with a star and half a dozen medals on his breast. Mr. Browne himself, the hero of the day, was the plainest and simplest man of all, — an exceedingly unpretending gentleman in black; small, white-haired, pale, quiet, and respectable. I rather wondered why he chose to be the centre of all this ceremony; for he did not seem either particularly to enjoy it, or to be at all incommoded by it, as a more nervous and susceptible man might have been.

The site of the projected edifice is on one of the streets bordering on St. George's Hall; and when we came within the enclosure, the corner-stone, a large square of red freestone, was already suspended over its destined place. It has a brass plate let into it, with an inscription, which will perhaps not be seen again till the present English type has grown as antique as black letter is now. Two or three photographs were now taken of the site, the corner-stone, Mr. Browne, the distinguished guests, and the crowd at large; then ensued a prayer from the Bishop of Chester, and speeches from Mr. Holme, Mr. Browne, Lord ——, Sir John Pakington, Sir Henry Smith, and as many others as there was time for. Lord —— acquitted himself very creditably, though brought out unexpectedly, and with evident reluctance. I am convinced that men, liable to be called on to address the public, keep a constant supply of commonplaces in their minds, which, with little variation, can be adapted to one subject about as well as to another; and thus they are always ready to do well enough, though seldom to do particularly well.

From the scene of the corner-stone, we went to St. George's Hall, where a drawing-room and dressing-room had been prepared for the principal guests. Before the banquet, I had some conversation with Sir James Kay Shuttleworth, who had known Miss Brontë very intimately, and bore testimony to the wonderful fidelity of Mrs. Gaskell's life of her. He seemed to have had an affectionate regard for her, and said that her marriage promised to have been productive of great happiness; her husband being not a remarkable man, but with the merit of an exceeding love for her.

Mr. Browne now took me up into the gallery, which by this time was full of ladies; and thence we had a fine view of the noble hall, with the tables laid, in readiness for the banquet. I cannot conceive of anything finer than this hall; it needs nothing but painted windows to make it perfect, and those I hope it may have one day or another.

At two o'clock we sat down to the banquet, which hardly justified that name, being only a cold collation, though sufficiently splendid in its way. In truth, it would have been impossible to provide a hot dinner for nine hundred people in a place remote from kitchens. The principal table extended lengthwise of the hall, and was a little elevated above the other tables, which stretched across, about twenty in all. Before each guest, besides the bill of fare, was laid a programme of the expected toasts, among which appeared my own name, to be proposed by Mr. Monckton Milnes. These things do not trouble me quite as much as they used, though still it sufficed to prevent much of the enjoyment which I might have had if I could have felt myself merely a spectator. My left-hand neighbor was Colonel Campbell of the Artillery; my right-hand one was Mr. Picton, of the Library Committee; and I found them both companionable men, especially the Colonel, who had served in China and in the Crimea, and owned that he hated the French. We did not make a very long business of the eatables, and then came the usual toasts of ceremony, and afterwards those more peculiar to the occasion, one of the first of which was "The House of Stanley," to which Lord —— responded. It was a noble subject, giving scope for as much eloquence as any man could have brought to bear upon it, and capable of being so wrought out as to develop and illustrate any sort of conservative or liberal tendencies which the speaker might entertain. There could not be a richer opportunity for reconciling and making friends betwixt the old system of society and the new; but Lord —— did not seem to make anything of it. I remember nothing that he said excepting his statement that the family had been five hundred years connected with the town of Liverpool. I wish I could have responded to "The House of Stanley," and his Lordship could have spoken in my behalf. None of the speeches were remarkably good; the Bishop of Chester's perhaps the best, though he is but a little man in aspect, not at all filling up one's idea of a bishop, and the rest were on an indistinguishable level, though, being all practised speakers, they were less hum-y and ha-y than English orators ordinarily are.

I was really tired to death before my own turn came, sitting all that time, as it were, on the scaffold, with the rope round my neck. At last Monckton Milnes was called up and made a speech, of which, to my dismay, I could hardly hear a single word, owing to his being at a considerable distance, on the other side of the chairman, and flinging his voice, which is a bass one, across the hall, instead of adown it, in my direction. I could not distinguish one word of any allusions to my works, nor even when he came to the toast, did I hear the terms in which he put it, nor whether I was toasted on my own basis, or as representing American literature, or as Consul of the United States. At all events, there was a vast deal of clamour; and uprose peers and bishop, general, mayor, knights and gentlemen, everybody in the hall greeting me with all the honors. I had uprisen, too, to commence my speech; but had to sit down again till matters grew more quiet, and then I got up, and proceeded to deliver myself with as much composure as I ever felt at my own fireside. It is very strange, this self-possession and clear-sightedness which I have experienced when standing before an audience, showing me my way through all the difficulties resulting from my not having heard Monckton Milnes's speech; and on since reading the latter, I do not see how I could have answered it better. My speech certainly was better cheered than any other; especially one passage, where I made a colossus of Mr. Browne, at which the audience grew so tumultuous in their applause that they drowned my figure of speech before it was half out of my mouth.

After rising from table, Lord —— and I talked about our respective oratorical performances; and he appeared to have a perception that he is not naturally gifted in this respect. I like Lord ——, and wish that it were possible that we might know one another better. If a nobleman has any true friend out of his own class, it ought to be a republican. Nothing farther of interest happened at the banquet, and the next morning came out the newspapers with vile reports of my speech, attributing to me a variety of forms of ragged nonsense, which, poor speaker as I am, I was quite incapable of uttering.

May 10th. — The winter is over, but as yet we scarcely have what ought to be called spring; nothing but cold east winds, accompanied with sunshine, however, as east winds generally are in this country. All milder winds seem to bring rain. The grass has been green for a month, — indeed, it has never been entirely brown, — and now the trees and hedges are beginning to be in foliage. Weeks ago the daisies bloomed, even in the sandy grass-plot bordering on the promenade beneath our front windows; and in the progress of the daisy, and towards its consummation, I saw the propriety of Burns's epithet, "wee, modest, *crimson-tipped* flower," — its little white petals in the bud being fringed all round with crimson, which fades into pure white when the flower blooms. At the beginning of this month I saw fruit-trees in blossom, stretched out flat against stone walls, reminding me of a dead bird nailed against the side of a barn. But it has been a backward and dreary spring; and I think Southport, in the course of it, has lost its advantage over the rest of the Liverpool neighborhood in point of milder atmosphere. The east wind feels even rawer here than in the city.

Nevertheless, the columns of the Southport Visitor begin to be well replenished with the names of guests, and the town is assuming its aspect of summer life. To say the truth, except where cultivation has done its utmost, there is very little difference between winter and summer in the mere material aspect of Southport; there being nothing but a waste of sand, intermixed with plashy pools to seaward, and a desert of sand-hillocks on the land side. But now the brown, weather-hardened donkey-women haunt people that stray along the reaches, and delicate persons face the cold, rasping, ill-tempered blast on the promenade, and children dig in the sands; and, for want of something better, it seems to be determined that this shall be considered spring.

Southport is as stupid a place as I ever lived in;

and I cannot but bewail our ill fortune to have been compelled to spend so many months on these barren sands, when almost every other square yard of England contains something that would have been historically or poetically interesting. Our life here has been a blank. There was, indeed, a shipwreck, a month or two ago, when a large ship came ashore within a mile from our windows; the larger portion of the crew landing safely on the hither sands, while six or seven betook themselves to the boat, and were lost in attempting to gain the shore, on the other side of the Ribble. After a lapse of several weeks, two or three of their drowned bodies were found floating in this vicinity, and brought to Southport for burial; so that it really is not at all improbable that Milton's Lycidas floated hereabouts, in the rise and lapse of the tides, and that his bones may still be whitening among the sands.

In the same gale that wrecked the above-mentioned vessel, a portion of a ship's mast was driven ashore, after evidently having been a very long time in and under water; for it was covered with great barnacles, and torn sea-weed, insomuch that there was scarcely a bare place along its whole length; clusters of sea-anemones were sticking to it, and I know not what strange marine productions besides. J—— at once recognized the sea-anemones, knowing them by his much reading of Gosse's Aquarium; and though they must now have been two or three days high and dry out of water, he made an extempore aquarium out of a bowl, and put in above a dozen of these strange creatures. In a little while they bloomed out wonderfully, and even seemed to produce young anemones;

but, from some fault in his management, they afterwards grew sickly and died. S—— thinks that the old storm-shattered mast, so studded with the growth of the ocean depths, is a relic of the Spanish Armada which strewed its wrecks along all the shores of England; but I hardly think it would have taken three hundred years to produce this crop of barnacles and sea-anemones. A single summer might probably have done it.

Yesterday we all of us except R—— went to Liverpool to see the performances of an American circus company. I had previously been, a day or two before, with J——, and had been happy to perceive that the fact of its being an American establishment really induced some slight swelling of the heart within me. It is ridiculous enough, to be sure, but I like to find myself not wholly destitute of this noble weakness, patriotism. As for the circus, I never was fond of that species of entertainment, nor do I find in this one the flash and glitter and whirl which I remember in other American exhibitions.

[Here follow the visits to Lincoln and Boston, printed in Our Old Home. — Ed.]

May 27th. — We left Boston by railway at noon, and arrived in

PETERBOROUGH

in about an hour and a quarter, and have put up at the Railway Hotel. After dinner we walked into the town to see

THE CATHEDRAL,

of the towers and arches of which we had already had a glimpse from our parlor window.

Our journey from Boston hitherward was through a perfectly level country, — the fens of Lincolnshire, — green, green, and nothing else, with old villages and farm-houses and old church-towers; very pleasant and rather wearisomely monotonous. To return to Peterborough. It is a town of ancient aspect; and we passed, on our way towards the market-place, a very ancient-looking church, with a very far projecting porch, opening in front and on each side through arches of broad sweep. The street by which we approached from our hotel led us into the market-place, which had what looked like an old Guildhall on one side. On the opposite side, above the houses, appeared the towers of the cathedral, and a street leads from the market-place to its front, through an arched gateway, which used to be the external entrance of the abbey, I suppose, of which the cathedral was formerly the church. The front of the cathedral is very striking, and unlike any other that I have seen; being formed by three lofty and majestic arches in a row, with three gable peaks above them, forming a sort of colonnade, within which is the western entrance of the nave. The towers are massive, but low in proportion to their bulk. There are no spires, but pinnacles and statues, and all the rich detail of Gothic architecture, the whole of a venerable gray hue. It is in perfect repair, and has not suffered externally, except by the loss of multitudes of statues, gargoyles, and miscellaneous eccentricities of sculpture, which used to smile, frown, laugh, and weep over the faces of these old fabrics.

We entered through a side portal, and sat down on a bench in the nave, and kept ourselves quiet; for the organ was sounding, and the choristers were chanting in the choir. The nave and transepts are very noble, with clustered pillars and Norman arches, and a great height under the central tower; the whole, however, being covered with plaster and whitewash, except the roof, which is of painted oak. This latter adornment has the merit, I believe, of being veritably ancient; but certainly I should prefer the oak of its native hue, for the effect of the paint is to make it appear as if the ceiling were covered with imitation mosaic work or an oil-cloth carpet.

After sitting awhile, we were invited by a verger, who came from within the screen, to enter the choir and hear the rest of the service. We found the choristers there in their white garments, and an audience of half a dozen people, and had time to look at the interior of the choir. All the carved wood-work of the tabernacle, the Bishop's throne, the prebends' stalls, and whatever else, is modern; for this cathedral seems to have suffered wofully from Cromwell's soldiers, who hacked at the old oak, and hammered and pounded upon the marble tombs till nothing of the first and very few of the latter remain. It is wonderful how suddenly the English people lost their sense of the sanctity of all manner of externals in religion, without losing their religion too. The French, in their Revolution, underwent as sudden a change; but they became pagans and atheists, and threw away the substance with the shadow.

I suspect that the interior arrangement of the choir and the chancel has been greatly modernized; for it is quite unlike anything that I have seen elsewhere. Instead of one vast eastern window, there are rows of windows lighting the Lady Chapel, and seen through rows of arches in the screen of the chancel; the effect being, whoever is to have the credit of it, very rich and beautiful. There is, I think, no stained glass in the windows of the nave, though in the windows of the chancel there is some of recent date, and some fragments of veritable antique. The effect of the whole interior is grand, expansive, and both ponderous and airy; not dim, mysterious, and involved, as Gothic interiors often are, the roundness and openness of the arches being opposed to this latter effect.

When the chanting came to a close, one verger took his stand at the entrance of the choir, and another stood farther up the aisle, and then the door of a stall opened, and forth came a clerical dignity of much breadth and substance, aged and infirm, and was ushered out of the choir with a great deal of ceremony. We took him for the bishop, but he proved to be only a canon. We now engaged an attendant to show us through the Lady Chapel and the other penetralia, which it did not take him long to accomplish. One of the first things he showed us was the tombstone, in the pavement of the southern aisle, beneath which Mary, Queen of Scots, had been originally buried, and where she lay for a quarter of a century, till borne to her present resting-place in Westminster Abbey. It is a plain marble slab, with no inscription. Near this, there was a Saxon monument of the date 870, with sculpture in relief upon it, — the memorial of an Abbot Hedda, who was killed by the Danes when they destroyed the monastery that preceded the abbey and church. I remember, likewise, the recumbent figure of a prelate, whose face has been quite obliterated by puritanic violence; and I think that there is not a single tomb older than the parliamentary wars, which has not been in like manner battered and shattered, except the Saxon abbot's just mentioned. The most pretentious monument remaining is that of a Mr. Deacon, a gentleman of George I.'s time, in wig and breeches, leaning on his elbow, and resting one hand upon a skull. In the north aisle, precisely opposite to that of Queen Mary, the attendant pointed out to us the slab beneath which lie the ashes of Catharine of Arragon, the divorced queen of Henry VIII.

In the nave there was an ancient font, a venerable and beautiful relic, which has been repaired not long ago, but in such a way as not to lessen its individuality. This sacred vessel suffered especial indignity from Cromwell's soldiers; insomuch that if anything could possibly destroy its sanctity, they would have effected that bad end. On the eastern wall of the nave, and near the entrance, hangs the picture of old Scarlet, the sexton who buried both Mary of Scotland and Catharine of Arragon, and not only these two queens, but everybody else in Peterborough, twice over. I think one feels a sort of enmity and spite against these grave-diggers, who live so long, and seem to contract a kindred and partnership with Death, being boon companions with him, and taking his part against mankind.

In a chapel, or some side apartment, there were two pieces of tapestry wretchedly faded, the handiwork of two nuns, and copied from two of Raphael's cartoons.

. . . . .

N

We now emerged from the cathedral, and walked round its exterior, admiring it to our utmost capacity, and all the more because we had not heard of it beforehand, and expected to see nothing so huge, majestic, grand, and gray. And of all the lovely closes that I ever beheld, that of Peterborough Cathedral is to me the most delightful; so quiet it is, so solemnly and nobly cheerful, so verdant, so sweetly shadowed, and so presided over by the stately minster, and surrounded by ancient and comely habitations of Christian men. The most enchanting place, the most enviable as a residence in all this world, seemed to me that of the Bishop's secretary, standing in the rear of the cathedral, and bordering on the churchyard; so that you pass through hallowed precincts in order to come at it, and find it a Paradise, the holier and sweeter for the dead men who sleep so near. We looked through the gateway into the lawn, which really seemed hardly to belong to this world, so bright and soft the sunshine was, so fresh the grass, so lovely the trees, so trained and refined and mellowed down was the whole nature of the spot, and so shut in and guarded from all intrusion. It is in vain to write about it; nowhere but in England can there be such a spot, nor anywhere but in the close of Peterborough Cathedral.

May 28th. — I walked up into the town this morning, and again visited the cathedral. On the way, I observed the Falcon Inn, a very old-fashioned hostelry, with a thatched roof, and what looked like the barn door or stable door in a side front. Very likely it may have been an inn ever since Queen Elizabeth's time.

The Guildhall, as I supposed it to be, in the market-place, has a basement story entirely open on all sides, but from its upper story it communicates with a large old house in the rear. I have not seen an older-looking town than Peterborough; but there is little that is picturesque about it, except within the domain of the cathedral. It was very fortunate for the beauty and antiquity of these precincts, that Henry VIII. did not suffer the monkish edifices of the abbey to be overthrown and utterly destroyed, as was the case with so many abbeys, at the Reformation; but, converting the abbey church into a cathedral, he preserved much of the other arrangement of the buildings connected with it. And so it happens that to this day we have the massive and stately gateway, with its great pointed arch, still keeping out the world from those who have inherited the habitations of the old monks; for though the gate is never closed, one feels himself in a sacred seclusion the instant he passes under the archway. And everywhere there are old houses that appear to have been adapted from the monkish residences, or from their spacious offices, and made into convenient dwellings for ecclesiastics, or vergers, or great or small people connected with the cathedral; and with all modern comfort they still retain much of the quaintness of the olden time, — arches, even rows of arcades, pillars, walls, beautified with patches of Gothic sculpture, not wilfully put on by modern taste, but lingering from a long past; deep niches, let into the fronts of houses, and occupied by images of saints; a growth of ivy, overspreading walls, and just allowing the windows to peep through, — so that no novelty, nor anything of our hard, ugly, and actual life comes into these limits, through the defences of the gateway, without being mollified and modified. Except in some of the old colleges of Oxford, I have not seen any other place that impressed me in this way; and the grounds of Peterborough Cathedral have the advantage over even the Oxford colleges, insomuch that the life is here domestic, — that of the family, that of the affections, — a natural life, which one deludes himself with imagining may be made into something sweeter and purer in this beautiful spot than anywhere else. Doubtless the inhabitants find it a stupid and tiresome place enough, and get morbid and sulky, and heavy and obtuse of head and heart, with the monotony of their life. But still I must needs believe that a man with a full mind, and objects to employ his affection, ought to be very happy here. And perhaps the forms and appliances of human life are never fit to make people happy until they cease to be used for the purposes for which they were directly intended, and are taken, as it were, in a sidelong application. I mean that the monks, probably, never enjoyed their own edifices while they were a part of the actual life of the day, so much as these present inhabitants now enjoy them when a new use has grown up apart from the original one.

Towards noon we all walked into the town again, and on our way went into the old church with the projecting portal, which I mentioned yesterday. A woman came hastening with the keys when she saw us looking up at the door. The interior had an exceeding musty odor, and was very ancient, with side aisles opening by a row of pointed arches into the nave, and a gallery of wood on each side, and built across the two rows of arches. It was paved with tombstones, and I suppose the dead people contributed to the musty odor. Very naked and unadorned it was, except with a few mural monuments of no great interest. We stayed but a little while, and amply rewarded the poor woman with a sixpence. Thence we proceeded to the cathedral, pausing by the way to look at the old Guildhall, which is no longer a Guildhall, but a butter-market; and then we bought some prints of exterior and interior views of the Minster, of which there are a great variety on note-paper, letter-sheets, large engravings, and lithographs. It is very beautiful; there seems to be nothing better than to say this over again. We found the doors most hospitably open, and every part entirely free to us, — a kindness and liberality which we have nowhere else experienced in England, whether as regards cathedrals or any other public buildings. My wife sat down to draw the font, and I walked through the Lady Chapel meanwhile, pausing over the empty bed of Queen Mary, and the grave of Queen Catharine, and looking at the rich and sumptuous roof, where a fountain, as it were, of groins of arches spouts from numberless pilasters, intersecting one another in glorious intricacy. Under the central tower, opening to either transept, to the nave and to the choir, are four majestic arches, which I think must equal in height those of which I saw the ruins, and one, all but perfect, at Furness Abbey. They are about eighty feet high.

I may as well give up Peterborough here, though I hate to leave it undescribed even to the tufts of yellow flowers, which grow on the projections high out of reach, where the winds have sown their seeds in soil made by the aged decay of the edifice. I could write a page, too, about the rooks or jackdaws that flit and clamor about the pinnacles, and dart in and out of the eyelet-holes, the piercings, — whatever they are called, — in the turrets and buttresses. On our way back to the hotel, J—— saw an advertisement of some knights in armor that were to tilt to-day; so he and I waited, and by and by a procession appeared, passing through the antique market-place, and in front of the abbey gateway, which might have befitted the same spot three hundred years ago. They were about twenty men-at-arms on horseback, with lances and banners. We were a little too near for the full enjoyment of the spectacle; for, though some of the armor was real, I could not help observing that other suits were made of silver paper or gold tinsel. A policeman (a queer anomaly in reference to such a mediæval spectacle) told us that they were going to joust and run at the ring, in a field a little beyond the bridge.

TO NOTTINGHAM.

May 28*th*. — We left Peterborough this afternoon, and, however reluctant to leave the cathedral, we were glad to get away from the hotel; for though outwardly pretentious, it is a wretched and uncomfortable place, with scanty table, poor attendance, and enormous charges. The first stage of our journey to-day was to Grantham, through a country the greater part of which was as level as the Lincolnshire landscapes have been, throughout our experience of them. We saw several old villages, gathered round their several churches; and one of these little communities, "Little Byforth," had a very primitive appearance, — a group of twenty or thirty dwellings of stone and thatch, without a house among them that could be so modern as a hundred years. It is a little wearisome to think of people living from century to century in the same spot, going in and out of the same doors, cultivating the same fields, meeting the same faces and marrying one another over and over again; and going to the same church, and lying down in the same churchyard, — to appear again, and go through the same monotonous round in the next generation.

At Grantham, our route branches off from the main line; and there was a delay of about an hour, during which we walked up into the town, to take a nearer view of a tall gray steeple which we saw from the railway station. The streets that led from the station were poor and commonplace; and, indeed, a railway seems to have the effect of making its own vicinity mean. We noticed nothing remarkable until we got to the market-place, in the centre of which there is a cross, doubtless of great antiquity, though it is in too good condition not to have been recently repaired. It consists of an upright pillar, with a pedestal of half a dozen stone steps, which are worn hollow by the many feet that have scraped their hobnailed shoes upon them. Among these feet, it is highly probable, may have been those of Sir Isaac Newton, who was a scholar of the free school of this town; and when J—— scampered up the steps, we told him so. Visible from the market-place also stands the Angel Inn, which seems to be a wonderfully old inn, being adorned with gargoyles and other antique sculpture, with projecting windows, and an arched entrance, and presenting altogether a frontispiece of so much venerable state that I feel curious to know its history. Had I been aware that the chief hotel of Grantham were such a time-honored establishment, I should have arranged to pass the night there, especially as there were interesting objects enough in the town to occupy us pleasantly. The church — the steeple of which is seen over the market-place, but is removed from it by a street or two — is very fine ; the tower and spire being adorned with arches, canopies, and niches, — twelve of the latter for the twelve Apostles, all of whom have now vanished, — and with fragments of other Gothic ornaments. The jackdaws have taken up their abodes in the crevices and crannies of the upper half of the steeple.

We left Grantham at nearly seven, and reached

NOTTINGHAM

just before eight. The castle, situated on a high and precipitous rock, directly over the edge of which look the walls, was visible, as we drove from the station to our hotel. We followed the advice of a railway attendant in going first to the May Pole, which proved to be a commercial inn, with the air of a drinking-shop, in a by-alley; and, furthermore, they could not take us in. So we drove to the George the Fourth, which seems to be an excellent house; and here I have remained quiet, the size of the town discouraging me from going out in the twilight which was fast coming on after tea. These are glorious long days for travel; daylight fairly between four in the morning and nine at night, and a margin of twilight on either side.

May 29th. — After breakfast, this morning, I wandered out and lost myself; but at last found the post-office, and a letter from Mr. Wilding, with some perplexing intelligence. Nottingham is an unlovely and uninteresting town. The castle I did not see; but I happened upon a large and stately old church, almost cathedralic in its dimensions. On returning to the hôtel, we deliberated on the mode of getting to Newstead Abbey, and we finally decided upon taking a fly; in which conveyance, accordingly, we set out before twelve. It was a slightly overcast day, about half intermixed of shade and sunshine, and rather cool, but not so cool that we could exactly wish it warmer. Our drive to Newstead lay through what was once a portion of Sherwood Forest, though all of it, I believe, has now become private property, and is converted into fertile fields, except where the owners of estates have set out plantations. We have now passed out of the fen-country, and the land rises and falls in gentle swells, presenting a pleasant, but not striking, character of scenery. I remember no remarkable object on the road, — here and there an old inn, a gentleman's seat of moderate pretension, a great deal of tall and continued hedge, a quiet English greenness and rurality, — till, drawing near

NEWSTEAD ABBEY,

we began to see copious plantations, principally of firs, larches, and trees of that order, looking very sombre, though with some intermingling of lighter foliage. It was after one when we reached "The Hut," — a small, modern wayside inn, almost directly across the road from the entrance-gate of Newstead. The post-boy calls the distance ten miles from Nottingham. He also averred that it was forbidden to drive visitors within the gates; so we left the fly at the inn, and set out to walk from the entrance to the house. There is no porter's lodge; and the grounds, in this outlying region, had not the appearance of being very primly kept, but were well wooded with evergreens, and much overgrown with ferns, serving for cover for hares, which scampered in and out of their hiding-places. The road went winding gently along, and, at the distance of nearly a mile, brought us to a second gate, through which we likewise passed, and walked onward a good way farther, seeing much wood, but as yet nothing of the Abbey. At last, through the trees, we caught a glimpse of its battlements, and saw, too, the gleam of water, and then appeared the Abbey's venerable front. It comprises the western wall of the church, which is all that remains of that fabric, — a great, central window, entirely empty, without tracery or mullions; the ivy clambering up on the inside of the wall, and hanging over in front. The front of the inhabited part of the house extends along on a line with this church wall, rather low, with battlements along its top, and all in good keeping with the ruinous remnant. We met a servant, who replied civilly to our inquiries about the mode of gaining admittance, and bade us ring a bell at the corner of the principal porch. We rang accordingly, and were forthwith admitted into a low, vaulted basement, ponderously wrought with intersecting arches, dark and rather chilly, just like what I remember to have seen at Battle Abbey; and, after waiting here a little while, a respectable elderly gentlewoman appeared, of whom we requested to be shown round the Abbey. She courteously acceded, first presenting us to a book in which to inscribe our names.

I suppose ten thousand people, three fourths of them Americans, have written descriptions of Newstead Abbey; and none of them, so far as I have read, give any true idea of the place; neither will my description, if I write one. In fact, I forget very much that I saw, and especially in what order the objects came. In the basement was Byron's bath, — a dark and cold and cellar-like hole, which it must have required good courage to plunge into; in this region, too, or near it, was the chapel, which Colonel Wildman has decorously fitted up, and where service is now regularly performed, but which was used as a dog's kennel in Byron's time.

After seeing this, we were led to Byron's own bedchamber, which remains just as when he slept in it, — the furniture and all the other arrangements being religiously preserved. It was in the plainest possible style, homely, indeed, and almost mean, — an ordinary paper-hanging, and everything so commonplace that it was only the deep embrasure of the window that made it look unlike a bedchamber in a middling-class lodging-house. It would have seemed difficult, beforehand, to fit up a room in that picturesque old edifice so that it should be utterly void of picturesqueness; but it was effected in this apartment, and I suppose it is a specimen of the way in which old mansions used to be robbed of their antique character, and adapted to modern tastes, before mediæval antiquities came into fashion. Some prints of the Cambridge colleges, and other pictures indicating Byron's predilections at the time, and which he himself had hung there, were on the walls. This, the housekeeper told us, had been the Abbot's chamber, in the monastic time. Adjoining it, is the haunted room, where the ghostly monk, whom Byron introduces into Don Juan, is said to have his lurking-place. It is fitted up in the same style as Byron's, and used to be occupied by his valet or page. No doubt in his Lordship's day, these were the only comfortable bedrooms in the Abbey; and by the housekeeper's account of what Colonel Wildman has done, it is to be inferred that the place must have been in a most wild, shaggy, tumble-down condition, inside and out, when he bought it.

It is very different now. After showing us these two apartments of Byron and his servant, the housekeeper led us from one to another and another magnificent chamber, fitted up in antique style, with oak panelling, and heavily carved bedsteads, of Queen Elizabeth's time, or of the Stuarts, hung with rich tapestry curtains of similar date, and with beautiful old cabinets of carved wood, sculptured in relief, or tortoise-shell and ivory. The very pictures and realities, these rooms were, of stately comfort; and they were called by the name of kings, — King Edward's, King Charles II.'s, King Henry VII.'s chamber; and they were hung with beautiful pictures, many of them portraits of these kings. The chimney-pieces were carved and emblazoned; and all, so far as I could judge, was in perfect keeping, so that if a prince or noble of three centuries ago were to come to lodge at Newstead Abbey, he would hardly know that he had strayed out of his own century. And yet he might have known by some token, for there are volumes of poetry and light literature on the tables in these royal bedchambers, and in that of Henry VII. I saw The House of the Seven Gables and The Scarlet Letter in Routledge's edition.

Certainly the house is admirably fitted up; and there must have been something very excellent and comprehensive in the domestic arrangements of the monks, since they adapt themselves so well to a state of society entirely different from that in which they originated. The library is a very comfortable room, and provocative of studious ideas, though lounging and luxurious. It is long, and rather low, furnished with soft couches, and, on the whole, though a man might dream of study, I think he would be most likely to read nothing but novels there. I know not what the room was in monkish times, but it was waste and ruinous in Lord Byron's. Here, I think, the housekeeper unlocked a beautiful cabinet, and took out the famous skull which Lord Byron transformed into a drinking-goblet. It has a silver rim and stand, but still the ugly skull is bare and evident, and the naked inner bone receives the wine. I should think it would hold at least a quart, — enough to overpower any living head into which this death's head should transfer its contents; and a man must be either very drunk or very thirsty, before he would taste wine out of such a goblet. I think Byron's freak was outdone by that of a cousin of my own, who once solemnly assured me that he had a spittoon made out of the skull of his enemy. The ancient coffin in which the goblet-skull was found was shown us in the basement of the Abbey.

There was much more to see in the house than I had any previous notion of; but except the two chambers already noticed, nothing remained the least as Byron left it. Yes, another place there was, — his own small dining-room, with a table of moderate size, where, no doubt, the skull-goblet has often gone its rounds. Colonel Wildman's dining-room was once Byron's shooting-gallery, and the original refectory of the monks. It is now magnificently arranged, with a vaulted roof, a music-gallery at one end, suits of armor and weapons on the walls, and mailed arms extended, holding candelabras. There are one or two painted windows, commemorative of the Peninsular war, and the battles in which the Colonel and his two brothers fought, — for these Wildmen seem to have been mighty troopers, and Colonel Wildman is represented as a fierce-looking mustachioed hussar at two different ages. The housekeeper spoke of him affectionately, but says that he is now getting into years, and that they fancy him failing. He has no children. He appears to have been on good terms with Byron, and had the latter ever returned to England, he was under promise to make his first visit to his old home and it was in such an expectation that Colonel Wildman had kept Byron's private apartments in the same condition in which he found them. Byron was informed of all the Colonel's fittings up and restorations, and when he introduces the Abbey in Don Juan, the poet describes it, not as he himself left it, but as Colonel Wildman has restored it. There is a beautiful drawing-room, and all these apartments are adorned with pictures, the collection being especially rich in portraits by Sir Peter Lely, — that of Nell Gwynn being one, who is one of the few beautiful women whom I have seen on canvas.

We parted with the housekeeper, and I with a good many shillings, at the door by which we entered; and our next business was to see the private grounds and gardens. A little boy attended us through the first part of our progress, but soon appeared the veritable gardener, — a shrewd and sensible old man, who has been very many years on the place. There was nothing of special interest as concerning Byron until we entered the original old monkish garden, which is still laid out in the same fashion as the monks left it, with a large, oblong piece of water in the centre, and terraced banks rising at two or three different stages with perfect regularity around it; so that the sheet of water looks like the plate of an immense looking-glass, of which the terraces form the frame. It seems as if, were there any giant large enough, he might raise up this mirror and set it on end. In the monks' garden, there is a marble statue of Pan, which, the gardener told us, was brought by the "Wicked Lord" (great-uncle of Byron) from Italy, and was supposed by the country people to represent the Devil, and to be the object of his worship, — a natural idea enough, in view of his horns and cloven feet and tail, though this indicates, at all events, a very jolly devil. There is also a female statue, beautiful from the waist upward, but shaggy and cloven-footed below, and holding a little cloven-footed child by the hand. This, the old gardener assured us, was Pandora, wife of the above-mentioned Pan, with her son. Not far from this spot, we came to the tree on which Byron carved his own name and that of his sister Augusta. It is a tree of twin stems, — a birch-tree, I think, growing up side by side. One of the stems still lives and flourishes, but that on which he carved the two names is quite dead, as if there had been something fatal in the inscription that has made it forever famous. The names are still very legible, although the letters had been closed up by the growth of the bark before the tree died. They must have been deeply cut at first.

There are old yew-trees of unknown antiquity in this garden, and many other interesting things; and among them may be reckoned a fountain of very pure water, called the "Holy Well," of which we drank. There are several fountains, besides the large mirror in the centre of the garden; and these are mostly inhabited by carp, the genuine descendants of those which peopled the fish-ponds in the days of the monks. Coming in front of the Abbey, the gardener showed us the oak that Byron planted, now a vigorous young tree; and the monument which he erected to his Newfoundland dog, and which is larger than most Christians get, being composed of a marble, altar-shaped tomb, surrounded by a circular area of steps, as much as twenty feet in diameter. The gardener said, however, that Byron intended this, not merely as the burial-place of his dog, but for himself too, and his sister. I know not how this may have been, but this inconvenience would have attended his being buried there, that, on transfer of the estate, his mortal remains would have become the property of some other man.

We had now come to the empty space, — a smooth green lawn, where had once been the Abbey church. The length had been sixty-four yards, the gardener said, and within his remembrance there had been many remains of it, but now they are quite removed, with the exception of the one ivy-grown western wall, which, as I mentioned, forms a picturesque part of the present front of the Abbey. Through a door in this wall the gardener now let us out. . . . .

In the evening our landlady, who seems to be a very intelligent woman, of a superior class to most landladies, came into our parlor, while I was out, and talked about the present race of Byrons and Lovelaces, who have often been at this house. There seems to be a taint in the Byron blood which makes those who inherit it wicked, mad, and miserable. Even Colonel Wildman comes in for a share of this ill luck, for he has almost ruined himself by his expenditure on the estate, and by his lavish hospitality, especially to the Duke of Sussex, who liked the Colonel, and used often to visit him during his lifetime, and his Royal Highness's gentlemen ate and drank Colonel Wildman almost up. So says our good landlady. At any rate, looking at this miserable race of Byrons, who held the estate so long, and at Colonel Wildman, whom it has ruined in forty years, we might see grounds for believing in the evil fate which is supposed to attend confiscated church property. Nevertheless, I would accept the estate, were it offered me.

. . . . Glancing back, I see that I have omitted some items that were curious in describing the house; for instance, one of the cabinets had been the personal property of Queen Elizabeth. It seems to me that the fashion of modern furniture has nothing to equal these old cabinets for beauty and convenience. In the state apartments, the floors were so highly waxed and polished that we slid on them as if on ice, and could only make sure of our footing by treading on strips of carpeting that were laid down.

June 7th. — We left Nottingham a week ago, and made our first stage to Derby, where we had to wait an hour or two at a great, bustling, pell-mell, crowded railway station. It was much thronged with second and third class passengers, coming and departing in continual trains; for these were the Whitsuntide holidays, which set all the lower orders of English people astir. This time of festival was evidently the origin of the old "Election" holidays in Massachusetts; the latter occurring at the same period of the year, and being celebrated (so long as they could be so) in very much the same way, with games, idleness, merriment of set purpose, and drunkenness. After a weary while we took the train for

MATLOCK,

via Ambergate, and arrived at the former place late in the afternoon. The village of Matlock is situated on the banks of the Derwent, in a delightful little nook among the hills, which rise above it in steeps, and in precipitous crags, and shut out the world so effectually that I wonder how the railway ever found it out. Indeed, it does make its approach to this region through a long tunnel. It was a beautiful, sunny afternoon when we arrived, and my present impressions are, that I have never seen anywhere else such exquisite scenery as that which surrounds the village. The street itself, to be sure, is commonplace enough, and hot, dusty, and disagreeable; but if you look above it, or on either side, there are green hills descending abruptly down, and softened with woods, amid which are seen villas, cottages, castles; and beyond the river is a line of crags, perhaps three hundred feet high, clothed with shrubbery in some parts from top to bottom, but in other places presenting a sheer precipice of rock, over which tumbles, as it were, a cascade of ivy and creeping plants. It is very beautiful, and, I might almost say, very wild; but it has those characteristics of finish, and of being redeemed from nature, and converted into a portion of the adornment of a great garden, which I find in all English scenery. Not that I complain of this; on the contrary, there is nothing that delights an American more, in contrast with the roughness and ruggedness of his native scenes, — to which, also, he might be glad to return after a while.

We put up at the old Bath Hotel, — an immense house, with passages of such extent that at first it seemed almost a day's journey from parlor to bedroom. The house stands on a declivity, and after ascending one pair of stairs, we came, in travelling along the passage-way, to a door that opened upon a beautifully arranged garden, with arbors and grottos, and the hillside rising steep above. During all the time of our stay at Matlock there was brilliant sunshine, and, the grass and foliage being in their freshest and most luxuriant phase, the place has left as bright a picture as I have anywhere in my memory.

The morning after our arrival we took a walk, and, following the sound of a church-bell, entered what appeared to be a park, and, passing along a road at the base of a line of crags, soon came in sight of a beautiful church. I rather imagine it to be the place of worship of the Arkwright family, whose seat is in this vicinity, — the descendants of the famous Arkwright who contributed so much towards turning England into a cotton-manufactory. We did not enter the church, but passed beyond it, and over a bridge, and along a road that ascended among the hills and finally brought us out by a circuit to the other end of Matlock village, after a walk of three or four miles. In the afternoon we took a boat across the Derwent, — a passage which half a dozen strokes of the oars accomplished, — and reached a very pleasant seclusion called "The Lovers' Walk." A ferriage of twopence pays for the transit across the river, and gives the freedom of these grounds, which are threaded with paths that meander and zigzag to the top of the precipitous ridge, amid trees and shrubbery, and the occasional ease of rustic seats. It is a sweet walk for lovers, and was so for us; although J——, with his scramblings and disappearances, and shouts from above, and headlong scamperings down the precipitous paths, occasionally frightened his mother. After gaining the heights, the path skirts along the precipice, allowing us to see down into the village street, and, nearer, the Derwent winding through the valley so close beneath us that we might have flung a stone into it. These crags would be very rude and harsh if left to themselves, but they are quite softened and made sweet and tender by the great deal of foliage that clothes their sides, and creeps and clambers over them, only letting a stern face of rock be seen here and there, and with a smile rather than a frown.

The next day, Monday, we went to see the grand cavern. The entrance is high up on the hillside, whither we were led by a guide, of whom there are many, and they all pay tribute to the proprietor of the cavern. There is a small shed by the side of the cavern mouth, where the guide provided himself and us with tallow candles, and then led us into the darksome and ugly pit, the entrance of which is not very imposing, for it has a door of rough pine boards, and is kept under lock and key. This is the disagreeable phase — one of the disagreeable phases — of man's conquest over nature in England, — cavern mouths shut up with cellar doors, cataracts under lock and key, precipitous crags compelled to figure in ornamented gardens, — and all accessible at a fixed amount of shillings or pence. It is not possible to draw a full free breath under such circumstances. When you think of it, it makes the wildest scenery look like the artificial rock-work which Englishmen are so fond of displaying in the little bit of grass-plot under their suburban parlor windows. However, the cavern was dreary enough and wild enough, though in a mean sort of way; for it is but a long series of passages and crevices, generally so narrow that you scrape your elbows, and so low that you hit your head. It has nowhere a lofty height, though sometimes it broadens out into ample space, but not into grandeur, the roof being always within reach, and in most places smoky with the tallow candles that have been held up to it. A very dirty, sordid, disagreeable burrow, more like a cellar gone mad than anything else; but it served to show us how the crust of the earth is moulded. This cavern was known to the Romans, and used to be worked by them as a lead-mine. Derbyshire spar is now taken from it; and in some of its crevices the gleam of the tallow candles is faintly reflected from the crystallizations; but, on the whole, I felt like a mole, as I went creeping along, and was glad when we came into the sunshine again. I rather think my idea of a cavern is taken from the one in the Forty Thieves, or in Gil Blas, — a vast, hollow womb, roofed and curtained with obscurity. This reality is very mean.

Leaving the cavern, we went to the guide's cottage, situated high above the village, where he showed us specimens of ornaments and toys manufactured by himself from Derbyshire spar and other materials. There was very pretty mosaic work, flowers of spar, and leaves of malachite, and miniature copies of Cleopatra's Needle, and other Egyptian monuments, and vases of graceful pattern, brooches, too, and many other things. The most valuable spar is called Blue John, and is only to be found in one spot, where, also, the supply is said to be growing scant. We bought a number of articles, and then came homeward, still with our guide, who showed us, on the way, the Romantic Rocks. These are some crags which have been rent away, and stand insulated from the hillside, affording a pathway between it and them; while the places can yet be seen where the sundered rocks would fit into the craggy hill if there were but a Titan strong enough to adjust them again. It is a very picturesque spot, and the price for seeing it is twopence; though in our case it was included in the four shillings which we had paid for seeing the cavern. The representative men of England are the showmen and the policemen; both very good people in their way.

Returning to the hotel, J—— and his mother went through the village to the river, near the railway, where J—— set himself to fishing, and caught three minnows. I followed, after a while, to fetch them back, and we called into one or two of the many shops in the village, which have articles manufactured of the spar for sale. Some of these are nothing short of magnificent. There was an inlaid table, valued at sixty guineas, and a splendid ornament for any drawing-room; another, inlaid with the squares of a chessboard. We heard of a table in the possession of the Marquis of Westminster, the value of which is three hundred guineas. It would be easy and pleasant to spend a great deal of money in such things as we saw there; but all our purchases in Matlock did not amount to more than twenty shillings, invested in brooches, shawl-pins, little vases and toys, which will be valuable to us as memorials on the other side of the water. After this, we visited a petrifying cave, of which there are several hereabouts. The process of petrifaction requires some months, or perhaps a year or two, varying with the size of the article to be operated upon. The articles are placed in the cave, under the drippings from the roof, and a hard deposit is formed upon them, and sometimes, as in the case of a bird's-nest, causes a curious result, — every straw and hair being immortalized and stiffened into stone. A horse's head was in process of petrifaction; and J—— bought a broken eggshell for a penny, though larger articles are expensive. The process would appear to be entirely superficial, — a mere crust on the outside of things, — but we saw some specimens of petrified oak, where the stony substance seemed to be intimately incorporated with the wood, and to have really changed it into stone. These specimens were immensely ponderous, and capable of a high polish, which brought out beautiful streaks and shades.

One might spend a very pleasant summer in Matlock, and I think there can be no more beautiful place in the world; but we left it that afternoon, and railed to Manchester, where we arrived between ten and eleven at night. The next day I left S—— to go to the Art Exhibition, and took J—— with me to Liverpool, where I had an engagement that admitted of no delay. Thus ended our tour, in which we had seen but a little bit of England, yet rich with variety and interest. What a wonderful land! It is our forefathers' land; our land, for I will not give up such a precious inheritance. We are now back again in flat and sandy Southport, which, during the past week, has been thronged with Whitsuntide people, who crowd the streets, and pass to and fro along the promenade, with a universal and monotonous air of nothing to do, and very little enjoyment. It is a pity that poor folks cannot employ their little hour of leisure to better advantage, in a country where the soil is so veined with gold.

These are delightfully long days. Last night, at half past nine, I could read with perfect ease in parts of the room remote from the window; and at nearly half past eleven there was a broad sheet of daylight in the west, gleaming brightly over the plashy sands. I question whether there be any total night at this season.

June 21*st.* — Southport, I presume, is now in its most vivid aspect; there being a multitude of visitors here, principally of the middling classes, and a frequent crowd, whom I take to be working-people from Manchester and other factory towns. It is the strangest place to come to for the pleasures of the sea, of which we scarcely have a glimpse from month's end to month's end, nor any fresh, exhilarating breath from it, but a lazy, languid atmosphere, brooding over the waste of sands; or even if there be a sulky and bitter wind blowing along the promenade, it still brings no salt elixir. I never was more weary of a place in all my life, and never felt such a disinterested pity as of the people who come here for pleasure. Nevertheless, the town has its amusements; in the first place, the day-long and perennial one of donkey-riding along the sands, large parties of men and girls pottering along together; the Flying Dutchman trundles hither and thither when there is breeze enough; an archery-man sets up his targets on the beach; the bathing-houses stand by scores and fifties along the shore, and likewise on the banks of the Ribble, a mile seaward; the hotels have their billiard-rooms; there is a theatre every evening; from morning till night comes a succession of organ-grinders, playing interminably under your window; and a man with a bassoon and a monkey, who takes your pennies and pulls off his cap in acknowledgment; and wandering minstrels, with guitar and voice; and a Highland bagpipe, squealing out a tangled skein of discord, together with a Highland maid, who dances a hornpipe; and Punch and Judy, — in a word, we have specimens of all manner of vagrancy that infests England. In these long days, and long and pleasant ones, the promenade is at its liveliest about nine o'clock, which is but just after sundown; and our little R—— finds it difficult to go to sleep amid so much music as comes to her ears from bassoon, bagpipe, organ, guitar, and now and then a military band. One feature of the place is the sick and infirm people, whom we see dragged along in bath-chairs, or dragging their own limbs languidly; or sitting on benches; or meeting in the streets, and making acquaintance on the strength of mutual maladies, — pale men leaning on their ruddy wives; cripples, three or four together in a ring, and planting their crutches in the centre. I don't remember whether I have ever mentioned among the notabilities of Southport the Town Crier, — a meek-looking old man, who sings out his messages in a most doleful tone, as if he took his title in a literal sense, and were really going to cry, or crying in the world's behalf; one other stroller, a foreigner with a dog, shaggy round the head and shoulders, and closely shaven behind. The poor little beast jumped through hoops, ran about on two legs of one side, danced on its hind legs, or on its fore paws, with its hind ones straight up in the air, — all the time keeping a watch on his master's eye, and evidently mindful of many a beating.

June 25th. — The war-steamer Niagara came up the Mersey a few days since, and day before yesterday Captain Hudson called at my office, — a somewhat meagre, elderly gentleman, of simple and hearty manners and address, having his purser, Mr. Eldredge, with him, who, I think, rather prides himself upon having a Napoleonic profile. The captain is an old acquaintance of Mrs. Blodgett, and has come ashore principally with a view to calling on her; so, after we had left our cards for the Mayor, I showed these naval gentlemen the way to her house. Mrs. Blodgett and Miss W—— were prodigiously glad to see him; and they all three began to talk of old times and old acquaintances; for when Mrs. Blodgett was a rich lady at Gibraltar, she used to have the whole navy-list at her table,—young midshipmen and lieutenants then perhaps, but old, gouty, paralytic commodores now, if still even partly alive. It was arranged that Mrs. Blodgett, with as many of the ladies of her family as she chose to bring, should accompany me on my official visit to the ship the next day; and yesterday we went accordingly,—Mrs. Blodgett, Miss W——, and six or seven American captains' wives, their husbands following in another boat. I know too little of ships to describe one, or even to feel any great interest in the details of this or of any other ship; but the nautical people seemed to see much to admire. She lay in the Sloyne, in the midst of a broad basin of the Mersey, with a pleasant landscape of green England, now warm with summer sunshine, on either side, with churches and villa residences, and suburban and rural beauty. The officers of the ship are gentlemanly men, externally very well mannered, although not polished and refined to any considerable extent. At least, I have not found naval men so, in general; but still it is pleasant to see Americans who are not stirred by such motives as usually interest our countrymen,—no hope nor desire of growing rich, but planting their claims to respectability on other grounds, and therefore acquiring a certain nobleness, whether it be inherent in their nature or no. It always seems to me they look down upon civilians with quiet and not ill-natured scorn, which one has the choice of smiling or being provoked at. It is not a true life which they lead, but shallow and aimless; and unsatisfactory it must be to the better minds among them; nor do they appear to profit by what would seem the advantages presented to them in their world-wide, though not world-deep experience. They get to be very clannish too.

After seeing the ship, we landed, all of us, ladies and captain, and went to the gardens of the Rock Ferry Hotel, where J—— and I stayed behind the rest.

TO SCOTLAND.

June 28th. — On the 26th my wife, J——, and I left Southport, taking the train for Preston, and as we had to stop an hour or two before starting for Carlisle, I walked up into the town. The street through which most of my walk lay was brick-built, lively, bustling, and not particularly noteworthy; but, turning a little way down another street, the town had a more ancient aspect. The day was intensely hot, the sun lying bright and broad as ever I remember it in an American city; so that I was glad to get back again to the shade and shelter of the station. The heat and dust, moreover, made our journey to Carlisle very uncomfortable. It was through very pretty, and sometimes picturesque, scenery, being on the confines of the hill-country, which we could see on our left, dim and blue; and likewise we had a refreshing breath from the sea in passing along the verge of Morecambe Bay. We reached

Carlisle at about five o'clock, and, after taking tea at the Bush Hotel, set forth to look at the town.

The notable objects were a castle and a cathedral; and we first found our way to the castle, which stands on elevated ground, on the side of the city towards Scotland. A broad, well-constructed path winds round the castle at the base of the wall, on the verge of a steep descent to the plain beneath, through which winds the river Eden. Along this path we walked quite round the castle, a circuit of perhaps half a mile, — pleasant, being shaded by the castle's height and by the foliage of trees. The walls have been so much rebuilt and restored that it is only here and there that we see an old buttress, or a few time-worn stones intermixed with the new facing with which the aged substance is overlaid. The material is red freestone, which seems to be very abundant in this part of the country. We found no entrance to the castle till the path had led us from the free and airy country into a very mean part of the town, where the wretched old houses thrust themselves between us and the castle wall, and then, passing through a narrow street, we walked up what appeared like a by-lane, and the portal of the castle was before us. There was a sentry-box just within the gate, and a sentinel was on guard, for Carlisle Castle is a national fortress, and has usually been a depot for arms and ammunition. The sergeant, or corporal of the guard, sat reading within the gateway, and, on my request for admittance, he civilly appointed one of the soldiers to conduct us to the castle. As I recollect, the chief gateway of the castle, with the guard-room in the thickness of the wall, is situated some twenty yards behind the first entrance where we met the sentinel.

It was an intelligent young soldier who showed us round the castle, and very civil, as I always find soldiers to be. He had not anything particularly interesting to show, nor very much to say about it; and what he did say, so far as it referred to the history of the castle, was probably apocryphal.

The castle has an inner and outer ward on the descent of the hill, and included within the circuit of the exterior wall. Having been always occupied by soldiers, it has not been permitted to assume the picturesque aspect of a ruin, but the buildings of the interior have either been constantly repaired, as they required it, or have been taken down when past repair. We saw a small part of the tower where Mary, Queen of Scots, was confined on her first coming to England; these remains consist only of a portion of a winding stone staircase, at which we glanced through a window. The keep is very large and massive, and, no doubt, old in its inner substance. We ascended to the castle walls, and looked out over the river towards the Scottish hills, which are visible in the distance, — the Scottish border being not more than eight or nine miles off. Carlisle Castle has stood many sieges, and witnessed many battles under its walls. There are now, on its ramparts, only some half a dozen old-fashioned guns, which our soldier told us had gone quite out of use in these days. They were long iron twelve-pounders, with one or two carronades. The soldier was of an artillery regiment, and wore the Crimean medal. He said the garrison now here consists only of about twenty men, all of whom had served in the Crimea, like himself. They seem to lead a very dull and monotonous life, as indeed it must be, without object or much hope, or any great employment of the present, like prisoners, as indeed they are. Our guide showed us on the rampart a place where the soldiers had been accustomed to drop themselves down at night, hanging by their hands from the top of the wall, and alighting on their feet close beside the path on the outside. The height seemed at least that of an ordinary house, but the soldier said that nine times out of ten the fall might be ventured without harm; and he spoke from experience, having himself got out of the castle in this manner. The place is now boarded up, so as to make egress difficult or impossible.

The castle, after all, was not particularly worth seeing. The soldier's most romantic story was of a daughter of Lord Scroope, a former governor of the castle, when Mary of Scotland was confined here. She attempted to assist the Queen in escaping, but was shot dead in the gateway by the warder; and the soldier pointed out the very spot where the poor young lady fell and died; — all which would be very interesting were there a word of truth in the story. But we liked our guide for his intelligence, simplicity, and for the pleasure which he seemed to take, as an episode of his dull daily life, in talking to strangers. He observed that the castle walls were solid, and, indeed, there was breadth enough to drive a coach and four along the top; but the artillery of the Crimea would have shelled them into ruins in a very few hours. When we got back to the guard-house, he took us inside, and showed the dismal and comfortless rooms where soldiers are confined for drunkenness, and other offences against military laws, telling us that he himself had been confined there, and almost perished with cold. I should not much wonder if he were to get into durance again, through misuse of the fee which I put into his hand at parting.

The cathedral is at no great distance from the castle; and though the streets are mean and sordid in the vicinity, the close has the antique repose and shadowy peace, at once domestic and religious, which seem peculiar and universal in cathedral closes. The foundation of this cathedral church is very ancient, it having been the church portion of an old abbey, the refectory and other remains of which are still seen around the close. But the whole exterior of the building, except here and there a buttress, and one old patch of gray stones, seems to have been renewed within a very few years with red freestone; and, really, I think it is all the more beautiful for being new, — the ornamental parts being so sharply cut, and the stone, moreover, showing various shadings, which will disappear when it gets weather-worn. There is a very large and fine east window, of recent construction, wrought with delicate stone tracery. The door of the south transept stood open, though barred by an iron grate. We looked in, and saw a few monuments on the wall, but found nobody to give us admittance. The portal of this entrance is very lovely with wreaths of stone foliage and flowers round the arch, recently carved; yet not so recently but that the swallows have given their sanction to it, as if it were a thousand years old, and have built their nests in the deeply carved recesses. While we were looking, a little bird flew into the small opening between two of these petrified flowers, behind which was his nest, quite out of sight. After some attempts to find the verger, we went back to the hotel. . . . .

In the morning my wife and J—— went back to see the interior of the cathedral, while I strayed at large about the town, again passing round the castle site, and thence round the city, where I found some inconsiderable portions of the wall which once girt it about. It was market-day in Carlisle, and the principal streets were much thronged with human life and business on that account; and in as busy a street as any stands a marble statue, in robes of antique state, fitter for a niche in Westminster Abbey than for the thronged street of a town. It is a statue of the Earl of Lonsdale, Lord Lieutenant of Cumberland, who died about twenty years ago.

[Here follows the record of the visits to the "Haunts of Burns," already published in Our Old Home. — Ed.]

GLASGOW.

July 1st. — Immediately after our arrival yesterday, we went out and inquired our way to the cathedral, which we reached through a good deal of Scotch dirt, and a rabble of Scotch people of all sexes and ages. The women of Scotland have a faculty of looking exceedingly ugly as they grow old. The cathedral I have already noticed in the record of my former visit to Scotland. I did it no justice then, nor shall do it any better justice now; but it is a fine old church, although it makes a colder and severer impression than most of the Gothic architecture which I have elsewhere seen. I do not know why this should be so;

for portions of it are wonderfully rich, and everywhere there are arches opening beyond arches, and clustered pillars and groined roofs, and vistas, lengthening along the aisles. The person who shows it is an elderly man of jolly aspect and demeanor; he is enthusiastic about the edifice, and makes it the thought and object of his life; and being such a merry sort of man, always saying something mirthfully, and yet, in all his thoughts, words, and actions, having reference to this solemn cathedral, he has the effect of one of the corbels or gargoyles, — those ludicrous, strange sculptures which the Gothic architects appended to their arches.

The upper portion of the minster, though very stately and beautiful, is not nearly so extraordinary as the crypts. Here the intricacy of the arches, and the profound system on which they are arranged, is inconceivable, even when you see them, — a whole company of arches uniting in one keystone; arches uniting to form a glorious canopy over the shrine or tomb of a prelate; arches opening through and beyond one another, whichever way you look, — all amidst a shadowy gloom, yet not one detail wrought out the less beautifully and delicately because it could scarcely be seen. The wreaths of flowers that festoon one of the arches are cut in such relief that they do but just adhere to the stone on which they grow. The pillars are massive, and the arches very low, the effect being a twilight, which at first leads the spectator to imagine himself underground; but by and by I saw that the sunshine came in through the narrow windows, though it scarcely looked liked sunshine then. For many years these crypts were used as burial-ground, and earth was brought in, for the purpose of making graves; so that the noble columns were half buried, and the beauty of the architecture quite lost and forgotten. Now the dead men's bones and the earth that covered them have all been removed, leaving the original pavement of the crypt, or a new one in its stead, with only the old relics of saints, martyrs, and heroes underneath, where they have lain so long that they have become a part of the spot. . . . . I was quite chilled through, and the old verger regretted that we had not come during the late hot weather, when the everlasting damp and chill of the spot would have made us entirely comfortable. These crypts originated in the necessity of keeping the floor of the upper cathedral on one level, the edifice being built on a declivity, and the height of the crypt being measured by the descent of the site.

After writing the above, we walked out and saw something of the newer portion of Glasgow; and, really, I am inclined to think it the stateliest of cities. The Exchange and other public buildings, and the shops in Buchanan Street, are very magnificent; the latter, especially, excelling those of London. There is, however, a pervading sternness and grimness resulting from the dark gray granite, which is the universal building material both of the old and new edifices. Later in the forenoon we again walked out, and went along Argyle Street, and through the Trongate and the Salt-Market. The two latter were formerly the principal business streets, and, together with High Street, the abode of the rich merchants and other great people of the town. High Street, and, still more, the Salt-Market, now swarm with the lower orders to a degree which I never witnessed elsewhere; so that it is difficult to make one's way among the sullen and unclean crowd, and not at all pleasant to breathe in the noisomeness of the atmosphere. The children seem to have been unwashed from birth. Some of the gray houses appear to have once been stately and handsome, and have their high gable ends notched at the edges, like a flight of stairs. We saw the Tron steeple, and the statue of King William III., and searched for the Old Tolbooth. . . . . Wandering up the High Street, we turned once more into the quadrangle of the University, and mounted a broad stone staircase which ascends square, and with right-angular turns on one corner, on the outside of the edifices. It is very striking in appearance, being ornamented with a balustrade, on which are large globes of stone, and a great lion and unicorn curiously sculptured on the opposite side. While we waited here, staring about us, a man approached, and offered to show us the interior. He seemed to be in charge of the College buildings. We accepted his offer, and were led first up this stone staircase, and into a large and stately hall, panelled high towards the ceiling with dark oak, and adorned with elaborately carved cornices, and other wood-work. There was a long reading-table towards one end of the hall, on which were laid pamphlets and periodicals; and a venerable old gentleman, with white head and bowed shoulders, sat there reading a newspaper. This was the Principal of the University, and as he looked towards us graciously, yet as if expecting some explanation of our entrance, I approached and apologized for intruding on the plea of our being strangers and anxious to see the College. He made a courteous response, though in exceedingly decayed and broken accents, being now eighty-six years old, and gave us free leave to inspect everything that was to be seen. This hall was erected two years after the Restoration of Charles II., and has been the scene, doubtless, of many ceremonials and high banquetings since that period; and, among other illustrious personages, Queen Victoria has honored it with her presence. Thence we went into several recitation or lecture rooms in various parts of the buildings; but they were all of an extreme plainness, very unlike the rich old Gothic libraries and chapels and halls which we saw in Oxford. Indeed, the contrast between this Scotch severity and that noble luxuriance, and antique majesty, and rich and sweet repose of Oxford, is very remarkable, both within the edifices and without. But we saw one or two curious things, — for instance, a chair of mahogany, elaborately carved with the arms of Scotland and other devices, and having a piece of the kingly stone of Scone inlaid in its seat. This chair is used by the Principal on certain high occasions, and we ourselves, of course, sat down in it. Our guide assigned to it a date preposterously earlier than could have been the true one, judging either by the character of the carving or by the fact that mahogany has not been known or used much more than a century and a half.

Afterwards he led us into the Divinity Hall, where, he said, there were some old portraits of historic people, and among them an original picture of Mary, Queen of Scots. There was, indeed, a row of old portraits at each end of the apartment, — for instance, Zachariah

Boyd, who wrote the rhyming version of the Bible, which is still kept, safe from any critical eye, in the library of the University, to which he presented this, besides other more valuable benefactions, — for which they have placed his bust in a niche in the principal quadrangle; also, John Knox makes one of the row of portraits; and a dozen or two more of Scotch worthies, all very dark and dingy. As to the picture of Mary of Scotland, it proved to be not hers at all, but a picture of Queen Mary, the consort of William III., whose portrait, together with that of her sister, Queen Anne, hangs in the same row. We told our guide this, but he seemed unwilling to accept it as a fact. There is a museum belonging to the University; but this, for some reason or other, could not be shown to us just at this time, and there was little else to show. We just looked at the gardens, but, though of large extent, they are so meagre and bare — so unlike that lovely shade of the Oxford gardens — that we did not care to make further acquaintance with them.

Then we went back to our hotel, and if there were not already more than enough of description, both past and to come, I should describe George's Square, on one side of which the hotel is situated. A tall column rises in the grassy centre of it, lifting far into the upper air a fine statue of Sir Walter Scott, which we saw to great advantage last night, relieved against the sunset sky; and there are statues of Sir John Moore, a native of Glasgow, and of James Watt, at corners of the square. Glasgow is certainly a noble city.

After lunch we embarked on board the steamer, and came up the Clyde. Ben Lomond, and other Highland hills, soon appeared on the horizon; we passed Douglas Castle, on a point of land projecting into the river; and, passing under the precipitous height of Dumbarton Castle, which we had long before seen, came to our voyage's end at this village, where we have put up at the Elephant Hotel.

July 2d. — After tea, not far from seven o'clock, it being a beautiful decline of day, we set out to walk to

DUMBARTON CASTLE,

which stands apart from the town, and is said to have been once surrounded by the waters of the Clyde. The rocky height on which the castle stands is a very striking object, bulging up out of the Clyde, with abrupt decision, to the elevation of five hundred feet. The summit is cloven in twain, the cleft reaching nearly to the bottom on the side towards the river, but not coming down so deeply on the landward side. It is precipitous all around; and wherever the steepness admits, or does not make assault impossible, there are gray ramparts round the hill, with cannon threatening the lower world. Our path led us beneath one of these precipices several hundred feet sheer down, and with an ivied fragment of ruined wall at the top. A soldier who sat by the wayside told us that this was called the "Lover's Leap," because a young girl, in some love-exigency, had once jumped down from it, and came safely to the bottom. We reached the castle gate, which is near the shore of the Clyde, and there found another artillery soldier, who guided us through the fortress. He said that there were now but about a dozen soldiers stationed in the castle, and no officer.

The lowest battery looks towards the river, and consists of a few twelve-pound cannon; but probably the chief danger of attack was from the land, and the chief pains have been taken to render the castle defensible in that quarter. There are flights of stone stairs ascending up through the natural avenue, in the cleft of the double-summited rock; and about midway there is an arched doorway, beneath which there used to be a portcullis, — so that if an enemy had won the lower part of the fortress, the upper portion was still inaccessible. Where the cleft of the rock widens into a gorge, there are several buildings, old, but not appertaining to the ancient castle, which has almost entirely disappeared. We ascended both summits, and, reaching the loftiest point on the right, stood upon the foundation of a tower that dates back to the fifth century, whence we had a glorious prospect of Highlands and Lowlands; the chief object being Ben Lomond, with its great dome, among a hundred other blue and misty hills, with the sun going down over them; and, in another direction, the Clyde, winding far downward through the plain, with the headland of Dumbeck close at hand, and Douglas Castle at no great distance. On the ramparts beneath us the soldier pointed out the spot where Wallace scaled the wall, climbing an apparently inaccessible precipice, and taking the castle. The principal parts of the ancient castle appear to have been on the other and lower summit of the hill, and thither we now went, and traced the outline of its wall, although none of it is now remaining. Here is the magazine, still containing some powder, and here is a battery of eighteen-pound guns, with pyramids of balls, all in readiness against an assault; which, however, hardly any turn of human affairs can hereafter bring about. The appearance of a fortress is kept up merely for ceremony's sake; and these cannon have grown antiquated. Moreover, as the soldier told us, they are seldom or never fired, even for purposes of rejoicing or salute, because their thunder produces the singular effect of depriving the garrison of water. There is a large tank, and the concussion causes the rifts of the stone to open, and thus lets the water out. Above this battery, and elsewhere about the fortress, there are warders' turrets of stone, resembling great pepper-boxes. When Dr. Johnson visited the castle, he introduced his bulky person into one of these narrow receptacles, and found it difficult to get out again. A gentleman who accompanied him was just stepping forward to offer his assistance, but Boswell whispered him to take no notice, lest Johnson should be offended; so they left him to get out as he could. He did finally extricate himself, else we might have seen his skeleton in the turret. Boswell does not tell this story, which seems to have been handed down by local tradition.

The less abrupt declivities of the rock are covered with grass, and afford food for a few sheep, who scamper about the heights, and seem to have attained the dexterity of goats in clambering. I never knew a purer air than this seems to be, nor a lovelier golden sunset.

Descending into the gorge again, we went into the armory, which is in one of the buildings occupying the space between the two hill-tops. It formerly contained a large collection of arms; but these have been removed to the Tower of London, and there are now only some tattered banners, of which I do not know the history, and some festoons of pistols, and grenades, shells, and grape and canister shot, kept merely as curiosities; and, far more interesting than the above, a few battle-axes, daggers, and spear-heads from the field of Bannockburn; and, more interesting still, the sword of William Wallace. It is a formidable-looking weapon, made for being swayed with both hands, and, with its hilt on the floor, reached about to my chin; but the young girl who showed us the armory said that about nine inches had been broken off the point. The blade was not massive, but somewhat thin, compared with its great length; and I found that I could brandish it, using both hands, with perfect ease. It is two-edged, without any gaps, and is quite brown and lustreless with old rust, from point to hilt.

These were all the memorables of our visit to Dumbarton Castle, which is a most interesting spot, and connected with a long series of historical events. It was first besieged by the Danes, and had a prominent share in all the warfare of Scotland, so long as the old warlike times and manners lasted. Our soldier was very intelligent and courteous, but, as usual with these guides, was somewhat apocryphal in his narrative; telling us that Mary, Queen of Scots, was confined here before being taken to England, and that the cells in which she then lived are still extant, under one of the ramparts. The fact is, she was brought here when a child of six years old, before going to France, and doubtless scrambled up and down these heights as freely and merrily as the sheep we saw.

We now returned to our hotel, a very nice one, and found the street of Dumbarton all alive in the summer evening with the sports of children and the gossip of grown people. There was almost no night, for at twelve o'clock there was still a golden daylight, and Yesterday, before it died, must have met the Morrow.

In the lower part of the fortress there is a large sun-dial of stone, which was made by a French officer imprisoned here during the Peninsular war. It still numbers faithfully the hours that are sunny, and it is a lasting memorial of him, in the stronghold of his enemies.

INVERANNAN.

Evening. — After breakfast at Dumbarton, I went out to look at the town, which is of considerable size, and possesses both commerce and manufactures. There was a screw-steamship at the pier, and many sailor-looking people were seen about the streets. There are very few old houses, though still the town retains an air of antiquity which one does not well see how to account for, when everywhere there is a modern front, and all the characteristics of a street built to-day. Turning from the main thoroughfare I crossed a bridge over the Clyde, and gained from it the best view of the cloven crag of Dumbarton Castle that I had yet found. The two summits are wider apart, more fully relieved from each other, than when seen from other points; and the highest ascends into a perfect pyramid, the lower one being obtusely rounded. There seem to be iron-works, or some kind of manufactory, on the farther side of the bridge; and I noticed a quaint, chateau-like mansion, with hanging turrets standing apart from the street, probably built by some person enriched by business.

We left Dumbarton at noon, taking the rail to Balloch, and the steamer to the head of Loch Lomond.

Wild mountain scenery is not very good to describe, nor do I think any distinct impressions are ever conveyed by such attempts; so I mean to be brief in what I saw about this part of our tour, especially as I suspect that I have said whatever I knew how to say in the record of my former visit to the Highlands. As for Loch Lomond, it lies amidst very striking scenery, being poured in among the gorges of steep and lofty mountains, which nowhere stand aside to give it room, but, on the contrary, do their best to shut it in. It is everywhere narrow, compared with its length of thirty miles; but it is the beauty of a lake to be of no greater width than to allow of the scenery of one of its shores being perfectly enjoyed from the other. The scenery of the Highlands, so far as I have seen it, cannot properly be called rich, but stern and impressive, with very hard outlines, which are unsoftened, mostly, by any foliage, though at this season they are green to their summits. They have hardly flesh enough to cover their bones, — hardly earth enough to lie over their rocky substance, — as may be seen by the minute variety, — the notched and jagged appearance of the profile of their sides and tops; this being caused by the scarcely covered rocks wherewith these great hills are heaped together.

Our little steamer stopped at half a dozen places on its voyage up the lake, most of them being stations where hotels have been established. Morally, the Highlands must have been more completely sophisticated by the invention of railways and steamboats than almost any other part of the world; but physically it can have wrought no great change. These mountains, in their general aspect, must be very much the same as they were thousands of years ago; for their sides never were capable of cultivation, nor even with such a soil and so bleak an atmosphere could they have been much more richly wooded than we see them now. They seem to me to be among the unchangeable things of Nature, like the sea and sky; but there is no saying what use human ingenuity may hereafter put them to. At all events, I have no doubt in the world that they will go out of fashion in due time; for the taste for mountains and wild scenery is, with most people, an acquired taste, and it was easy to see to-day that nine people in ten care nothing about them. One group of gentlemen and ladies — at least, men and women — spent the whole time in listening to a trial for murder, which was read aloud by one of their number from a newspaper. I rather imagine that a taste for trim gardens is the most natural and universal taste as regards landscape. But perhaps it is necessary for the health of the human mind and heart that there should be a possibility of taking refuge in what is wild and uncontaminated by any meddling of man's hand, and so it has been ordained that science shall never alter the aspect of the sky, whether stern, angry, or beneficent, — nor of the awful sea, either in calm or tempest, — nor of these rude Highlands. But they will go out of general fashion, as I have said, and perhaps the next fashionable taste will be for cloud land, — that is, looking skyward, and observing the wonderful variety of scenery, that now constantly passes unnoticed, among the clouds.

At the head of the lake, we found that there was only a horse-cart to convey our luggage to the hotel at Inverannan, and that we ourselves must walk, the distance being two miles. It had sprinkled occasionally during our voyage, but was now sunshiny, and not excessively warm; so we set forth contentedly enough, and had an agreeable walk along an almost perfectly level road; for it is one of the beauties of these hills, that they descend abruptly down, instead of undulating away forever. There were lofty heights on each side of us, but not so lofty as to have won a distinctive name; and adown their sides we could see the rocky pathways of cascades, which, at this season, are either quite dry, or mere trickles of a rill. The hills and valleys abound in streams, sparkling through pebbly beds, and forming here and there a dark pool; and they would be populous with trout if all England, with one fell purpose, did not come hither to fish them. A fisherman must find it difficult to gratify his propensities in these days; for even the lakes and streams in Norway are now preserved. J——, by the way, threatens ominously to be a fisherman. He rode the latter portion of the way to the hotel on the luggage-cart; and when we arrived, we found that he had already gone off to catch fish, or to attempt it (for there is as much chance of his catching a whale as a trout), in a mountain stream near the house. I went in search of him, but without success, and was somewhat startled at the depth and blackness of some of the pools into which the stream settled itself and slept. Finally, he came in while we were at dinner. We afterwards walked out with him, to let him play at fishing again, and discovered on the bank of the stream a wonderful oak, with as many as a dozen boles springing either from close to the ground or within a foot or two of it, and looking like twelve separate trees, at least, instead of one.

INVERSNAID.

July 3d. — Last night seemed to close in clear, and even at midnight it was still light enough to read; but this morning rose on us misty and chill, with spattering showers of rain. Clouds momentarily settled and shifted on the hill-tops, shutting us in even more completely than these steep and rugged green walls would be sure to do, even in the clearest weather. Often these clouds came down and enveloped us in a drizzle, or rather a shower, of such minute drops that they had not weight enough to fall. This, I suppose, was a genuine Scotch mist; and as such it is well enough to have experienced it, though I would willingly never see it again. Such being the state of the weather, my wife did not go out at all, but I strolled about the premises, in the intervals of rain-drops, gazing up at the hillsides, and recognizing that there is a vast variety of shape, of light and shadow, and incidental circumstance, even in what looks so monotonous at first as the green slope of a hill. The little rills that come down from the summits were rather more distinguishable than yesterday, having been refreshed by the night's rain; but still they were very much out of proportion with the wide pathways of bare rock adown which they ran. These little rivulets, no doubt, often lead through the wildest scenery that is to be found in the Highlands, or anywhere else, and to the formation and wildness of which they have greatly contributed by sawing away for countless ages, and thus deepening the ravines.

I suspect the American clouds are more picturesque than those of Great Britain, whatever our mountains may be; at least, I remember the Berkshire hills looking grander, under the influence of mist and cloud, than the Highlands did to-day. Our clouds seem to be denser and heavier, and more decided, and form greater contrasts of light and shade. I have remarked in England that the cloudy firmament, even on a day of settled rain, always appears thinner than those I had been accustomed to at home, so as to deceive me with constant expectations of better weather. It has been the same to-day. Whenever I looked upward, I thought it might be going to clear up; but, instead of that, it began to rain more in earnest after midday, and at half past two we left Inverannan in a smart shower. At the head of the lake, we took the steamer, with the rain pouring more heavily than ever, and landed at Inversnaid under the same dismal auspices. We left a very good hotel behind us, and have come to another that seems also good. We are more picturesquely situated at this spot than at Inverannan, our hotel being within a short distance of the lake shore, with a glen just across the water, which will doubtless be worth looking at when the mist permits us to see it. A good many tourists were standing about the door when we arrived, and looked at us with the curiosity of idle and weather-bound people. The lake is here narrow, but a hundred fathoms deep; so that a great part of the height of the mountains which beset it round is hidden beneath its surface.

July 4th. — This morning opened still misty, but with a more hopeful promise than yesterday, and when I went out, after breakfast, there were gleams of sunshine here and there on the hillsides, falling, one did not exactly see how, through the volumes of cloud. Close beside the hotel of Inversnaid is the waterfall; all night, my room being on that side of the house, I had heard its voice, and now I ascended beside it to a point where it is crossed by a wooden bridge. There is thence a view, upward and downward, of the most striking descents of the river, as I believe they call it, though it is but a mountain-stream, which tumbles down an irregular and broken staircase in its headlong haste to reach the lake. It is very picturesque, however, with its ribbons of white foam over the precipitous steps, and its deep black pools, overhung by black rocks, which reverberate the rumble of the falling water. J—— and I ascended a little distance along the cascade, and then turned aside; he going up the hill, and I taking a path along its side which gave me a view across the lake. I rather think this particular stretch of Loch Lomond, in front of Inversnaid, is the most beautiful lake and mountain view that I have ever seen. It is so shut in that you can see nothing beyond, nor would suspect anything more to exist than this watery vale among the hills; except that, directly opposite, there is the beautiful glen of Inveruglass, which winds away among the feet of Ben Crook, Ben Ein, Ben Vain and Ben Voirlich, standing mist-inwreathed together. The mists, this morning, had a very soft and beautiful effect, and made the mountains tenderer than I have hitherto felt them to be; and they lingered about their heads like morning-dreams, flitting and retiring, and letting the sunshine in, and snatching it away again. My wife came up, and we enjoyed it together, till the steamer came smoking its pipe along the loch, stopped to land some passengers, and steamed away again. While we stood there, a Highlander passed by us, with a very dark tartan, and bare shanks, most enormously calved. I presume he wears the dress for the sole purpose of displaying those stalwart legs; for he proves to be no genuine Gael, but a manufacturer, who has a shooting-box, or a share in one, on the hill above the hotel.

We now engaged a boat, and were rowed to Rob Roy's cave, which is perhaps half a mile distant up the lake. The shores look much more striking from a row-boat, creeping along near the margin, than from a steamer in the middle of the loch; and the ridge, beneath which Rob's cave lies, is precipitous with gray rocks, and clothed, too, with thick foliage. Over the cave itself there is a huge ledge of rock, from which immense fragments have tumbled down, ages and ages ago, and fallen together in such a way as to leave a large irregular crevice in Rob Roy's cave. We scrambled up to its mouth by some natural stairs, and scrambled down into its depths by the aid of a ladder. I suppose I have already described this hole in the record of my former visit. Certainly, Rob Roy, and Robert Bruce, who is said to have inhabited it before him, were not to be envied their accommodations; yet these were not so very intolerable when compared with a Highland cabin, or with cottages such as Burns lived in.

J—— had chosen to remain to fish. On our return

from the cave, we found that he had caught nothing; but just as we stepped into the boat, a fish drew his float far under water, and J—— tugging at one end of the line, and the fish at the other, the latter escaped, with the hook in his mouth. J—— avers that he saw the fish, and gives its measurement as about eighteen inches; but the fishes that escape us are always of tremendous size. The boatman thought, however, that it might have been a pike.

THE TROSACHS' HOTEL.—ARDCHEANOCHROCHAN.

July 5th.—. . . . Not being able to get a post-chaise, we took places in the omnibus for the head of Loch Katrine. Going up to pay a parting visit to the waterfall before starting, I met with Miss C——, as she lately was, who is now on her wedding tour as Mrs. B——. She was painting the falls in oil, with good prospect of a successful picture. She came down to the hotel to see my wife, and soon afterwards J—— and I set out to ascend the steep hill that comes down upon the lake of Inversnaid, leaving the omnibus to follow at leisure. The Highlander who took us to Rob Roy's cave had foreboded rain, from the way in which the white clouds hung about the mountain-tops; nor was his augury at fault, for just at three o'clock, the time he foretold, there were a few rain-drops, and a more defined shower during the afternoon, while we were on Loch Katrine. The few drops, however, did not disturb us; and, reaching the top of the hill, J—— and I turned aside to examine the old stone fortress which was erected in this mountain pass to bridle the Highlanders after the rebellion of 1745. It stands in a very desolate and dismal situation, at the foot of long bare slopes, on mossy ground, in the midst of a disheartening loneliness, only picturesque because it is so exceedingly ungenial and unlovely. The chief interest of this spot is the fact that Wolfe, in his earlier military career, was stationed here. The fortress was a very plain structure, built of rough stones, in the form of a parallelogram, one side of which I paced, and found it between thirty and forty of my paces long. The two ends have fallen down; the two sides that remain are about twenty feet high, and have little port-holes for defence, but no openings of the size of windows. The roof is gone, and the interior space overgrown with grass. Two little girls were at play in one corner, and, going round to the rear of the ruin, I saw that a small Highland cabin had been built against the wall. A dog sat in the doorway, and gave notice of my approach, and some hens kept up their peculiarly domestic converse about the door.

We kept on our way, often looking back towards Loch Lomond, and wondering at the grandeur which Ben Vain and Ben Voirlich, and the rest of the Ben fraternity, had suddenly put on. The mists which had hung about them all day had now descended lower, and lay among the depths and gorges of the hills, where also the sun shone softly down among them, and filled those deep mountain laps, as it were, with a dimmer sunshine. Ben Vain, too, and his brethren, had a veil of mist all about them, which seemed to render them really transparent; and they had unaccountably grown higher, vastly higher, than when we viewed them from the shore of the lake. It was as if we were looking at them through the medium of a poet's imagination. All along the road, since we left Inversnaid, there had been the stream, which there formed the waterfall, and which here was brawling down little declivities, and sleeping in black pools, which we disturbed by flinging stones into them from the roadside. We passed a drunken old gentleman, who civilly bade me "good day"; and a man and woman at work in a field, the former of whom shouted to inquire the hour; and we had come in sight of little Loch Arklet before the omnibus came up with us. It was about five o'clock when we reached the head of

LOCH KATRINE,

and went on board the steamer Rob Roy; and, setting forth on our voyage, a Highland piper made music for us the better part of the way.

We did not see Loch Katrine, perhaps, under its best presentment; for the surface was roughened with a little wind, and darkened even to inky blackness by the clouds that overhung it. The hill-tops, too, wore a very dark frown. A lake of this size cannot be terrific, and is therefore seen to best advantage when it is beautiful. The scenery of its shores is not altogether so rich and lovely as I had preimagined; not equal, indeed, to the best parts of Loch Lomond, — the hills being lower and of a more ridgy shape, and exceedingly bare, at least towards the lower end. But they turn the lake aside with headland after headland, and shut it in closely, and open one vista after another, so that the eye is never weary, and, least of all, as we approach the end. The length of the loch is ten miles, and at its termination it meets the pass of the Trosachs, between Ben An and Ben Venue, which are the rudest and shaggiest of hills. The steamer passes Ellen's Isle, but to the right, which is the side opposite to that on which Fitz-James must be supposed to have approached it. It is a very small island, situated where the loch narrows, and is perhaps less than a quarter of a mile distant from either shore. It looks like a lump of rock, with just soil enough to support a crowd of dwarf oaks, birches, and firs, which do not grow so high as to be shadowy trees. Our voyage being over, we landed, and found two omnibuses, one of which took us through the famous pass of the Trosachs, a distance of a mile and a quarter, to a hotel, erected in castellated guise by Lord Willoughby d'Eresby. We were put into a parlor within one of the round towers, panelled all round, and with four narrow windows, opening through deep embrasures. No play-castle was ever more like the reality, and it is a very good hotel, like all that we have had experience of in the Highlands. After tea we walked out, and visited a little kirk that stands near the shore of Loch Achray, at a good point of view for seeing the hills round about.

This morning opened cloudily; but after breakfast I set out alone, and walked through the pass of the Trosachs, and thence by a path along the right shore of the lake. It is a very picturesque and beautiful path, following the windings of the lake, — now along the beach, now over an impending bank, until it comes opposite to Ellen's Isle, which on this side looks more worthy to be the island of the poem than as we first saw it. Its shore is craggy and precipitous, but there was a point where it seemed possible to land, nor was it too much to fancy that there might be a rustic habitation among the shrubbery of this rugged spot. It is foolish to look into these matters too strictly. Scott evidently used as much freedom with his natural scenery as he did with his historic incidents; and he could have made nothing of either one or the other if he had been more scrupulous in his arrangement and adornment of them. In his description of the Trosachs, he has produced something very beautiful, and as true as possible, though certainly its beauty has a little of the scene-painter's gloss on it. Nature is better, no doubt, but Nature cannot be exactly reproduced on canvas or in print; and the artist's only resource is to substitute something that may stand instead of and suggest the truth.

The path still kept onward, after passing Ellen's Isle, and I followed it, finding it wilder, more shadowy with overhanging foliage of trees, old and young, — more like a mountain-path in Berkshire or New Hampshire, yet still with an old-world restraint and cultivation about it, — the farther I went. At last I came upon some bars, and though the track was still seen beyond, I took this as a hint to stop, especially as I was now two or three miles from the hotel, and it just then began to rain. My umbrella was a poor one at best, and had been tattered and turned inside out, a day or two ago, by a gust on Loch Lomond; but I spread it to the shower, and, furthermore, took shelter under the thickest umbrage I could find. The rain came straight down, and bubbled in the loch; the little rills gathered force, and plashed merrily over the stones;

the leaves of the trees condensed the shower into large drops, and shed them down upon me where I stood. Still I was comfortable enough in a thick Skye Tweed, and waited paitently till the rain abated; then took my way homeward, and admired the pass of the Trosachs more than when I first traversed it. If it has a fault, it is one that few scenes in Great Britain share with it, — that is, the trees and shrubbery, with which the precipices are shagged, conceal them a little too much. A crag, streaked with black and white, here and there shows its head aloft, or its whole height from base to summit, and suggests that more of such sublimity is hidden than revealed. I think, however, that it is this unusual shagginess which made the scene a favorite with Scott, and with the people on this side of the ocean generally. There are many scenes as good in America, needing only the poet.

July 6th. — We dined yesterday at the *table d'hôte*, at the suggestion of the butler, in order to give less trouble to the servants of the hotel, and afford them an opportunity to go to kirk. The dining-room is in accordance with the rest of the architecture and fittings up of the house, and is a very good reproduction of an old baronial hall, with high panellings and a roof of dark, polished wood. There were about twenty guests at table; and if they and the waiters had been dressed in mediæval costume, we might have imagined ourselves banqueting in the Middle Ages.

After dinner we all took a walk through the Trosachs' pass again, and by the right-hand path along the lake, as far as Ellen's Isle. It was very pleasant, there being gleams of calm evening sunshine gilding the mountain-sides, and putting a golden crown occasionally on the head of Ben Venue. It is wonderful how many aspects a mountain has, — how many mountains there are in every single mountain! — how they vary too, in apparent attitude and bulk. When we reached the lake, its surface was almost unruffled, except by now and then the narrow pathway of a breeze, as if the wing of an unseen spirit had just grazed it in flitting across. The scene was very beautiful, and, on the whole, I do not know that Walter Scott has overcharged his description, although he has symbolized the reality by types and images which it might not precisely suggest to other minds. We were reluctant to quit the spot, and cherish still a hope of seeing it again, though the hope does not seem very likely to be gratified.

This was a lowering and sullen morning, but soon after breakfast I took a walk in the opposite direction to Loch Katrine, and reached the Brig of Turk, a little beyond which is the new Trosachs' Hotel, and the little rude village of Duncraggan, consisting of a few hovels of stone, at the foot of a bleak and dreary hill. To the left, stretching up between this and other hills, is the valley of Glenfinlass, — a very awful region in Scott's poetry and in Highland tradition, as the haunt of spirits and enchantments. It presented a very desolate prospect. The walk back to the Trosachs showed me Ben Venue and Ben An under new aspects, — the bare summit of the latter rising in a perfect pyramid, whereas from other points of view it looks like quite a different mountain. Sometimes a gleam of sunshine came out upon the rugged side of Ben Venue, but his prevailing mood, like that of the rest of the landscape, was stern and gloomy. I wish I could give an idea of the variety of surface upon one of these hillsides, — so bulging out and hollowed in, so bare where the rock breaks through, so shaggy in other places with heath, and then, perhaps, a thick umbrage of birch, oak, and ash ascending from the base high upward. When I think I have described them, I remember quite a different aspect, and find it equally true, and yet lacking something to make it the whole or an adequate truth.

J—— had gone with me part of the way, but stopped to fish with a pin-hook in Loch Achray, which bordered along our path. When I returned, I found him much elated at having caught a fish, which, however, had got away, carrying his pin-hook along with it. Then he had amused himself with taking some lizards by the tail, and had collected several in a small hollow of the rocks. We now walked home together, and at half past three we took our seats in a genuine old-fashioned stage-coach, of which there are few specimens now to be met with. The coachman was smartly dressed in the Queen's scarlet, and was a very pleasant and affable personage, conducting himself towards the passengers with courteous authority. Inside we were four, including J——, but on the top there were at least a dozen, and I would willingly have been there too, but had taken an inside seat, under apprehension of rain, and was not allowed to change it. Our drive was not marked by much describable incident. On changing horses at Callender, we alighted, and saw Ben

Ledi behind us, making a picturesque background to the little town, which seems to be the meeting-point of the Highlands and Lowlands. We again changed horses at Doune, an old town, which would doubtless have been well worth seeing, had time permitted. Thence we kept on till the coach drew up at a spacious hotel, where we alighted, fancying that we had reached Stirling, which was to have been our journey's end; but, after fairly establishing ourselves, we found that it was the

BRIG OF ALLAN.

The place is three miles short of Stirling. Nevertheless, we did not much regret the mistake, finding that the Brig of Allan is the principal Spa of Scotland, and a very pleasant spot, to all outward appearance. After tea we walked out, both up and down the village street, and across the bridge, and up a gentle eminence beyond it, whence we had a fine view of a glorious plain, out of which rose several insulated headlands. One of these was the height on which stands Stirling Castle, and which reclines on the plain like a hound or a lion or a sphinx, holding the castle on the highest part, where its head should be. A mile or two distant from this picturesque hill rises another, still more striking, called the Abbey Craig, on which is a ruin, and where is to be built the monument to William Wallace. I cannot conceive a nobler or more fitting pedestal. The sullenness of the day had vanished, the air was cool but invigorating, and the cloud scenery was as fine as that below it.

. . . . Though it was nearly ten o'clock, the boys of the village were in full shout and play, for these long and late summer evenings keep the children out of bed interminably.

STIRLING.

July 7th. — We bestirred ourselves early this morning, ... and took the rail for Stirling before eight. It is but a few minutes' ride, so that doubtless we were earlier on the field than if we had slept at Stirling. After our arrival our first call was at the post-office, where I found a large package containing letters from America, but none from U——. We then went to a bookseller's shop, and bought some views of Stirling and the neighborhood; and it is surprising what a quantity and variety of engravings there are of every noted place that we have visited. You seldom find two sets alike. It is rather nauseating to find that what you came to see has already been looked at in all its lights, over and over again, with thousand-fold repetition; and, beyond question, its depictment in words has been attempted still oftener than with the pencil. It will be worth while to go back to America, were it only for the chance of finding a still virgin scene.

We climbed the steep slope of the Castle Hill, sometimes passing an antique-looking house, with a high, notched gable, perhaps with an ornamented front, until we came to the sculptures and battlemented wall, with an archway, that stands just below the castle. . . . . A shabby-looking man now accosted us, and could hardly be shaken off. I have met with several such boors in my experience of sight-seeing. He kept along with us, in spite of all hints to the contrary, and insisted on pointing out objects of interest. He showed us a house in Broad Street, below the castle and cathedral, which he said had once been inhabited by Henry Darnley, Queen Mary's husband. There was little or nothing peculiar in its appearance; a large, gray, gabled house standing lengthwise to the street, with three windows in the roof, and connected with other houses on each side. Almost directly across the street, he pointed to an archway, through the side of a house, and, peeping through it, we found a soldier on guard in a court-yard, the sides of which were occupied by an old mansion of the Argyle family, having towers at the corners, with conical tops, like those reproduced in the hotel at the Trosachs. It is now occupied as a military hospital. Shaking off our self-inflicted guide, we now made our way to the castle parade, and to the gateway, where a soldier with a tremendously red nose and two medals at once took charge of us.

Beyond all doubt, I have written quite as good a description of the castle and Cärse of Stirling in a former portion of my journal as I can now write. We passed through the outer rampart of Queen Anne; through the old round gate-tower of an earlier day, and beneath the vacant arch where the portcullis used to fall, thus reaching the inner region, where stands the old palace on one side, and the old Parliament House on the other. The former looks aged, ragged, and rusty, but makes a good appearance enough pictorially, being adorned all round about with statues, which may have been white marble once, but are as gray as weather-beaten granite now, and look down from between the windows above the basement story. A photograph would give the idea of very rich antiquity, but as it really stands, looking on a gravelled court-yard, and with "CANTEEN" painted on one of its doors, the spectator does not find it very impressive. The great hall of this palace is now partitioned off into two or three rooms, and the whole edifice is arranged to serve as barracks. Of course, no trace of ancient magnificence, if anywise destructible, can be left in the interior. We were not shown into this palace, nor into the Parliament House, nor into the tower, where King James stabbed the Earl of Douglas. When I was here a year ago, I went up the old staircase and into the room where the murder was committed, although it had recently been the scene of a fire, which consumed as much of it as was inflammable. The window whence the Earl's body was thrown then remained; but now the whole tower seems to have been renewed, leaving only the mullions of the historic window.

We merely looked up at the new, light-colored freestone of the restored tower in passing, and ascended to the ramparts, where we found one of the most splendid views, morally and materially, that this world can show. Indeed, I think there cannot be such a landscape as the Carse of Stirling, set in such a frame as it is, — the Highlands, comprehending our friends, Ben Lomond, Ben Venue, Ben An, and the whole Ben brotherhood, with the Grampians surrounding it to the westward and northward, and in other directions some range of prominent objects to shut it in; and the plain itself, so worthy of the richest setting, so fertile, so beautiful, so written over and over again with histories. The silver Links of Forth are as sweet and gently picturesque an object as a man sees in a lifetime. I do not wonder that Providence caused great things to happen on this plain; it was like choosing a good piece of canvas to paint a great picture upon. The battle of Bannockburn (which we saw beneath us, with the Gillie's Hill on the right) could not have been fought upon a meaner plain, nor Wallace's victory gained; and if any other great historic act still remains to be done in this country, I should imagine the Cärse of Stirling to be the future scene of it. Scott seems to me hardly to have done justice to this landscape, or to have bestowed pains enough to put it in strong relief before the world; although it is from the lights shed on it, and so much other Scottish scenery, by his mind, that we chiefly see it, and take an interest in it. . . . .

I do not remember seeing the hill of execution before, — a mound on the same level as the castle's base, looking towards the Highlands. A solitary cow was now feeding upon it. I should imagine that no person could ever have been unjustly executed there; the spot is too much in the sight of heaven and earth to countenance injustice.

Descending from the ramparts, we went into the Armory, which I did not see on my former visit. The superintendent of this department is an old soldier of very great intelligence and vast communicativeness, and quite absorbed in thinking of and handling weapons; for he is a practical armorer. He had few things to show us that were very interesting, — a helmet or two, a bomb and grenade from the Crimea; also some muskets from the same quarter, one of which, with a sword at the end, he spoke of admiringly, as the best weapon in the collection, its only fault being its extreme weight. He showed us, too, some Minie rifles, and whole ranges of the old-fashioned Brown Bess, which had helped to win Wellington's victories; also the halberts of sergeants now laid aside, and some swords that had been used at the battle of Sheriffmuir. These latter were very short, not reaching to the floor, when I held one of them, point downward, in my hand. The shortness of the blade and consequent closeness of the encounter, must have given the weapon a most dagger-like murderousness. Hanging in the hall of arms, there were two tattered banners that had gone through the Peninsular battles, one of them belonging to the gallant 42d Regiment. The armorer gave my wife a rag from each of these banners, consecrated by so much battle smoke; also a piece of old oak, half burned to charcoal, which had been rescued from the panelling of the Douglas Tower. We saw better things, more-over, than all these rusty weapons and ragged flags; namely, the pulpit and communion-table of John Knox. The frame of the former, if I remember aright, is complete; but one or two of the panels are knocked out and lost, and, on the whole, it looks as if it had been shaken to pieces by the thunder of his holdings forth, — much worm-eaten, too, is the old oak wood, as well it may be, for the letters MD (1500) are carved on its front. The communion-table is polished, and in much better preservation.

Then the armorer showed us a Damascus blade, of the kind that will cut a delicate silk handkerchief while floating in the air; and some inlaid matchlock guns. A child's little toy-gun was lying on a work-bench among all this array of weapons; and when I took it up and smiled, he said that it was his son's.

So he called in a little fellow of four years' old, who was playing in the castle yard, and made him go through the musket exercise, which he did with great good-will. This small Son of a Gun, the father assured us, cares for nothing but arms, and has attained all his skill with the musket merely by looking at the soldiers on parade. . . . .

Our soldier, who had resigned the care of us to the armorer, met us again at the door, and led us round the remainder of the ramparts, dismissing us finally at the gate by which we entered. All the time we were in the castle there had been a great discordance of drums and fifes, caused by the musicians who were practising just under the walls; likewise the sergeants were drilling their squads of men, and putting them through strange gymnastic motions. Most, if not all, of the garrison belongs to a Highland regiment, and those whom we saw on duty, in full costume, looked very martial and gallant. Emerging from the castle, we took the broad and pleasant footpath, which circles it about midway on the grassy steep which descends from the rocky precipice on which the walls are built. This is a very beautiful walk, and affords a most striking view of the castle, right above our heads, the height of its wall forming one line with the precipice. The grassy hillside is almost as precipitous as the dark gray rock that rises out of it, to form the foundations of the castle; but wild rose-bushes, both of a white and red variety, are abundant here, and all in bloom; nor are these the only flowers. There is also shrubbery in some spots, tossing up green waves against the precipice; and broad sheets of ivy here and there mantle the headlong rock, which also has a growth of weeds in its crevices. The castle walls above, however, are quite bare of any such growth. Thus, looking up at the old storied fortress, and looking down over the wide, historic plain, we wandered half-way round the castle, and then, retracing our steps, entered the town close by an old hospital.

A hospital it was, or had been intended for; but the authorities of the town had made some convenient arrangement with those entitled to its charity, and had appropriated the ancient edifice to themselves. So said a boy who showed us into the Guildhall, — an apartment with a vaulted oaken roof, and otherwise of antique aspect and furniture; all of which, however, were modern restorations. We then went into an old church or cathedral, which was divided into two parts; one of them, in which I saw the royal arms, being probably for the Church-of-England service, and the other for the Kirk of Scotland. I remember little or nothing of this edifice, except that the Covenanters had uglified it with pews and a gallery, and whitewash; though I doubt not it was a stately Gothic church, with innumerable enrichments and incrustations of beauty, when it passed from popish hands into theirs. Thence we wandered downward, through a back street, amid very shabby houses, some of which bore tokens of having once been the abodes of courtly and noble personages. We paused before one that displayed, I think, the sign of a spirit-retailer, and looked as disreputable as a house could, yet was built of stalwart stone, and had two circular towers in front, once, doubtless, crowned with conical tops. We asked an elderly man whether he knew anything of the history of this house; and he said that he had been acquainted with it for almost fifty years, but never knew anything noteworthy about it. Reaching the foot of the hill, along whose back the streets of Stirling run, and which blooms out into the Castle Craig, we returned to the railway, and at noon took leave of Stirling.

I forgot to tell of the things that awakened rather more sympathy in us than any other objects in the castle armory. These were some rude weapons — pikes, very roughly made; and old rusty muskets, broken and otherwise out of order; and swords, by no means with Damascus blades — that had been taken from some poor weavers and other handicraft men who rose against the government in 1820. I pitied the poor fellows much, seeing how wretched were their means of standing up against the cannon, bayonets, swords, shot, shell, and all manner of murderous facilities possessed by their oppressors. Afterwards, our guide showed, in a gloomy quadrangle of the castle, the low windows of the dungeons where two of the leaders of the insurrectionists had been confined before their execution. I have not the least shadow of doubt that these men had a good cause to fight for; but what availed it with such weapons! and so few even of those!

. . . . . I believe I cannot go on to recount any further this evening the experiences of to-day. It has been a very rich day; only that I have seen more than my sluggish powers of reception can well take in at once. After quitting Stirling, we came in somewhat less than an hour to

LINLITHGOW,

and, alighting, took up our quarters at the Star and Garter Hotel, which, like almost all the Scottish caravansaries of which we have had experience, turns out a comfortable one. . . . . We stayed within doors for an hour or two, and I busied myself with writing up my journal. At about three, however, the sky brightened a little, and we set forth through the ancient, rusty, and queer-looking town of Linlithgow, towards the palace and the ancient church, which latter was one of St. David's edifices, and both of which stand close together, a little removed from the long street of the village. But I can never describe them worthily, and shall make nothing of the description if I attempt it now.

July 8th. — At about three o'clock yesterday, as I said, we walked forth through the ancient street of Linlithgow, and, coming to the market-place, stopped to look at an elaborate and heavy stone fountain, which we found by an inscription to be a fac-simile of an old one that used to stand on the same site. Turning to the right, the outer entrance to the palace fronts on this market-place, if such it be; and close to it, a little on one side, is the church. A young woman, with a key in her hand, offered to admit us into the latter; so we went in, and found it divided by a wall across the middle into two parts. The hither portion, being the nave, was whitewashed, and looked as bare and uninteresting as an old Gothic church of St. David's epoch possibly could do. The interior portion, being the former choir, is covered with pews over the whole floor, and further defaced by galleries, that unmercifully cut midway across the stately and beautiful arches. It is likewise whitewashed. There were, I believe, some mural monuments of Bailies and other such people stuck up about the walls, but nothing that much interested me, except an ancient oaken chair, which the girl said was the chair of St. Crispin, and it was fastened to the wall, in the holiest part of the church. I know not why it was there; but as it had been the chair of so distinguished a personage, we all sat down in it. It was in this church that the apparition of St. James appeared to King James IV., to warn him against engaging in that war which resulted in the battle of Flodden, where he and the flower of his nobility were slain. The young woman showed us the spot where the apparition spake to him, — a side chapel, with a groined roof, at the end of the choir next the nave. The Covenanters seem to have shown some respect to this one chapel, by refraining from drawing the gallery across its height; so that, except for the whitewash, and the loss of the painted glass in the window, and probably of a good deal of rich architectural detail, it looks as it did when the ghostly saint entered beneath its arch, while the king was kneeling there.

We stayed but a little while in the church, and then proceeded to the palace, which, as I said, is close at hand. On entering the outer enclosure through an ancient gateway, we were surprised to find how entire the walls seemed to be; but the reason is, I suppose, that the ruins have not been used as a stone-quarry, as has almost always been the case with old abbeys and castles. The palace took fire and was consumed, so far as consumable, in 1745, while occupied by the soldiers of General Hawley; but even yet the walls appear so stalwart that I should imagine it quite possible to rebuild and restore the stately rooms on their original plan. It was a noble palace, one hundred and seventy-five feet in length by one hundred and sixty-five in breadth, and though destitute of much architectural beauty externally, yet its aspect from the quadrangle which the four sides enclose is venerable and sadly beautiful. At each of the interior angles there is a circular tower, up the whole height of the edifice and overtopping it, and another in the centre of one of the sides, all containing winding staircases. The walls facing upon the enclosed quadrangle are pierced with many windows, and have been ornamented with sculpture, rich traces of which still remain over the arched entrance-ways; and in the grassy centre of the court there is the ruin and broken fragments of a fountain, which once used to play for the delight of the king and queen, and lords and ladies, who looked down upon it from hall and chamber. Many old carvings that belonged to it are heaped together there; but the water has disappeared, though, had it been a natural spring, it would have outlasted all the heavy stonework.

As far as we were able, and could find our way, we went through every room of the palace, all round the four sides. From the first floor upwards it is entirely roofless. In some of the chambers there is an accumulation of soil, and a goodly crop of grass; in others there is still a flooring of flags or brick tiles, though damp and moss-grown, and with weeds sprouting between the crevices. Grass and weeds, indeed, have found soil enough to flourish in, even on the highest ranges of the walls, though at a dizzy height above the ground; and it was like an old and trite touch of romance, to see how the weeds sprouted on the many hearth-stones and aspired under the chimney-flues, as if in emulation of the long-extinguished flame. It was very mournful, very beautiful, very delightful, too, to see how Nature takes back the palace, now that kings have done with it, and adopts it as a part of her great garden.

On one side of the quadrangle we found the roofless chamber where Mary, Queen of Scots, was born, and in the same range the bedchamber that was occupied by several of the Scottish Jameses; and in one corner of the latter apartment there is a narrow, winding staircase, down which I groped, expecting to find a door, either into the enclosed quadrangle or to the outside of the palace. But it ends in nothing, unless it be a dungeon; and one does not well see why the bedchamber of the king should be so convenient to a dungeon. It is said that King James III. once escaped down this secert stair, and lay concealed from some conspirators who had entered his chamber to murder him. This range of apartments is terminated, like the other sides of the palace, by a circular tower enclosing a staircase, up which we mounted, winding round and round, and emerging at various heights, until at last we found ourselves at the very topmost point of the edifice; and here there is a small pepper-box of a turret, almost as entire as when the stones were first laid. It is called Queen Margaret's bower, and looks forth on a lovely prospect of mountain and plain, and on the old red roofs of Linlithgow town, and on the little loch that lies within the palace grounds. The cold north-wind blew chill upon us through the empty window-frames, which very likely were never glazed; but it must be a delightful nook in a calmer and warmer summer evening.

Descending from this high perch, we walked along ledges and through arched corridors, and stood, contemplative, in the dampness of the banqueting-hall, and sat down on the seats that still occupy the embrasures of the deep windows. In one of the rooms, the sculpture of a huge fireplace has recently been imitated and restored, so as to give an idea of what the richness of the adornments must have been when the building was perfect. We burrowed down, too, a little way, in the direction of the cells, where prisoners used to be confined; but these were too ugly and too impenetrably dark to tempt us far. One vault, exactly beneath a queen's very bedchamber, was designated as a prison. I should think bad dreams would have winged up, and made her pillow an uncomfortable one.

There seems to be no certain record as respects the date of this palace, except that the most recent part was built by James I., of England, and bears the figures 1620 on its central tower. In this part were the kitchens and other domestic offices. In Robert Bruce's time there was a castle here, instead of a palace, and an ancestor of our friend Bennoch was the means of taking it from the English by a stratagem in which valor went halves. Four centuries afterwards, it was a royal residence, and might still have been nominally so, had not Hawley's dragoons lighted their fires on the floors of the magnificent rooms; but, on the whole, I think it more valuable as a ruin than if it were still perfect. Scotland, and the world, needs only one Holyrood; and Linlithgow, were it still a perfect palace, must have been second in interest to that, from its lack of association with historic events so grand and striking.

After tea we took another walk, and this time went along the High Street, in quest of the house whence Bothwellhaugh fired the shot that killed the Regent Murray. It has been taken down, however; or, if any part of it remain, it has been built into and incorporated with a small house of dark stone, which forms one range with two others that stand a few feet back from the general line of the street. It is as mean-looking and commonplace an edifice as is anywhere to be seen, and is now occupied by one Steele, a tailor. We went under a square arch (if an arch can be square) that goes quite through the house, and found ourselves in a little court; but it was not easy to identify anything as connected with the historic event, so we did but glance about us, and returned into the street. It is here narrow, and as Bothwellhaugh stood in a projecting gallery, the Regent must have been within a few yards of the muzzle of his carbine. The street looks as old as any that I have seen, except, perhaps, a vista here and there in Chester, — the houses all of stone, many of them tall, with notched gables, and with stone staircases going up outside, the steps much worn by feet now dust; a pervading ugliness, which yet does not fail to be picturesque; a general filth and evil odor of gutters and people, suggesting sorrowful ideas of what the inner houses must be, when the outside looks and smells so badly; and, finally, a great rabble of the inhabitants, talking, idling, sporting, staring about their own thresholds and those of dram-shops, the town being most alive in the long twilight of the summer evening. There was nothing uncivil in the deportment of these dirty people, old or young; but they did stare at us most unmercifully.

We walked very late, entering, after all that we had seen, into the palace grounds, and skirting along Linlithgow Loch, which would be very beautiful if its banks were made shadowy with trees, instead of being almost bare. We viewed the palace on the outside, too, and saw what had once been the principal entrance, but now looked like an arched window, pretty high in the wall; for it had not been accessible except by a drawbridge. I might write pages in telling how venerable the ruin looked, as the twilight fell deeper and deeper around it; but we have had enough of Linlithgow, especially as there have been so many old palaces and old towns to write about, and there will still be more. We left Linlithgow early this morning, and reached Edinburgh in half an hour. To-morrow I suppose I shall try to set down what I see; at least, some points of it.

July 9th. — Arriving at

EDINBURGH,

and acting under advice of the cabman, we drove to Addison's Alma Hotel, which we find to be in Prince's Street, having Scott's monument a few hundred yards below, and the Castle Hill about as much above.

The Edinburgh people seem to be accustomed to climb mountains within their own houses; so we had to mount several staircases before we reached our parlor, which is a very good one, and commands a beautiful view of Prince's Street, and of the picturesque old town, and the valley between, and of the castle on its hill.

Our first visit was to the castle, which we reached by going across the causeway that bridges the valley, and has some edifices of Grecian architecture on it, contrasting strangely with the nondescript ugliness of the old town, into which we immediately pass. As this is my second visit to Edinburgh, I surely need not dwell upon describing it at such length as if I had never been here before. After climbing up through various wards of the castle to the topmost battery, where Mons Meg holds her station, looking like an uncouth dragon,—with a pile of huge stone balls beside her for eggs,—we found that we could not be admitted to Queen Mary's apartments, nor to the crown-room, till twelve o'clock; moreover, that there was no admittance to the crown-room without tickets from the crown-office, in Parliament Square. There being no help for it, I left my wife and J—— to wander through the fortress, and came down through High Street in quest of Parliament Square, which I found after many inquiries of policemen, and after first going to the Justiciary Court, where there was a great throng endeavoring to get in; for the trial of Miss Smith for the murder of her lover is causing great excitement just now. There was no difficulty made about the tickets, and, returning, found S—— and J——; but J——

grew tired of waiting, and set out to return to our hotel, through the great, strange city, all by himself. Through means of an attendant, we were admitted into Queen Margaret's little chapel, on the top of the rock; and then we sat down, in such shelter as there was, to avoid the keen wind, blowing through the embrasures of the ramparts, and waited as patiently as we could.

Twelve o'clock came, and we went into the crown-room, with a throng of other visitors, — so many that they could only be admitted in separate groups. The Regalia of Scotland lie on a circular table within an iron railing, round and round which the visitors pass, gazing with all their eyes. The room was dark, however, except for the dim twinkle of a candle or gas-light; and the regalia did not show to any advantage, though there are some rich jewels, set in their ancient gold. The articles consist of a two-handed sword, with a hilt and scabbard of gold, ornamented with gems, and a mace, with a silver handle, all very beautifully made; besides the golden collar and jewelled badge of the Garter, and something else which I forget. Why they keep this room so dark I cannot tell; but it is a poor show, and gives the spectator an idea of the poverty of Scotland, and the minuteness of her sovereignty, which I had not gathered from her royal palaces.

Thence we went into Queen Mary's room, and saw that beautiful portrait — that very queen and very woman — with which I was so much impressed at my last visit. It is wonderful that this picture does not drive all the other portraits of Mary out of the field, whatever may be the comparative proofs of their authenticity. I do not know the history of this one, except that it is a copy by Sir William Gordon of a picture by an Italian, preserved at Dunrobin Castle.

After seeing what the castle had to show, which is but little except itself, its rocks, and its old dwellings of princes and prisoners, we came down through the High Street, inquiring for John Knox's house. It is a strange-looking edifice, with gables on high, projecting far, and some sculpture, and inscriptions referring to Knox. There is a tobacconist's shop in the basement story, where I learned that the house used to be shown to visitors till within three months, but it is now closed, for some reason or other. Thence we crossed a bridge into the new town, and came back through Prince's Street to the hotel, and had a good dinner, as preparatory to fresh wearinesses; for there is no other weariness at all to be compared to that of sight-seeing.

In mid afternoon we took a cab and drove to Holyrood Palace, which I have already described, as well as the chapel, and do not mean to meddle with either of them again. We looked at our faces in the old mirrors that Queen Mary brought from France with her, and which had often reflected her own lovely face and figure; and I went up the winding stair through which the conspirators ascended. This, I think, was not accessible at my former visit. Before leaving the palace, one of the attendants advised us to see some pictures in the apartments occupied by the Marquis of Breadalbane during the queen's residence here. We found some fine old portraits and other paintings by Vandyke, Sir Peter Lely, Sir Godfrey Kneller, and a strange head by Rubens, amid all which I walked wearily, wishing that there were nothing worth looking at in the whole world. My wife differs altogether from me in this matter; . . . . but we agreed, on this occasion, in being tired to death. Just as we got through with the pictures, I became convinced of what I had been dimly suspecting all the while, namely, that at my last visit to the palace I had seen these self-same pictures, and listened to the self-same woman's civil answers, in just the self-same miserable weariness of mood.

We left the palace, and toiled up through the dirty Canongate, looking vainly for a fly, and employing our time, as well as we could, in looking at the squalid mob of Edinburgh, and peeping down the horrible vistas of the closes, which were swarming with dirty life, as some mouldy and half-decayed substance might swarm with insects, — vistas down alleys where sin, sorrow, poverty, drunkenness, all manner of sombre and sordid earthly circumstances, had imbued the stone, brick, and wood of the habitations for hundreds of years. And such a multitude of children too; that was a most striking feature.

After tea I went down into the valley between the old town and the new, which is now laid out as an ornamental garden, with grass, shrubbery, flowers, gravelled walks, and frequent seats. Here the sun was setting, and gilded the old town with its parting rays, making it absolutely the most picturesque scene possible to be seen. The mass of tall, ancient houses, heaped densely together, looked like a Gothic dream; for there seemed to be towers and all sorts of stately architecture, and spires ascended out of the mass; and above the whole was the castle, with a diadem of gold on its topmost turret. It wanted less than a quarter of nine when the last gleam faded from the windows of the old town, and left the crowd of buildings dim and indistinguishable, to reappear on the morrow in squalor, lifting their meanness skyward, the home of layer upon layer of unfortunate humanity. The change symbolized the difference between a poet's imagination of life in the past — or in a state which he looks at through a colored and illuminated medium — and the sad reality.

This morning we took a cab, and set forth between ten and eleven to see Edinburgh and its environs; driving past the University, and other noticeable objects in the old town, and thence out to Arthur's Seat. Salisbury Crags are a very singular feature of the outskirts. From the heights, beneath Arthur's Seat, we had a fine prospect of the sea, with Leith and Portobello in the distance, and of a fertile plain at the foot of the hill. In the course of our drive our cabman pointed out Dumbiedike's house; also the cottage of Jennie Deans, — at least, the spot where it formerly stood; and Muschat's Cairn, of which a small heap of stones is yet remaining. Near this latter object are the ruins of St. Anthony's Chapel, a roofless gable, and other remains, standing on the abrupt hillside. We drove homeward past a parade-ground on which a body of cavalry was exercising, and we met a company of infantry on their route thither. Then we drove near Calton Hill, which seems to be not a burial-ground, although the site of stately monuments. In fine, we passed through the Grass-Market, where we saw the cross in the pavement in the street, marking the spot, as I recorded before, where Porteous was executed. Thence we passed through the Cowgate, all the latter part of our drive being amongst the tall, quaint edifices of the old town, alike venerable and squalid. From the Grass-Market the rock of the castle looks more precipitous than as we had hitherto seen it, and its prisons, palaces, and barracks approach close to its headlong verge, and form one steep line with its descent. We drove quite round the Castle Hill, and returned down Prince's Street to our hotel. There can be no other city in the world that affords more splendid scenery, both natural and architectural, than Edinburgh.

Then we went to St. Giles's Cathedral, which I shall not describe, it having been kirkified into three interior divisions by the Covenanters; and I left my wife to take drawings, while J—— and I went to Short's Observatory, near the entrance of the castle. Here we saw a camera-obscura, which brought before us, without our stirring a step, almost all the striking objects which we had been wandering to and fro to see. We also saw the mites in cheese, gigantically magnified by a solar microscope; likewise some dioramic views, with all which J—— was mightily pleased, and for myself, being tired to death of sights, I would as lief see them as anything else. We found, on calling for mamma at St. Giles's, that she had gone away; but she rejoined us between four and five o'clock at our hotel, where the next thing we did was to dine. Again after dinner we walked out, looking at the shop-windows of jewellers, where ornaments made of cairngorm pebbles are the most peculiar attraction. As it was our wedding-day, ... I gave S—— a golden and amethyst-bodied cairngorm beetle with a ruby head; and after sitting awhile in Prince's Street Gardens, we came home.

July 10*th.* — Last evening I walked round the castle rock, and through the Grass-Market, where I stood on the inlaid cross in the pavement, thence down the High Street beyond John Knox's house. The throng in that part of the town was very great. There is a strange fascination in these old streets, and in the peeps down the closes; but it doubtless would be a great blessing were a fire to sweep through the whole of ancient Edinburgh. This system of living on flats, up to I know not what story, must be most unfavorable to cleanliness, since they have to fetch their water all that distance towards heaven, and how they get rid of their rubbish is best known to themselves.

My wife has gone to Roslin this morning, and since her departure it has been drizzly, so that J—— and I, after a walk through the new part of the town, are imprisoned in our parlor with little resource except to look across the valley to the castle, where Mons Meg is plainly visible on the upper platform, and the lower ramparts, zigzagging about the edge of the precipice, which nearly in front of us is concealed or softened by a great deal of shrubbery, but farther off descends steeply down to the grass below. Somewhere on this side of the rock was the point where Claverhouse, on quitting Edinburgh before the battle of Killiecrankie, clambered up to hold an interview with the Duke of Gordon. What an excellent thing it is to have such striking and indestructible land-marks and time-marks that they serve to affix historical incidents to, and thus, as it were, nail down the Past for the benefit of all future ages!

The old town of Edinburgh appears to be situated, in its densest part, on the broad back of a ridge, which rises gradually to its termination in the precipitous rock, on which stands the castle. Between the old town and the new is the valley, which runs along at the base of this ridge, and which, in its natural state, was probably rough and broken, like any mountain gorge. The lower part of the valley, adjacent to the Canongate, is now a broad hollow space, fitted up with dwellings, shops, or manufactories; the next portion, between two bridges, is converted into an ornamental garden free to the public, and contains Scott's beautiful monument, — a canopy of Gothic arches and a fantastic spire, beneath which he sits, thoughtful and observant of what passes in the contiguous street; the third portion of the valley, above the last bridge, is another ornamental garden, open only to those who have pass-keys. It is an admirable garden, with a great variety of surface, and extends far round the castle rock, with paths that lead up to its very base, among leafy depths of shrubbery, and winds beneath the sheer, black precipice. J—— and I walked there this forenoon, and took refuge from a shower beneath an overhanging jut of the rock, where a bench had been placed, and where a curtain of hanging ivy helped to shelter us. On our return to the hotel, we found mamma just alighting from a cab. She had had very bad fortune in her excursion to Roslin, having had to walk a long distance to the chapel, and being caught in the rain; and, after all, she could only spend seven minutes in viewing the beautiful Roslin architecture.

MELROSE.

July 11*th*. — We left Edinburgh, where we had found at Addison's, 87 Prince's Street, the most comfortable hotel in Great Britain, and went to Melrose, where we put up at the George. This is all travelled ground with me, so that I need not much perplex myself with further description, especially as it is impossible, by any repetition of attempts, to describe Melrose Abbey. We went thither immediately after tea, and were shown over the ruins by a very delectable old Scotchman, incomparably the best guide I ever met with. I think he must take pains to speak the Scotch dialect, he does it with such pungent felicity and effect, and it gives a flavor to everything he says, like the mustard and vinegar in a salad. This is not the man I saw when here before. The Scotch dialect is still, in a greater or less degree, universally prevalent in Scotland, insomuch that we generally find it difficult to comprehend the answers to our questions, though more, I think, from the unusual intonation than either from strange words or pronunciation. But this old man, though he spoke the most unmitigated Scotch, was perfectly intelligible, — perhaps because his speech so well accorded with the classic standard of the Waverley Novels. Moreover, he is thoroughly acquainted with the Abbey, stone by stone; and it was curious to see him, as we walked among its aisles, and over the grass beneath its roofless portions, pick up the withered leaves that had fallen there, and do other such little things, as a good housewife might do to a parlor. I have met with two or three instances where the guardian of an old edifice seemed really to love it, and this was one, although the old man evidently had a Scotch Covenanter's contempt and dislike of the faith that founded the Abbey. He repeated King David's dictum that King David the First was "a sair saint for the crown," as bestowing so much wealth on religious edifices; but really, unless it be Walter Scott, I know not any Scotchman who has done so much for his country as this same St. David. As the founder of Melrose and many other beautiful churches and abbeys, he left magnificent specimens of the only kind of poetry which the age knew how to produce; and the world is the better for him to this day, — which is more, I believe, than can be said of any hero or statesman in Scottish annals.

We went all over the ruins, of course, and saw the marble stone of King Alexander, and the spot where Bruce's heart is said to be buried, and the slab of Michael Scott, with the cross engraved upon it; also the exquisitely sculptured kail-leaves, and other foliage and flowers, with which the Gothic artists inwreathed this edifice, bestowing more minute and faithful labor than an artist of these days would do on the most delicate piece of cabinet-work. We came away sooner than we wished, but we hoped to return thither this morning; and, for my part, I cherish a presentiment that this will not be our last visit to Scotland and Melrose. . . . . J—— and I then walked to the Tweed, where we saw two or three people angling, with naked legs, or trousers turned up, and wading among the rude stones that make something like a dam over the wide and brawling stream. I did not observe that they caught any fish, but J—— was so fascinated with the spectacle that he pulled out his poor little fishing-line, and wished to try his chance forthwith. I never saw the angler's instinct stronger in anybody. We walked across the footbridge that here spans the Tweed; and J—— observed that he did not see how William of Deloraine could have found so much difficulty in swimming his horse across so shallow a river. Neither do I. It now began to sprinkle, and we hastened back to the hotel.

It was not a pleasant morning; but we started immediately after breakfast for

ABBOTSFORD,

which is but about three miles distant. The country between Melrose and that place is not in the least beautiful, nor very noteworthy, — one or two old irregular villages; one tower that looks principally domestic, yet partly warlike, and seems to be of some antiquity; and an undulation, or rounded hilly surface of the landscape, sometimes affording wide vistas between the slopes. These hills, which, I suppose, are some of them on the Abbotsford estate, are partly covered with woods, but of Scotch fir, or some tree of that species, which creates no softened undulation, but overspreads the hill like a tightly fitting wig. It is a cold, dreary, disheartening neighborhood, that of Abbotsford; at least, it has appeared so to me at both of my visits, — one of which was on a bleak and windy May morning, and this one on a chill, showery morning of midsummer.

The entrance-way to the house is somewhat altered since my last visit; and we now, following the direction of a painted finger on the wall, went round to a side door in the basement story, where we found an elderly man waiting as if in expectation of visitors. He asked us to write our names in a book, and told us that the desk on the leaf of which it lay was the one in which Sir Walter found the forgotten manuscript of Waverley, while looking for some fishing-tackle. There was another desk in the room, which had belonged to the Colonel Gardiner who appears in Waverley. The first apartment into which our guide showed us was Sir Walter's study, where I again saw his clothes, and remarked how the sleeve of his old green coat was worn at the cuff, — a minute circumstance that seemed to bring Sir Walter very near me. Thence into the library; thence into the drawing-room, whence, methinks, we should have entered the dining-room, the most interesting of all, as being the room where he died. But this room seems not to be shown now. We saw the armory, with the gun of Rob Roy, into the muzzle of which I put my finger, and found the bore very large; the beautifully wrought pistol of Claverhouse, and a pair of pistols that belonged to Napoleon; the sword of Montrose, which I grasped, and drew half out of the scabbard; and Queen Mary's iron jewel-box, six or eight inches long, and two or three high, with a lid rounded like that of a trunk, and much corroded with rust. There is no use in making a catalogue of these curiosities. The feeling in visiting Abbotsford is not that of awe; it is little more than going to a museum. I do abhor this mode of making pilgrimages to the shrines of departed great men. There is certainly something wrong in it, for it seldom or never produces (in me, at least) the right feeling. It is an odd truth, too, that a house is forever after spoiled and ruined as a home, by having been the abode of a great man. His spirit haunts it, as it were, with a malevolent effect, and takes hearth and hall away from the nominal possessors, giving all the world the right to enter there because he had such intimate relations with all the world.

We had intended to go to Dryburgh Abbey; but as the weather more than threatened rain, ... we gave up the idea, and so took the rail for Berwick, after one o'clock. On our road we passed several ruins in Scotland, and some in England, — one old castle in particular, beautifully situated beside a deep-banked stream. The road lies for many miles along the coast, affording a fine view of the German Ocean, which was now blue, sunny, and breezy, the day having risen out of its morning sulks. We waited an hour or more at Berwick, and J—— and I took a hasty walk into the town. It is a rough and rude assemblage of rather mean houses, some of which are thatched. There seems to have been a wall about the town at a former period, and we passed through one of the gates. The view of the river Tweed here is very fine, both above and below the railway bridge, and especially where it flows, a broad tide, and between high banks, into the sea. Thence we went onward along the coast, as I have said, pausing a few moments in smoky Newcastle, and reaching Durham about eight o'clock.

DURHAM.

I wandered out in the dusk of the evening, — for the

dusk comes on comparatively early as we draw southward, — and found a beautiful and shadowy path along the river-side, skirting its high banks, up and adown which grow noble elms. I could not well see, in that obscurity of twilight boughs, whither I was going, or what was around me; but I judged that the castle or cathedral, or both, crowned the highest line of the shore, and that I was walking at the base of their walls. There was a pair of lovers in front of me, and I passed two or three other tender couples. The walk appeared to go on interminably by the river-side, through the same sweet shadow; but I turned, and found my way into the cathedral close, beneath an ancient archway, whence, issuing again, I inquired my way to the Waterloo Hotel, where we had put up.

ITEMS. — We saw the Norham Castle of Marmion, at a short distance from the station of the same name. Viewed from the railway, it has not a very picturesque appearance, — a high, square ruin of what I suppose was the keep. — At Abbotsford, treasured up in a glass case in the drawing-room, were memorials of Sir Walter Scott's servants and humble friends, — for instance, a brass snuff-box of Tom Purdy, — there, too, among precious relics of illustrious persons. — In the armory, I grasped with some interest the sword of Sir Adam Ferguson, which he had worn in the Peninsular war. Our guide said, of his own knowledge, that "he was a very funny old gentleman." He died only a year or two since.

July 11th. — The morning after our arrival in Durham being Sunday, we attended service in the cathedral. . . . . We found a tolerable audience, seated on benches, within and in front of the choir; and people continually strayed in and out of the sunny churchyard and sat down, or walked softly and quietly up and down the side aisle. Sometimes, too, one of the vergers would come in with a handful of little boys, whom he had caught playing among the tombstones.

DURHAM CATHEDRAL

has one advantage over the others which I have seen, there being no organ-screen, nor any sort of partition between the choir and nave; so that we saw its entire length, nearly five hundred feet, in one vista. The pillars of the nave are immensely thick, but hardly of proportionate height, and they support the round Norman arch; nor is there, as far as I remember, a single pointed arch in the cathedral. The effect is to give the edifice an air of heavy grandeur. It seems to have been built before the best style of church architecture had established itself; so that it weighs upon the soul, instead of helping it to aspire. First, there are these round arches, supported by gigantic columns; then, immediately above, another row of round arches, behind which is the usual gallery that runs, as it were, in the thickness of the wall, around the nave of the cathedral; then, above all, another row of round arches, enclosing the windows of the clere-story. The great pillars are ornamented in various ways, — some with a great spiral groove running from bottom to top; others with two spirals, ascending in different directions, so as to cross over one another; some are fluted or channelled straight up and down; some are wrought with chevrons, like those on the sleeve of a police-inspector. There are zigzag cuttings and carvings, which I do not know how to name scientifically, round the arches of the doors and windows; but nothing that seems to have flowered out spontaneously, as natural incidents of a grand and beautiful design. In the nave, between the columns of the side aisles, I saw one or two monuments. . . . .

The cathedral service is very long; and though the choral part of it is pleasant enough, I thought it not best to wait for the sermon, especially as it would have been quite unintelligible, so remotely as I sat in the great space. So I left my seat, and after strolling up and down the aisle a few times, sallied forth into the churchyard. On the cathedral door there is a curious old knocker, in the form of a monstrous face, which was placed there, centuries ago, for the benefit of fugitives from justice, who used to be entitled to sanctuary here. The exterior of the cathedral, being huge, is therefore grand; it has a great central tower, and two at the western end; and reposes in vast and heavy length, without the multitude of niches, and crumbling statues, and richness of detail, that make the towers and fronts of some cathedrals so endlessly interesting. One piece of sculpture I remember, — a carving of a cow, a milk-maid, and a monk, in reference to the legend that the site of the cathedral was, in some way, determined by a woman bidding her cow go home to Dunholme. Cadmus was guided to the site of his destined city in some such way as this.

It was a very beautiful day, and though the shadow of the cathedral fell on this side, yet, it being about noontide, it did not cover the churchyard entirely, but left many of the graves in sunshine. There were not a great many monuments, and these were chiefly horizontal slabs, some of which looked aged, but on closer inspection proved to be mostly of the present century. I observed an old stone figure, however, half worn away, which seemed to have something like a bishop's mitre on its head, and may perhaps have lain in the proudest chapel of the cathedral before occupying its present bed among the grass. About fifteen paces from the central tower, and within its shadow, I found a weather-worn slab of marble, seven or eight feet long, the inscription on which interested me somewhat. It was to the memory of Robert Dodsley, the bookseller, Johnson's acquaintance, who, as his tombstone rather superciliously avers, had made a much better figure as an author than "could have been expected in his rank of life." But, after all, it is inevitable that a man's tombstone should look down on him, or, at all events, comport itself towards him "de haut en bas." I love to find the graves of men connected with literature. They interest me more, even though of no great eminence, than those of persons far more illustrious in other walks of life. I know not whether this is because I happen to be one of the literary kindred, or because all men feel themselves akin, and on terms of intimacy, with those whom they know, or might have known, in books. I rather believe that the latter is the case.

My wife had stayed in the cathedral, but she came out at the end of the sermon, and told me of two little birds, who had got into the vast interior, and were in great trouble at not being able to find their way out again. Thus, two winged souls may often have been imprisoned within a faith of heavy ceremonials.

We went round the edifice, and, passing into the close, penetrated through an arched passage into the crypt, which, methought, was in a better style of architecture than the nave and choir. At one end stood a crowd of venerable figures leaning against the wall, being stone images of bearded saints, apostles, patriarchs, kings, — personages of great dignity, at all events, who had doubtless occupied conspicuous niches in and about the cathedral till finally imprisoned in this cellar. I looked at every one, and found not an entire nose among them, nor quite so many heads as they once had.

Thence we went into the cloisters, which are entire, but not particularly interesting. Indeed, this cathedral has not taken hold of my affections, except in one aspect, when it was exceedingly grand and beautiful.

After looking at the crypt and the cloisters, we returned through the close and the churchyard, and went back to the hotel through a path by the river-side. This is the same dim and dusky path through which I wandered the night before, and in the sunshine it looked quite as beautiful as I knew it must, — a shadow of elm-trees clothing the high bank, and overarching the paths above and below; some of the elms growing close to the water-side, and flinging up their topmost boughs not nearly so high as where we stood, and others climbing upward and upward, till our way wound among their roots; while through the foliage the quiet river loitered along, with this lovely shade on both its banks, to pass through the centre of the town. The stately cathedral rose high above us, and farther onward, in a line with it, the battlemented walls of the old Norman castle, gray and warlike, though now it has become a University. This delightful walk terminates at an old bridge in the heart of the town; and the castle hangs immediately over its busiest street. On this bridge, last night, in the embrasure, or just over the pier, where there is a stone seat, I saw some old men seated, smoking their pipes and chatting. In my judgment, a river flowing through the centre of a town, and not too broad to make itself familiar, nor too swift, but idling along, as if it loved better to stay there than to go, is the pleasantest imaginable piece of scenery; so transient as it is, and yet enduring,—just the same from life's end to life's end; and this river Wear, with its sylvan wildness, and yet so sweet and placable, is the best of all little rivers,—not that it is so very small, but with a bosom broad enough to be crossed by a three-arched bridge. Just above the cathedral there is a mill upon its shore, as ancient as the times of the Abbey.

We went homeward through the market-place and one or two narrow streets; for the town has the irregularity of all ancient settlements, and, moreover, undulates upward and downward, and is also made more unintelligible to a stranger, in its points and bearings, by the tortuous course of the river.

After dinner J—— and I walked along the bank opposite to that on which the cathedral stands, and found the paths there equally delightful with those which I have attempted to describe. We went onward while the river gleamed through the foliage beneath us, and passed so far beyond the cathedral that we began to think we were getting into the country, and that it was time to return; when all at once we saw a bridge before us, and beyond that, on the opposite bank of the Wear, the cathedral itself! The stream had made a circuit without our knowing it. We paused upon the bridge, and admired and wondered at the beauty and glory of the scene, with those vast, ancient towers rising out of the green shade, and looking as if they were based upon it. The situation of Durham Cathedral is certainly a noble one, finer even than that of Lincoln, though the latter stands even at a more lordly height above the town. But as I saw it then, it was grand, venerable, and sweet, all at once; and I never saw so lovely and magnificent a scene, nor, being content with this, do I care to see a better. The castle beyond came also into the view, and the whole picture was mirrored in the tranquil stream below. And so, crossing the bridge, the path led us back through many a bower of hollow shade; and we then quitted the hotel, and took the rail for

YORK,

where we arrived at about half past nine. We put up at the Black Swan, with which we had already made acquaintance at our previous visit to York. It is a very ancient hotel; for in the coffee-room I saw on the wall an old printed advertisement, announcing that a stage-coach would leave the Black Swan in London, and arrive at the Black Swan in York, with God's permission, in four days. The date was 1706; and still, after a hundred and fifty years, the Black Swan receives travellers in Coney Street. It is a very good hotel, and was much thronged with guests when we arrived, as the Sessions come on this week. We found a very smart waiter, whose English faculties have been brightened by a residence of several years in America.

In the morning, before breakfast, I strolled out, and walked round the cathedral, passing on my way the sheriff's javelin-men, in long gowns of faded purple embroidered with gold, carrying halberds in their hands; also a gentleman in a cocked hat, gold lace, and breeches, who, no doubt, had something to do with the ceremonial of the Sessions. I saw, too, a procession of a good many old cabs and other carriages, filled with people, and a banner flaunting above each vehicle. These were the piano-forte makers of York, who were going out of town to have a jollification together.

After breakfast we all went to the cathedral, and no sooner were we within it than we found how much our eyes had recently been educated, by our greater power of appreciating this magnificent interior; for it impressed us both with a joy that we never felt before. J—— felt it too, and insisted that the cathedral must have been altered and improved since we were last here. But it is only that we have seen much splendid architecture since then, and so have grown in some degree fitted to enjoy it. York Cathedral (I say it now, for it is my present feeling) is the most wonderful work that ever came from the hands of man. Indeed, it seems like "a house not made with hands," but rather to have come down from above, bringing an awful majesty and sweetness with it; and it is so light and aspiring, with all its vast columns and pointed arches, that one would hardly wonder if it should ascend back to heaven again by its mere spirituality. Positively the pillars and arches of the choir are so very beautiful that they give the impression of being exquisitely polished, though such is not the fact; but their beauty throws a gleam around them. I thank God that I saw this cathedral again, and I thank him that he inspired the builder to make it, and that mankind has so long enjoyed it, and will continue to enjoy it.

July 14*th.* — We left York at twelve o'clock, and were delayed an hour or two at Leeds, waiting for a train. I strolled up into the town, and saw a fair, with puppet-shows, booths of penny actors, merry-go-rounds, clowns, boxers, and other such things as I saw, above a year ago, at Greenwich fair, and likewise at Tranmere, during the Whitsuntide holidays.

We resumed our journey, and reached Southport in pretty good trim at about nine o'clock. It has been a very interesting tour. We find Southport just as we left it, with its regular streets of little and big lodging-houses, where the visitors perambulate to and fro without any imaginable object. The tide, too, seems not to have been up over the waste of sands since we went away; and far seaward stands the same row of bathing-machines, and just on the verge of the horizon a gleam of water, — even this being not the sea, but the mouth of the river Ribble, seeking the sea amid the sandy desert. But we shall soon say good by to Southport.

OLD TRAFFORD, MANCHESTER.

July 22*d.* — We left Southport for good on the 20th, and have established ourselves in this place, in lodgings that had been provided for us by Mr. Swain; our principal object being to spend a few weeks in the proximity of the Arts' Exhibition. We are here, about three miles from the Victoria Railway station in Manchester on one side, and nearly a mile from the Exhibition on the other. This is a suburb of Manchester, and consists of a long street, called the Stratford Road, bordered with brick houses two stories high, such as are usually the dwellings of tradesmen or respectable mechanics, but which are now in demand for lodgings, at high prices, on account of the Exhibition. It seems to be rather a new precinct of the city, and the houses, though ranged along a continuous street, are but a brick border of the green fields in the rear. Occasionally you get a glimpse of this country aspect between two houses; but the street itself, even with its little grass-plots and bits of shrubbery under the front windows, is as ugly as it can be made. Some of the houses are better than I have described; but the brick used here in building is very unsightly in hue and surface.

Betimes in the morning the Exhibition omnibuses begin to trundle along, and pass at intervals of two and a half minutes through the day, — immense vehicles constructed to carry thirty-nine passengers, and generally with a good part of that number inside and out. The omnibuses are painted scarlet, bordered with white, have three horses abreast, and a conductor in a red coat. They perform the journey from this point into town in about half an hour; and yesterday morning, being in a hurry to get to the railway station, I found that I could outwalk them, taking into account their frequent stoppages.

We have taken the whole house (except some inscrutable holes, into which the family creeps), of respectable people, who never took lodgers until this juncture. Their furniture, however, is of the true lodging-house pattern, — sofas and chairs which have no possibility of repose in them; rickety tables; an old piano and old music, with "Lady Helen Elizabeth" somebody's name written on it. It is very strange how nothing but a genuine home can ever look homelike. They appear to be good people; a little girl of twelve, a daughter, waits on table; and there is an elder daughter, who yesterday answered the door-bell, looking very like a young lady, besides five or six smaller children, who make less uproar of grief or merriment than could possibly be expected. The husband is not apparent, though I see his hat in the hall. The house is new, and has a trim, light-colored interior of half-gentility. I suppose the rent, in ordinary times, might be £25 per annum; but we pay at the rate of £338 for the part which we occupy. This, like all the other houses in the neighborhood, was evidently built to be sold or let; the builder never thought of living in it himself, and so that subtile element, which would have enabled him to create a home, was entirely left out.

This morning, J—— and I set forth on a walk, first towards the palace of the Arts' Exhibition, which looked small compared with my idea of it, and seems to be of the Crystal Palace order of architecture, only with more iron to its glass. Its front is composed of three round arches in a row. We did not go in. . . . . Turning to the right, we walked onward two or three miles, passing the Botanic Garden, and thence along by suburban villas, Belgrave terraces, and other such prettinesses in the modern Gothic or Elizabethan style, with fancifully ornamented flower-plats before them; thence by hedgerows and fields, and through two or three villages, with here and there an old plaster and timber-built thatched house, among a street full of modern brick-fronts, — the ale-house, or rural inn, being generally the most ancient house in the village. It was a sultry, heavy day, and I walked without much enjoyment of the air and exercise. We crossed a narrow and swift river, flowing between deep banks. It must have been either the Mersey, still an infant stream, and little dreaming of the thousand mighty ships that float on its farther tide, or else the Irwell, which empties into the Mersey. We passed through the village beyond this stream, and went to the railway station, and then were brought back to Old Trafford, and deposited close by the Exhibition.

It has showered this afternoon; and I beguiled my time for half an hour by setting down the vehicles that went past; not that they were particularly numerous, but for the sake of knowing the character of the travel along the road.

. . . . .

July 26th. — Day before yesterday we went to the Arts' Exhibition, of which I do not think that I have a great deal to say. The edifice, being built more for convenience than show, appears better in the interior than from without, — long vaulted vistas, lighted from above, extending far away, all hung with pictures; and, on the floor below, statues, knights in armor, cabinets, vases, and all manner of curious and beautiful things, in a regular arrangement. Scatter five thousand people through the scene, and I do not know how to make a better outline sketch. I was unquiet, from a hopelessness of being able to enjoy it fully. Nothing is more depressing to me than the sight of a great many pictures together; it is like having innumerable books open before you at once, and being able to read only a sentence or two in each. They bedazzle one another with cross lights. There never should be more than one picture in a room, nor more than one picture to be studied in one day. Galleries of pictures are surely the greatest absurdities that ever were contrived, there being no excuse for them, except that it is the only way in which pictures can be made generally available and accessible.

We went first into the Gallery of British Painters, where there were hundreds of pictures, every one of which would have interested me by itself; but I could not fix my mind on one more than another, so I wandered about, to get a general idea of the Exhibition. Truly it is very fine; truly, also, every great show is a kind of humbug. I doubt whether there were half a dozen people there who got the kind of enjoyment that it was intended to create, — very respectable people they seemed to be, and very well behaved, but all skimming the surface, as I did, and none of them so feeding on what was beautiful as to digest it, and make it a part of themselves. Such a quantity of objects must be utterly rejected before you can get any real profit from one! It seemed like throwing away time to look twice even at whatever was most precious; and it was dreary to think of not fully enjoying this collection, the very flower of Time, which never bloomed before, and never, by any possibility, can bloom again. Viewed hastily, moreover, it is somewhat sad to think that mankind, after centuries of cultivation of the beautiful arts, can produce no more splendid spectacle than this. It is not so very grand, although, poor as it is, I lack capacity to take in even the whole of it.

What gave me most pleasure (because it required no trouble nor study to come at the heart of it) were the individual relics of antiquity, of which there are some very curious ones in the cases ranged along the principal saloon or nave of the building. For example, the dagger with which Felton killed the Duke of Buckingham, — a knife with a bone handle and a curved blade, not more than three inches long; sharp-pointed, murderous-looking, but of very coarse manufacture. Also, the Duke of Alva's leading staff of iron; and the target of the Emperor Charles V., which seemed to be made of hardened leather, with designs artistically engraved upon it, and gilt. I saw Wolsey's portrait, and, in close proximity to it, his veritable cardinal's hat in a richly ornamented glass case, on which was an inscription to the effect that it had been bought by Charles Kean at the sale of Horace Walpole's collection. It is a felt hat with a brim about six inches wide all round, and a rather high crown; the color was, doubtless, a bright red originally, but now it is mottled with a grayish hue, and there are cracks in the brim, as if the hat had seen a good deal of wear. I suppose a far greater curiosity than this is the signet-ring of one of the Pharaohs, who reigned over Egypt during Joseph's prime ministry, — a large ring to be worn on the thumb, if at all, — of massive gold, seal part and all, and inscribed with some characters that looked like Hebrew. I had seen this before in Mr. Mayer's collection in Liverpool. The mediæval and English relics, however, interested me more, — such as the golden and enamelled George worn by Sir Thomas More; or the embroidered shirt of Charles I., — the very one, I presume, which he wore at his execution. There are no blood marks on it, it being very nicely washed and folded. The texture of the linen cloth — if linen it be — is coarser than any peasant would wear at this day, but the needle-work is exceedingly fine and elaborate. Another relic of the same period, — the Cavalier General Sir Jacob Astley's buff coat, with his belt and sword; the leather of the buff coat, for I took it between my fingers, is about a quarter of an inch thick, of the same material as a wash-leather glove, and by no means smoothly dressed, though the sleeves are covered with silver lace. Of old armor, there are admirable specimens; and it makes one's head ache to look at the iron pots which men used to thrust their heads into. Indeed, at one period they seem to have worn an inner iron cap underneath the helmet. I doubt whether there ever was any age of chivalry. . . . . It certainly was no chivalric sentiment that made men case themselves in impenetrable iron, and ride about in iron prisons, fearfully peeping at their enemies through little slits and gimlet-holes. The unprotected breast of a private soldier must have shamed his leaders in those days. The point of honor is very different now.

I mean to go again and again, many times more, and will take each day some one department, and so endeavor to get some real use and improvement out of what I see. Much that is most valuable must be immitigably rejected; but something, according to the measure of my poor capacity, will really be taken into my mind. After all, it was an agreeable day, and I think the next one will be more so.

July 28th. — Day before yesterday I paid a second visit to the Exhibition, and devoted the day mainly to seeing the works of British painters, which fill a very large space, — two or three great saloons at the right side of the nave. Among the earliest are Hogarth's pictures, including the Sigismunda, which I remember to have seen before, with her lover's heart in her hand, looking like a monstrous strawberry; and the March to Finchley, than which, nothing truer to English life and character was ever painted, nor ever can be; and a large stately portrait of Captain Coram, and others, all excellent in proportion as they come near to ordinary life, and are wrought out through its forms. All English painters resemble Hogarth in this respect. They cannot paint anything high, heroic, and ideal, and their attempts in that direction are wearisome to look at; but they sometimes produce good effects by means of awkward figures in ill-made coats and small-clothes, and hard, coarse-complexioned faces, such as they might see anywhere in the street. They are strong in homeliness and ugliness, weak in their efforts at the beautiful. Sir Thomas Lawrence attains a sort of grace, which you feel to be a trick, and therefore get disgusted with it. Reynolds is not quite genuine, though certainly he has produced some noble and beautiful heads. But Hogarth is the only English painter, except in the landscape department; there are no others who interpret life to me at all, unless it be some of the modern Pre-Raphaelites. Pretty village scenes of common life, — pleasant domestic passages, with a touch of easy humor in them, — little pathoses and fancynesses, are abundant enough; and Wilkie, to be sure, has done more than this, though not a great deal more. His merit lies, not in a high aim, but in accomplishing his aim so perfectly. It is unaccountable that the English painters' achievements should be so much inferior to those of the English poets, who have really elevated the human mind; but, to be sure, painting has only become an English art subsequently to the epochs of the greatest poets, and since the beginning of the last century, during which England had no poets. I respect Haydon more than I once did, not for his pictures, they being detestable to see, but for his heroic rejection of whatever his countrymen and he himself could really do, and his bitter resolve to achieve something higher, — failing in which, he died.

No doubt I am doing vast injustice to a great many gifted men in what I have here written, — as, for instance, Copley, who certainly has painted a slain man to the life; and to a crowd of landscape painters, who have made wonderful reproductions of little English streams and shrubbery, and cottage doors and country lanes. And there is a picture called "The Evening Gun" by Danby, — a ship of war on a calm, glassy tide, at sunset, with the cannon-smoke puffing from her port-hole; it is very beautiful, and so effective that you can even hear the report breaking upon the stillness, with so grand a roar that it is almost like stillness too. As for Turner, I care no more for his light-colored pictures than for so much lacquered ware or painted gingerbread. Doubtless this is my fault, my own deficiency; but I cannot help it, — not, at least, without sophisticating myself by the effort. The only modern pictures that accomplish a higher end than that of pleasing the eye — the only ones that really take hold of my mind, and with a kind of acerbity, like unripe fruit — are the works of Hunt, and one or two other painters of the Pre-Raphaelite school. They seem wilfully to abjure all beauty, and to make their pictures disagreeable out of mere malice; but at any rate, for the thought and feeling which are ground up with the paint, they will bear looking at, and disclose a deeper value the longer you look. Never was anything so stiff and unnatural as they appear; although every single thing represented seems to be taken directly out of life and reality, and, as it were, pasted down upon the canvas. They almost paint even separate hairs. Accomplishing so much, and so perfectly, it seems unaccountable that the picture does not live; but Nature has an art beyond these painters, and they leave out some medium, — some enchantment that should intervene, and keep the object from pressing so baldly and harshly upon the spectator's eyeballs. With the most lifelike reproduction, there is no illusion. I think if a semi-obscurity were thrown over the picture after finishing it to this nicety, it might bring it nearer to Nature. I remember a heap of autumn leaves, every one of which seems to have been stiffened with gum and varnish, and then put carefully down into the stiffly disordered heap. Perhaps these artists may hereafter succeed in combining the truth of detail with a broader and higher truth. Coming from such a depth as their pictures do, and having really an idea as the seed of them, it is strange that they should look like the most made-up things imaginable. One picture by Hunt that greatly interested me was of some sheep that had gone astray among heights and precipices, and I could have looked all day at these poor, lost creatures, — so true was their meek alarm and hopeless bewilderment, their huddling together, without the slightest confidence of mutual help; all that the courage and wisdom of the bravest and wisest of them could do being to bleat, and only a few having spirits enough even for this.

After going through these modern masters, among whom were some French painters who do not interest me at all, I did a miscellaneous business, chiefly among the water-colors and photographs, and afterwards among the antiquities and works of ornamental art. I have forgotten what I saw, except the breastplate and helmet of Henry of Navarre, of steel, engraved with designs that have been half obliterated by scrubbing. I remember, too, a breastplate of an Elector of Saxony, with a bullet-hole through it. He received his mortal wound through that hole, and died of it two days afterwards, three hundred years ago.

There was a crowd of visitors, insomuch that it was difficult to get a satisfactory view of the most interesting objects. They were nearly all middling-class people; the Exhibition, I think, does not reach the lower classes at all; in fact, it could not reach them, nor their betters either, without a good deal of study to help it out. I shall go to-day, and do my best to get profit out of it.

July 30th. — We all, with R—— and Fanny, went to the Exhibition yesterday, and spent the day there; not J——, however, for he went to the Botanical Gardens. After some little skirmishing with other things, I devoted myself to the historical portraits, which hang on both sides of the great nave, and went through them pretty faithfully. The oldest are pictures of Richard II. and Henry IV. and Edward IV. and Jane Shore, and seem to have little or no merit as works of art, being cold and stiff, the life having, perhaps, faded out of them; but these older painters were trustworthy, inasmuch as they had no idea of making a picture, but only of getting the face before them on canvas as accurately as they could. All English history scarcely supplies half a dozen portraits before the time of Henry VIII.; after that period, and through the reigns of Elizabeth and James, there are many ugly pictures by Dutchmen and Italians; and the collection is wonderfully rich in portraits of the time of Charles I. and the Commonwealth. Vandyke seems to have brought portrait-painting into fashion; and very likely the king's love of art diffused a taste for it throughout the nation, and remotely suggested, even to his enemies, to get their pictures painted. Elizabeth has perpetrated her cold, thin visage on many canvases, and generally with some fantasy of costume that makes her ridiculous to all time. There are several of Mary of Scotland, none of which have a gleam of beauty; but the stiff old brushes of these painters could not catch the beautiful.

Of all the older pictures, the only one that I took pleasure in looking at was a portrait of Lord Deputy Falkland, by Vansomer, in James I.'s time, — a very stately, full-length figure in white, looking out of the picture as if he saw you. The catalogue says that this portrait suggested an incident in Horace Walpole's Castle of Otranto; but I do not remember it.

I have a haunting doubt of the value of portrait-painting; that is to say, whether it gives you a genuine idea of the person purporting to be represented. I do not remember ever to have recognized a man by having previously seen his portrait. Vandyke's pictures are full of grace and nobleness, but they do not look like Englishmen, — the burly, rough, wine-flushed and weather-reddened faces, and sturdy flesh and blood, which we see even at the present day, when they must naturally have become a good deal refined from either the country gentleman or the courtier of the Stuarts' age. There is an old, fat portrait of Gervoyse Holles, in a buff coat, — a coarse, hoggish, yet manly man. The painter is unknown; but I honor him, and Gervoyse Holles too, — for one was willing to be truly rendered, and the other dared to do it. It seems to be the aim of portrait-painters generally, especially of those who have been most famous, to make their pictures as beautiful and noble as can anywise consist with retaining the very slightest resemblance to the person sitting to them. They seldom attain even the grace and beauty which they aim at, but only hit some temporary or individual taste. Vandyke, however, achieved graces that rise above time and fashion, and so did Sir Peter Lely, in his female portraits; but the doubt is, whether the works of either are genuine history. Not more so, I suspect, than the narrative of a historian who should seek to make poetry out of the events which he relates, rejecting those which could not possibly be thus idealized.

I observe, furthermore, that a full-length portrait has seldom face enough; not that it lacks its fair proportion by measurement, but the artist does not often find it possible to make the face so intellectually prominent as to subordinate the figure and drapery. Vandyke does this, however. In his pictures of Charles I., for instance, it is the melancholy grace of the visage that attracts the eye, and it passes to the rest of the composition only by an effort. Earlier and later pictures are but a few inches of face to several feet of figure and costume, and more insignificant than the latter because seldom so well done; and I suspect the same would generally be the case now, only that the present simplicity of costume gives the face a chance to be seen.

I was interrupted here, and cannot resume the thread; but considering how much of his own conceit the artist puts into a portrait, how much affectation the sitter puts on, and then again that no face is the same to any two spectators; also, that these portraits are darkened and faded with age, and can seldom be more than half seen, being hung too high, or somehow or other inconvenient, — on the whole, I question whether there is much use in looking at them. The truest test would be, for a man well read in English history and biography, and himself an observer of insight, to go through the series without knowing what personages they represented, and write beneath each the name which the portrait vindicated for itself.

After getting through the portrait-gallery, I went among the engravings and photographs, and then glanced along the old masters, but without seriously looking at anything. While I was among the Dutch painters, a gentleman accosted me. It was Mr. J—— whom I once met at dinner with Bennoch. He told me that "the Poet Laureate" (as he called him) was in the Exhibition rooms; and as I expressed great interest, Mr. J—— was kind enough to go in quest of him. Not for the purpose of introduction, however, for he was not acquainted with Tennyson. Soon Mr. J—— returned, and said that he had found the Poet Laureate, — and, going into the saloon of the old masters, we saw him there, in company with Mr. Woolner, whose bust of him is now in the Exhibition.

• • • • •

Gazing at him with all my eyes, I liked him well, and rejoiced more in him than in all the other wonders of the Exhibition.

• • • • •

How strange that in these two or three pages I cannot get one single touch that may call him up hereafter!

I would most gladly have seen more of this one poet of our day, but forbore to follow him; for I must own that it seemed mean to be dogging him through the saloons, or even to look at him, since it was to be done stealthily, if at all.

• • • • •

He is as un-English as possible; indeed an English

man of genius usually lacks the national characteristics, and is great abnormally. Even the great sailor, Nelson, was unlike his countrymen in the qualities that constituted him a hero; he was not the perfection of an Englishman, but a creature of another kind, — sensitive, nervous, excitable, and really more like a Frenchman.

Un-English as he was, Tennyson had not, however, an American look. I cannot well describe the difference; but there was something more mellow in him, — softer, sweeter, broader, more simple than we are apt to be. Living apart from men as he does would hurt any one of us more than it does him. I may as well leave him here, for I cannot touch the central point.

August 2d. — Day before yesterday I went again to the Exhibition, and began the day with looking at the old masters. Positively, I do begin to receive some pleasure from looking at pictures; but as yet it has nothing to do with any technical merit, nor do I think I shall ever get so far as that. Some landscapes by Ruysdael, and some portraits by Murillo, Velasquez, and Titian, were those which I was most able to appreciate; and I see reason for allowing, contrary to my opinion, as expressed a few pages back, that a portrait may preserve some valuable characteristics of the person represented. The pictures in the English portrait-gallery are mostly very bad, and that may be the reason why I saw so little in them. I saw too, at this last visit, a Virgin and Child, which appeared to me to have an expression more adequate to the subject than most of the innumerable virgins and children, in which we see only repetitions of simple maternity; indeed, any mother, with her first child, would serve an artist for one of them. But in this picture the Virgin had a look as if she were loving the infant as her own child, and at the same time rendering him an awful worship, as to her Creator.

While I was sitting in the central saloon, listening to the music, a young man accosted me, presuming that I was so-and-so, the American author. He himself was a traveller for a publishing firm; and he introduced conversation by talking of Uttoxeter, and my description of it in an annual. He said that the account had caused a good deal of pique among the good people of Uttoxeter, because of the ignorance which I attribute to them as to the circumstance which connects Johnson with their town. The spot where Johnson stood can, it appears, still be pointed out. It is on one side of the market-place, and not in the neighborhood of the church. I forget whether I recorded, at the time, that an Uttoxeter newspaper was sent me, containing a proposal that a statue or memorial should be erected on the spot. It would gratify me exceedingly if such a result should come from my pious pilgrimage thither.

My new acquaintance, who was cockneyish, but very intelligent and agreeable, went on to talk about many literary matters and characters; among others, about Miss Brontë, whom he had seen at the Chapter Coffee-House, when she and her sister Anne first went to London. He was at that time connected with the house of —— and ——, and he described the surprise and incredulity of Mr. ——, when this little, commonplace-looking woman presented herself as the author of Jane Eyre. His story brought out the insignificance of

Charlotte Brontë's aspect, and the bluff rejection of her by Mr. ——, much more strongly than Mrs. Gaskell's narrative.

Chorlton Road, August 9th. — We have changed our lodgings since my last date, those at Old Trafford being inconvenient, and the landlady a sharp, peremptory housewife, better fitted to deal with her own family than to be complaisant to guests. We are now a little farther from the Exhibition, and not much better off as regards accommodation, but the housekeeper is a pleasant, civil sort of a woman, auspiciously named Mrs. Honey. The house is a specimen of the poorer middle-class dwellings as built nowadays, — narrow staircase, thin walls, and, being constructed for sale, very ill put together indeed, — the floors with wide cracks between the boards, and wide crevices admitting both air and light over the doors, so that the house is full of draughts. The outer walls, it seems to me, are but of one brick in thickness, and the partition walls certainly no thicker; and the movements, and sometimes the voices, of people in the contiguous house are audible to us. The Exhibition has temporarily so raised the value of lodgings here that we have to pay a high price for even such a house as this.

Mr. Wilding having gone on a tour to Scotland, I have had to be at the Consulate every day last week till yesterday; when I absented myself from duty, and went to the Exhibition. U—— and I spent an hour together, looking principally at the old Dutch masters, who seem to me the most wonderful set of men that ever handled a brush. Such lifelike representations of cabbages, onions, brass kettles, and kitchen crockery; such blankets, with the woollen fuzz upon them; such everything I never thought that the skill of man could produce! Even the photograph cannot equal their miracles. The closer you look, the more minutely true the picture is found to be, and I doubt if even the microscope could see beyond the painter's touch. Gerard Dow seems to be the master among these queer magicians. A straw mat, in one of his pictures, is the most miraculous thing that human art has yet accomplished; and there is a metal vase, with a dent in it, that is absolutely more real than reality. These painters accomplish all they aim at, — a praise, methinks, which can be given to no other men since the world began. They must have laid down their brushes with perfect satisfaction, knowing that each one of their million touches had been necessary to the effect, and that there was not one too few nor too many. And it is strange how spiritual and suggestive the commonest household article — an earthen pitcher, for example — becomes, when represented with entire accuracy. These Dutchmen got at the soul of common things, and so make them types and interpreters of the spiritual world.

Afterwards I looked at many of the pictures of the old masters, and found myself gradually getting a taste for them; at least, they give me more and more pleasure the oftener I come to see them. Doubtless I shall be able to pass for a man of taste by the time I return to America. It is an acquired taste, like that for wines; and I question whether a man is really any truer, wiser, or better for possessing it. From the old masters, I went among the English painters, and found myself more favorably inclined towards some of them than at my previous visits; seeing something wonderful even in Turner's lights and mists and yeasty waves, although I should like him still better if his pictures looked in the least like what they typify. The most disagreeable of English painters is Etty, who had a diseased appetite for woman's flesh, and spent his whole life, apparently, in painting them with enormously developed busts. I do not mind nudity in a modest and natural way; but Etty's women really thrust their nudity upon you with malice aforethought, ... and the worst of it is, they are not beautiful.

Among the last pictures that I looked at was Hogarth's March to Finchley; and surely nothing can be covered more thick and deep with English nature than that piece of canvas. The face of the tall grenadier in the centre, between two women, both of whom have claims on him, wonderfully expresses trouble and perplexity; and every touch in the picture meant something and expresses what it meant.

The price of admission, after two o'clock, being sixpence, the Exhibition was thronged with a class of people who do not usually come in such large numbers. It was both pleasant and touching to see how earnestly some of them sought to get instruction from what they beheld. The English are a good and simple people, and take life in earnest.

August 14*th.* — Passing by the gateway of the Manchester Cathedral the other morning, on my way to the station, I found a crowd collected, and, high overhead, the bells were chiming for a wedding. These chimes of bells are exceedingly impressive, so broadly gladsome as they are, filling the whole air, and every nook of one's heart with sympathy. They are good for a people to rejoice with, and good also for a marriage, because through all their joy there is something solemn, — a tone of that voice which we have heard so often at funerals. It is good to see how everybody, up to this old age of the world, takes an interest in weddings, and seems to have a faith that now, at last, a couple have come together to make each other happy. The high, black, rough old cathedral tower sent out its chime of bells as earnestly as for any bridegroom and bride that came to be married five hundred years ago. I went into the churchyard, but there was such a throng of people on its pavement of flat tombstones, and especially such a cluster along the pathway by which the bride was to depart, that I could only see a white dress waving along, and really do not know whether she was a beauty or a fright. The happy pair got into a post-chaise that was waiting at the gate, and immediately drew some crimson curtains, and so vanished into their Paradise. There were two other post-chaises and pairs, and all three had postilions in scarlet. This is the same cathedral where, last May, I saw a dozen couples married in the lump.

In a railway carriage, two or three days ago, an old merchant made rather a good point of one of the uncomfortable results of the electric telegraph. He said that formerly a man was safe from bad news, such as intelligence of failure of debtors, except at the hour of opening his letters in the morning; and then he was in some degree prepared for it, since, among (say) fifteen letters, he would be pretty certain to find some "queer" one. But since the telegraph has come into play, he is never safe, and may be hit with news of failure, shipwreck, fall of stocks, or whatever disaster, at all hours of the day.

I went to the Exhibition on Wednesday with U——, and looked at the pencil sketches of the old masters; also at the pictures generally, old and new. I particularly remember a spring landscape, by John Linnell the younger. It is wonderfully good; so tender and fresh that the artist seems really to have caught the evanescent April and made her permanent. Here, at last, is eternal spring.

I saw a little man, behind an immense beard, whom I take to be the Duke of Newcastle; at least, there was a photograph of him in the gallery, with just such a beard. He was at the Palace on that day.

August 16th.—I went again to the Exhibition day before yesterday, and looked much at both the modern and ancient pictures, as also at the water-colors. I am making some progress as a connoisseur, and have got so far as to be able to distinguish the broader differences of style,—as, for example, between Rubens and Rembrandt. I should hesitate to claim any more for myself thus far. In fact, however, I do begin to have a liking for good things, and to be sure that they are good. Murillo seems to me about the noblest and purest painter that ever lived, and his "Good Shepherd" the loveliest picture I have seen. It is a hopeful symptom, moreover, of improving taste, that I see more merit in the crowd of painters than I was at first competent to acknowledge. I could see some of their defects from the very first; but that is the earliest stage of connoisseurship, after a formal and ignorant admiration. Mounting a few steps higher, one sees beauties. But how much study, how many opportunities, are requisite to form and cultivate a taste! The Exhibition must be quite thrown away on the mass of spectators.

Both they and I are better able to appreciate the specimens of ornamental art contained in the Oriental Room, and in the numerous cases that are ranged up and down the nave. The gewgaws of all Time are here, in precious metals, glass, china, ivory, and every other material that could be wrought into curious and beautiful shapes; great basins and dishes of embossed gold from the Queen's sideboard, or from the beaufets of noblemen; vessels set with precious stones; the pastoral staffs of prelates, some of them made of silver or gold, and enriched with gems, and what have been found in the tombs of the bishops; state swords, and silver maces; the rich plate of colleges, elaborately wrought, — great cups, salvers, tureens, that have been presented by loving sons to their Alma Mater; the heirlooms of old families, treasured from generation to generation, and hitherto only to be seen by favored friends; famous historical jewels, some of which are painted in the portraits of the historical men and women that hang on the walls; numerous specimens of the beautiful old Venetian glass, some of which looks so fragile that it is a wonder how it could bear even the weight of the wine, that used to be poured into it, without breaking.

These are the glasses that tested poison, by being shattered into fragments at its touch. The strangest and ugliest old crockery, pictured over with monstrosities, — the Palissy ware, embossed with vegetables, fishes, lobsters, that look absolutely real; the delicate Sèvres china, each piece made inestimable by pictures from a master's hand; — in short, it is a despair and misery to see so much that is curious and beautiful, and to feel that far the greater portion of it will slip out of the memory, and be as if we had never seen it. But I mean to look again and again at these things. We soon perceive that the present day does not engross all the taste and ingenuity that has ever existed in the mind of man; that, in fact, we are a barren age in that respect.

August 20th. — I went to the Exhibition on Monday, and again yesterday, and measurably enjoyed both visits. I continue to think, however, that a picture cannot be fully enjoyed except by long and intimate acquaintance with it, nor can I quite understand what the enjoyment of a connoisseur is. He is not usually, I think, a man of deep, poetic feeling, and does not deal with the picture through his heart, nor set it in a poem, nor comprehend it morally. If it be a landscape, he is not entitled to judge of it by his intimacy with Nature; if a picture of human action, he has no experience nor sympathy of life's deeper passages. However, as my acquaintance with pictures increases, I find myself recognizing more and more the merit of the acknowledged masters of the art; but, possibly, it is only because I adopt the wrong principles which may have been laid down by the connoisseurs. But there can be no mistake about Murillo, — not that I am worthy to admire him yet, however.

Seeing the many pictures of Holy Families, and the Virgin and Child, which have been painted for churches and convents, the idea occurs, that it was in this way that the poor monks and nuns gratified, as far as they could, their natural longing for earthly happiness. It was not Mary and her heavenly Child that they really beheld, or wished for; but an earthly mother rejoicing over her baby, and displaying it probably to the world, as an object worthy to be admired by kings, — as Mary does, in the Adoration of the Magi. Every mother, I suppose, feels as if her first child deserved everybody's worship.

I left the Exhibition at three o'clock, and went to Manchester, where I sought out Mr. C—— S—— in his little office. He greeted me warmly, and at five we took the omnibus for his house, about four miles from town. He seems to be on pleasant terms with his neighbors, for almost everybody that got into the omnibus exchanged kindly greetings with him, and indeed his kindly, simple, genial nature comes out so evidently that it would be difficult not to like him. His house stands, with others, in a green park, — a small, pretty, semi-detached, suburban residence of brick, with a lawn and garden round it. In close vicinity, there is a deep clough or dell, as shaggy and wild as a poet could wish, and with a little stream running through it, as much as five miles long.

. . . . .

The interior of the house is very pretty, and nicely, even handsomely and almost sumptuously, furnished;

and I was very glad to find him so comfortable. His recognition as a poet has been hearty enough to give him a feeling of success, for he showed me various tokens of the estimation in which he is held, — for instance, a presentation copy of Southey's works, in which the latter had written " Amicus amico, — poeta poetæ." He said that Southey had always been most kind to him. . . . . There were various other testimonials from people of note, American as well as English. In his parlor there is a good oil-painting of himself, and in the drawing-room a very fine crayon sketch, wherein his face, handsome and agreeable, is lighted up with all a poet's ecstasy; likewise a large and fine engraving from the picture. The government has recognized his poetic merit by a pension of fifty pounds, — a small sum, it is true, but enough to mark him out as one who has deserved well of his country. . . . . The man himself is very good and lovable. . . . . I was able to gratify him by saying that I had recently seen many favorable notices of his poems in the American newspapers; an edition having been published a few months since on our side of the ocean. He was much pleased at this, and asked me to send him the notices. . . . .

August 30*th*. — I have been two or three times to the Exhibition since my last date, and enjoy it more as I become familiar with it. There is supposed to be about a third of the good pictures here which England contains; and it is said that the Tory nobility and gentry have contributed to it much more freely and largely than the Whigs. The Duke of Devonshire, for instance, seems to have sent nothing. Mr. Ticknor, the

Spanish historian, whom I met yesterday, observed that we should not think quite so much of this Exhibition as the English do after we have been to Italy, although it is a good school in which to gain a preparatory knowledge of the different styles of art. I am glad to hear that there are better things still to be seen. Nevertheless, I should suppose that certain painters are better represented here than they ever have been or will be elsewhere. Vandyke, certainly, can be seen nowhere else so well; Rembrandt and Rubens have satisfactory specimens; and the whole series of English pictorial achievement is shown more perfectly than within any other walls. Perhaps it would be wise to devote myself to the study of this latter, and leave the foreigners to be studied on their own soil. Murillo can hardly have done better than in the pictures by him which we see here. There is nothing of Raphael's here that is impressive. Titian has some noble portraits, but little else that I care to see. In all these old masters, Murillo only excepted, it is very rare, I must say, to find any trace of natural feeling and passion; and I am weary of naked goddesses, who never had any real life and warmth in the painter's imagination, — or, if so, it was the impure warmth of an unchaste woman, who sat for him.

Last week I dined at Mr. F. Heywood's, to meet Mr. Adolphus, the author of a critical work on the Waverley Novels, published long ago, and intended to prove, from internal evidence, that they were written by Sir Walter Scott. . . . . His wife was likewise of the party, ... and also a young Spanish lady, their niece, and daughter of a Spaniard of literary note.

She herself has literary tastes and ability, and is well known to Prescott, whom, I believe, she has assisted in his historical researches, and also to Professor Ticknor; and furthermore she is very handsome and unlike an English damsel, very youthful and maiden-like; and her manners have an ardor and enthusiasm that were pleasant to see, especially as she spoke warmly of my writings; and yet I should wrong her if I left the impression of her being forthputting and obtrusive, for it was not the fact in the least. She speaks English like a native, insomuch that I should never have suspected her to be anything else.

. . . . .

My nerves recently have not been in an exactly quiet and normal state. I begin to weary of England and need another clime.

. . . . .

September 6th. — I think I paid my last visit to the Exhibition, and feel as if I had had enough of it, although I have got but a small part of the profit it might have afforded me. But pictures are certainly quite other things to me now from what they were at my first visit; it seems even as if there were a sort of illumination within them, that makes me see them more distinctly. Speaking of pictures, the miniature of Anne of Cleves is here, on the faith of which Henry VIII. married her; also, the picture of the Infanta of Spain, which Buckingham brought over to Charles I. while Prince of Wales. This has a delicate, rosy prettiness.

One rather interesting portion of the Exhibition is

the Refreshment-room, or rather rooms; for very much space is allowed both to the first and second classes. I have looked most at the latter, because there John Bull and his wife may be seen in full gulp and guzzle, swallowing vast quantities of cold boiled beef, thoroughly moistened with porter or bitter ale; and very good meat and drink it is.

At my last visit, on Friday, I met Judge Pollock of Liverpool, who introduced me to a gentleman in a gray slouched hat as Mr. Du Val, an artist, resident in Manchester; and Mr. Du Val invited me to dine with him at six o'clock. So I went to Carlton Grove, his residence, and found it a very pretty house, with its own lawn and shrubbery about it. . . . . There was a mellow fire in the grate, which made the drawing-room very cosey and pleasant, as the dusk came on before dinner. Mr. Du Val looked like an artist, and like a remarkable man. . . . . We had very good talk, chiefly about the Exhibition, and Du Val spoke generously and intelligently of his brother-artists. He says that England might furnish five exhibitions, each one as rich as the present. I find that the most famous picture here is one that I have hardly looked at, "The Three Marys," by Annibal Caracci. In the drawing-room there were several pictures and sketches by Du Val, one of which I especially liked — a misty, moonlight picture of the Mersey, near Seacombe. I never saw painted such genuine moonlight. . . . .

I took my leave at half past ten, and found my cab at the door, and my cabman snugly asleep inside of it; and when Mr. Du Val awoke him, he proved to be quite drunk, insomuch that I hesitated whether to let him clamber upon the box, or to take post myself, and drive the cabman home. However, I propounded two questions to him: first, whether his horse would go of his own accord; and, secondly, whether he himself was invariably drunk at that time of night, because, if it were his normal state, I should be safer with him drunk than sober. Being satisfied on these points, I got in, and was driven home without accident or adventure; except, indeed, that the cabman drew up and opened the door for me to alight at a vacant lot on Stratford Road, just as if there had been a house and home and cheerful lighted windows in that vacancy. On my remonstrance he resumed the whip and reins, and reached Boston Terrace at last; and, thanking me for an extra sixpence as well as he could speak, he begged me to inquire for "Little John" whenever I next wanted a cab. Cabmen are, as a body, the most ill-natured and ungenial men in the world; but this poor little man was excellently good-humored.

Speaking of the former rudeness of manners, now gradually refining away, of the Manchester people, Judge —— said that, when he first knew Manchester, women, meeting his wife in the street, would take hold of her dress and say, "Ah, three and sixpence a yard!" The men were very rough, after the old Lancashire fashion. They have always, however, been a musical people, and this may have been a germ of refinement in them. They are still much more simple and natural than the Liverpool people, who love the aristocracy and whom they heartily despise. It is singular that the great Art-Exhibition should have come to pass in the rudest great town in England.

LEAMINGTON.

Lansdowne Circus, September 10th. — We have become quite weary of our small, mean, uncomfortable, and unbeautiful lodgings at Chorlton Road, with poor and scanty furniture within doors, and no better prospect from the parlor windows than a mud-puddle, larger than most English lakes, on a vacant building-lot opposite our house. The Exhibition, too, was fast becoming a bore; for you must really love a picture, in order to tolerate the sight of it many times. Moreover, the smoky and sooty air of that abominable Manchester affected my wife's throat disadvantageously; so, on a Tuesday morning, we struck our tent and set forth again, regretting to leave nothing except the kind disposition of Mrs. Honey, our housekeeper. I do not remember meeting with any other lodging-house keeper who did not grow hateful and fearful on short acquaintance; but I attribute this, not so much to the people themselves, as, primarily, to the unfair and ungenerous conduct of some of their English guests, who feel so sure of being cheated that they always behave as if in an enemy's country, and therefore they find it one.

The rain poured down upon us as we drove away in two cabs, laden with mountainous luggage, to the London Road Station; and the whole day was grim with cloud and moist with showers. We went by way of Birmingham, and stayed three hours at the great dreary station there, waiting for the train to Leamington, whither Fanny had gone forward the day before to secure lodgings for us (as she is English, and understands the matter). . . . . We all were tired and dull by the time we reached the Leamington station, where a note from Fanny gave us the address of our lodgings. Lansdowne Circus is really delightful, after that ugly and grimy suburb of Manchester. Indeed, there could not possibly be a greater contrast than between Leamington and Manchester, — the latter built only for dirty uses, and scarcely intended as a habitation for man; the former so cleanly, so set out with shade-trees, so regular in its streets, so neatly paved, its houses so prettily contrived and nicely stuccoed, that it does not look like a portion of the work-a-day world.

. . . . .

KENILWORTH.

September 13*th.* — The weather was very uncertain through the last week, and yesterday morning, too, was misty and sunless; notwithstanding which we took the rail for Kenilworth before eleven. The distance from Leamington is less than five miles, and at the Kenilworth station we found a little bit of an omnibus, into which we packed ourselves, together with two ladies, one of whom, at least, was an American. I begin to agree partly with the English, that we are not a people of elegant manners. At all events there is sometimes a bare, hard, meagre sort of deportment, especially in our women, that has not its parallel elsewhere. But perhaps what sets off this kind of behavior, and brings it into *alto relievo*, is the fact of such uncultivated persons travelling abroad, and going to see sights that would not be interesting except to people of some education and refinement.

We saw but little of the village of Kenilworth, passing through it sidelong fashion, in the omnibus; but I learn that it has between three and four thousand inhabitants, and is of immemorial antiquity. We saw a few, old, gabled, and timber-framed houses; but generally the town was of modern aspect, although less so in the immediate vicinity of the castle gate, across the road from which there was an inn, with bowling-greens, and a little bunch of houses and shops. Apart from the high road there is a gate-house, ancient, but in excellent repair, towered, turreted, and battlemented, and looking like a castle in itself. Until Cromwell's time, the entrance to the castle used to be beneath an arch that passed through this structure; but the gate-house being granted to one of the Parliament officers, he converted it into a residence, and apparently added on a couple of gables, which now look quite as venerable as the rest of the edifice. Admission within the outer grounds of the castle is now obtained through a little wicket close beside the gate-house, at which sat one or two old men, who touched their hats to us in humble willingness to accept a fee. One of them had guide-books for sale; and, finding that we were not to be bothered by a cicerone, we bought one of his books.

The ruins are perhaps two hundred yards from the gate-house and the road, and the space between is a pasture for sheep, which also browse in the inner court, and shelter themselves in the dungeons and state apartments of the castle. Goats would be fitter occupants, because they would climb to the tops of the crumbling towers, and nibble the weeds and shrubbery that grow there. The first part of the castle which we reach is called Cæsar's Tower, being the oldest portion of the ruins, and still very stalwart and massive, and built of red freestone, like all the rest. Cæsar's Tower being on the right, Leicester's Buildings, erected by the Earl of Leicester, Queen Elizabeth's favorite, are on the left; and between these two formerly stood other structures which have now as entirely disappeared as if they had never existed; and through the wide gap, thus opened, appears the grassy inner court, surrounded on three sides by half-fallen towers and shattered walls. Some of these were erected by John of Gaunt; and among these ruins is the Banqueting-Hall, — or rather was, — for it has now neither floor nor roof, but only the broken stonework of some tall, arched windows, and the beautiful, old ivied arch of the entrance-way, now inaccessible from the ground. The ivy is very abundant about the ruins, and hangs its green curtains quite from top to bottom of some of the windows. There are likewise very large and aged trees within the castle, there being no roof nor pavement anywhere, except in some dungeon-like nooks; so that the trees having soil and air enough, and being sheltered from unfriendly blasts, can grow as if in a nursery. Hawthorn, however, next to ivy, is the great ornament and comforter of these desolate ruins. I have not seen so much nor such thriving hawthorn anywhere else, — in the court, high up on crumbly heights, on the sod that carpets roofless rooms, — everywhere, indeed, and now rejoicing in plentiful crops of red berries. The ivy is even more wonderfully luxuriant; its trunks being, in some places, two or three feet in diameter, and forming real buttresses against the walls, which are actually supported and vastly strengthened by this parasite, that clung to them at first only for its own convenience, and now holds them up, lest it should be ruined by their fall. Thus an abuse has strangely grown into a use, and I think we may sometimes see the same fact, morally, in English matters. There is something very curious in the close, firm grip which the ivy fixes upon the wall, closer and closer for centuries. Neither is it at all nice as to what it clutches, in its necessity for support. I saw in the outer court an old hawthorn-tree, to which a plant of ivy had married itself, and the ivy trunk and the hawthorn trunk were now absolutely incorporated, and in their close embrace you could not tell which was which.

At one end of the Banqueting-Hall, there are two large bay-windows, one of which looks into the inner court, and the other affords a view of the surrounding country. The former is called Queen Elizabeth's Dressing-room. Beyond the Banqueting-Hall is what is called the Strong Tower, up to the top of which we climbed principally by the aid of the stones that have tumbled down from it. A lady sat half-way down the crumbly descent, within the castle, on a camp-stool, and before an easel, sketching this tower, on the summit of which we sat. She said it was Amy Robsart's Tower; and within it, open to the day, and quite accessible, we saw a room that we were free to imagine had been occupied by her. I do not find that these associations of real scenes with fictitious events greatly heighten the charm of them.

By this time the sun had come out brightly, and with such warmth that we were glad to sit down in the shadow. Several sight-seers were now rambling about, and among them some school-boys, who kept scrambling up to points whither no other animal, except a goat, would have ventured. Their shouts and the sunshine made the old castle cheerful; and what with the ivy and the hawthorn, and the other old trees, it was very beautiful and picturesque. But a castle does not make nearly so interesting and impressive a ruin as an abbey, because the latter was built for beauty, and on a plan in which deep thought and feeling were involved; and having once been a grand and beautiful work, it continues grand and beautiful through all the successive stages of its decay. But a castle is rudely piled together for strength and other material conveniences; and, having served these ends, it has nothing left to fall back upon, but crumbles into shapeless masses, which are often as little picturesque as a pile of bricks. Without the ivy and the shrubbery, this huge Kenilworth would not be a pleasant object, except for one or two window-frames, with broken tracery, in the Banqueting-Hall. . . . .

We stayed from eleven till two, and identified the various parts of the castle as well as we could by the guide-book. The ruins are very extensive, though less so than I should have imagined, considering that seven acres were included within the castle wall. But a large part of the structures have been taken away to build houses in Kenilworth village and elsewhere, and much, too, to make roads with, and a good deal lies under the green turf in the court-yards, inner and outer. As we returned to the gate, my wife and U—— went into the gate-house to see an old chimney-piece, and other antiquities, and J—— and I proceeded a little way round the outer wall, and saw the remains of the moat, and Lin's Tower, — a real and shattered fabric of John of Gaunt.

The omnibus now drove up, and one of the old men at the gate came hobbling up to open the door, and was rewarded with a sixpence, and we drove down to the King's Head. . . . . We then walked out and bought prints of the castle, and inquired our way to the church, and to the ruins of the Priory. The latter, so far as we could discover them, are very few and uninteresting, and the church, though it has a venerable exterior, and an aged spire, has been so modernized within, and in so plain a fashion, as to have lost what beauty it may once have had. There were a few brasses and mural monuments, one of which was a marble group of a dying woman and her family by Westmacott. The sexton was a cheerful little man, but knew very little about his church, and nothing of the remains of the Priory. The day was spent very pleasantly amid this beautiful green English scenery, these fine old Warwickshire trees, and broad, gently swelling fields.

LIVERPOOL.

September 17*th.* — I took the train for Rugby, and thence to Liverpool. The most noticeable character at Mrs. Blodgett's now is Mr. T——, a Yankee, who has seen the world, and gathered much information and experience already, though still a young man, — a handsome man, with black curly hair, a dark, intelligent, bright face, and rather cold blue eyes, but a very pleasant air and address. His observing faculties are very strongly developed in his forehead, and his reflective ones seem to be adequate to making some, if not the deepest, use of what he sees. He has voyaged and travelled almost all over the world, and has recently published a book of his peregrinations, which has been well received. He is of exceeding fluent talk, though rather too much inclined to unfold the secret springs of action in Louis Napoleon, and other potentates, and to tell of revolutions that are coming at some unlooked-for moment, but soon. Still I believe in his wisdom and foresight about as much as in any other man's. There are no such things. He is a merchant, and meditates settling in London, and making a colossal fortune there during the next ten or twenty years; that being the period during which London is to hold the exchanges of the world, and to continue its metropolis. After that, New York is to be the world's queen city.

There is likewise here a young American, named A——, who has been at a German University, and favors us with descriptions of his student life there, which seem chiefly to have consisted in drinking beer and fighting duels. He shows a cut on his nose as a trophy of these combats. He has with him a dog of St. Bernard, who is a much more remarkable character than himself, — an immense dog, a noble and gentle creature; and really it touches my heart that his master is going to take him from his native snow-mountain to a southern plantation to die. Mr. A—— says that there are now but five of these dogs extant at the convent; there having, within two or three years, been a disease among them, with which this dog also has suffered. His master has a certificate of his genuineness, and of himself being the rightful purchaser; and he says that as he descended the mountain, every peasant along the road stopped him, and would have compelled him to give up the dog had he not produced this proof of property. The neighboring mountaineers are very jealous of the breed being taken away, considering them of such importance to their own safety. This huge animal, the very biggest dog I ever saw, though only eleven months old, and not so high by two or three inches as he will be, allows Mr. —— to play with him, and take him on his shoulders (he weighs, at least, a hundred pounds) like any lap-dog.

LEAMINGTON.

Lansdowne Circus, October 10th. — I returned hither from Liverpool last week, and have spent the time idly since then, reposing myself after the four years of unnatural restraint in the Consulate. Being already pretty well acquainted with the neighborhood of Leamington, I have little or nothing to record about the prettiest, cheerfullest, cleanest of English towns.

. . . . .

On Saturday we took the rail for Coventry, about a half-hour's travel distant. I had been there before, more than two years ago. . . . . No doubt I described it on my first visit; and it is not remarkable enough to be worth two descriptions, — a large town of crooked and irregular streets and lanes, not looking nearly so ancient as it is, because of new brick and stuccoed fronts which have been plastered over its antiquity; although still there are interspersed the peaked gables of old-fashioned, timber-built houses; or an archway of worn stone, which, if you pass through it, shows like an avenue from the present to the past; for just in the rear of the new-fangled aspect lurks the old arrangement of court-yards, and rustiness, and grimness, that would not be suspected from the exterior.

. . . . . .

Right across the narrow street stands St. Michael's Church with its tall, tall tower and spire. The body of the church has been almost entirely recased with stone since I was here before; but the tower still retains its antiquity, and is decorated with statues that look down from their lofty niches seemingly in good preservation. The tower and spire are most stately and beautiful, the whole church very noble. We went in, and found that the vulgar plaster of Cromwell's time has been scraped from the pillars and arches, leaving them all as fresh and splendid as if just made.

We looked also into Trinity Church, which stands close by St. Michael's, separated only, I think, by the churchyard. We also visited St. John's Church, which is very venerable as regards its exterior, the stone being worn and smoothed — if not roughened, rather — by centuries of storm and fitful weather. This wear and tear, however, has almost ceased to be a charm to my mind, comparatively to what it was when I first began to see old buildings. Within, the church is spoiled by wooden galleries, built across the beautiful pointed arches.

We saw nothing else particularly worthy of remark except Ford's Hospital, in Grey Friars' Street. It has an Elizabethan front of timber and plaster, facing on the street, with two or three peaked gables in a row, beneath which is a low, arched entrance, giving admission into a small paved quadrangle, open to the sky above, but surrounded by the walls, lozenge-paned windows, and gables of the Hospital. The quadrangle is but a few paces in width, and perhaps twenty in length; and, through a half-closed doorway, at the farther end, there was a glimpse into a garden. Just within the entrance, through an open door, we saw the neat and comfortable apartment of the Matron of the Hospital; and, along the quadrangle, on each side, there were three or four doors, through which we glanced into little rooms, each containing a fireplace, a bed, a chair or two, — a little, homely, domestic scene, with one old woman in the midst of it; one old woman in each room. They are destitute widows, who have their lodging and home here, — a small room for each one to sleep, cook, and be at home in, — and three and sixpence a week to feed and clothe themselves with, — a cloak being the only garment bestowed on them. When one of the sisterhood dies, each old woman has to pay twopence towards the funeral; and so they slowly starve and wither out of life, and claim each their twopence contribution in turn. I am afraid they have a very dismal time.

There is an old man's hospital in another part of the town, on a similar plan. A collection of sombre and lifelike tales might be written on the idea of giving the experiences of these Hospitallers, male and female; and they might be supposed to be written by the Matron of one, who had acquired literary taste and practice as a governess, — and by the Master of the other, a retired school-usher.

It was market-day in Coventry, and far adown the street leading from it there were booths and stalls, and apples, pears, toys, books, — among which I saw my Twice-Told Tales, with an awful portrait of myself as frontispiece, — and various country produce, offered for sale by men, women, and girls. The scene looked lively, but had not much vivacity in it.

. . . . .

October 27th. — The autumn has advanced progressively, and is now fairly established, though still there is much green foliage, in spite of many brown trees, and an enormous quantity of withered leaves, too damp to rustle, strewing the paths, —whence, however, they are continually swept up and carried off in wheelbarrows, either for neatness or for the agricultural worth, as manure, of even a withered leaf. The pastures look just as green as ever, — a deep, bright verdure, that seems almost sunshine in itself, however sombre the sky may be. The little plats of grass and flowers, in front of our circle of houses, might still do credit to an American midsummer; for I have seen beautiful roses here within a day or two; and dahlias, asters, and such autumnal flowers, are plentiful; and I have no doubt that the old year's flowers will bloom till those of the new year appear. Really, the English winter is not so terrible as ours.

. . . . .

October 30th. — Wednesday was one of the most beautiful of all days, and gilded almost throughout with the precious English sunshine, — the most delightful sunshine ever made, both for its positive fine qualities and because we seldom get it without too great an admixture of water. We made no use of this lovely day, except to walk to an Arboretum and Pinetum on the outskirts of the town. U—— and Mrs. Shepard made an excursion to Guy's Cliff.

[Here comes in the visit to Leicester's Hospital and Redfern's Shop, and St. Mary's Church, printed in Our Old Home. — Ed.]

From Redfern's we went back to the market-place, expecting to find J—— at the Museum, but the keeper said he had gone away. We went into this museum, which contains the collections in Natural History, &c. of a county society. It is very well arranged, and is rich in specimens of ornithology, among which was an albatross, huge beyond imagination. I do not think that Coleridge could have known the size of the fowl when he caused it to be hung round the neck of his Ancient Mariner. There were a great many humming-birds from various parts of the world, and some of their breasts actually gleamed and shone as with the brightest lustre of sunset. Also, many strange fishes, and a huge pike taken from the river Avon, and so long that I wonder how he could turn himself about in such a little river as the Avon is near Warwick. A great curiosity was a bunch of skeleton leaves and flowers, prepared by a young lady, and preserving all the most delicate fibres of the plant, looking like inconceivably fine lace-work, white as snow, while the substance was quite taken away. In another room there were minerals, shells, and a splendid collection of fossils, among which were remains of antediluvian creatures, several feet long.

In still another room, we saw some historical curiosities, — the most interesting of which were two locks of reddish-brown hair, one from the head and one from the beard of Edward IV. They were fastened to a manuscript letter which authenticates the hair as having been taken from King Edward's tomb in 1789. Near these relics was a seal of the great Earl of Warwick, the mighty king-maker; also a sword from Bosworth Field, smaller and shorter than those now in use; for, indeed, swords seem to have increased in length, weight, and formidable aspect, now that the weapon has almost ceased to be used in actual warfare. The short Roman sword was probably more murderous than any weapon of the same species, except the bowie-knife. Here, too, were Parliamentary cannon-balls, &c. . . . .

[The visit to Whitnash intervenes here. — ED.]

LONDON.

24 *Great Russell Street, November 10th.* — We have been thinking and negotiating about taking lodgings in London lately, and this morning we left Leamington and reached London with no other misadventure than that of leaving the great bulk of our luggage behind us, — the van which we hired to take it to the railway station having broken down under its prodigious weight, in the middle of the street. On our journey we saw nothing particularly worthy of note, — but everywhere the immortal verdure of England, scarcely less perfect than in June, so far as the fields are concerned, though the foliage of the trees presents pretty much the same hues as those of our own forests, after the gayety and gorgeousness have departed from them.

Our lodgings are in close vicinity to the British Museum, which is the great advantage we took them for.

I felt restless and uncomfortable, and soon strolled forth, without any definite object, and walked as far as Charing Cross. Very dull and dreary the city looked, and not in the least lively, even where the throng was thickest and most brisk. As I trudged along, my reflection was, that never was there a dingier, uglier, less picturesque city than London; and that it is really wonderful that so much brick and stone, for centuries together, should have been built up with so poor a result. Yet these old names of the city — Fleet Street, Ludgate Hill, the Strand — used to throw a glory over these homely precincts when I first saw them, and still do so in a less degree. Where Farrington Street opens upon Fleet Street, moreover, I had a glimpse of St. Paul's, along Ludgate Street, in the gathering dimness, and felt as if I saw an old friend. In that neighborhood — speaking of old friends — I met Mr. Parker of Boston, who told me sad news of a friend whom I love as much as if I had known him for a lifetime, though he is, indeed, but of two or three years' standing. He said that my friend's bankruptcy is in to-day's Gazette. Of all men on earth, I had rather this misfortune should have happened to any other; but I hope and think he has sturdiness and buoyancy enough to rise up beneath it. I cannot conceive of his face otherwise than with a glow on it, like that of the sun at noonday.

Before I reached our lodgings, the dusk settled into the streets, and a mist bedewed and bedamped me, and I went astray, as is usual with me, and had to inquire my way; indeed, except in the principal thoroughfares,

London is so miserably lighted that it is impossible to recognize one's whereabouts. On my arrival I found our parlor looking cheerful with a brisk fire; . . . . but the first day or two in new lodgings is at best an uncomfortable time. Fanny has just come in with more unhappy news about ——. Pray Heaven it may not be true! . . . . Troubles are a sociable brotherhood; they love to come hand in hand, or sometimes, even, to come side by side, with long looked-for and hoped-for good fortune. . . . .

November 11th. — This morning we all went to the British Museum, always a most wearisome and depressing task to me. I strolled through the lower rooms with a good degree of interest, looking at the antique sculptures, some of which were doubtless grand and beautiful in their day. . . . . The Egyptian remains are, on the whole, the more satisfactory; for, though inconceivably ugly, they are at least miracles of size and ponderosity, — for example, a hand and arm of polished granite, as much as ten feet in length. The upper rooms, containing millions of specimens of Natural History, in all departments, really made my heart ache with a pain and woe that I have never felt anywhere but in the British Museum, and I hurried through them as rapidly as I could persuade J—— to follow me. We had left the rest of the party still intent on the Grecian sculptures; and though J—— was much interested in the vast collection of shells, he chose to quit the Museum with me in the prospect of a stroll about London. He seems to have my own passion for thronged streets, and the utmost bustle of human life.

We went first to the railway station, in quest of our luggage, which we found. Then we made a pretty straight course down to Holborn, and through Newgate Street, stopping a few moments to look through the iron fence at the Christ's Hospital boys, in their long blue coats and yellow petticoats and stockings. It was between twelve and one o'clock; and I suppose this was their hour of play, for they were running about the enclosed space, chasing and overthrowing one another, without their caps, with their yellow petticoats tucked up, and all in immense activity and enjoyment. They were eminently a healthy and handsome set of boys.

Then we went into Cheapside, where I called at Mr. Bennett's shop, to inquire what are the facts about ——. When I mentioned his name, Mr. Bennett shook his head and expressed great sorrow; but, on further talk, I found that he referred only to the failure, and had heard nothing about the other rumor. It cannot, therefore, be true; for Bennett lives in his neighborhood, and could not have remained ignorant of such a calamity. There must be some mistake; none, however, in regard to the failure, it having been announced in the Times.

From Bennett's shop, — which is so near the steeple of Bow Church that it would tumble upon it if it fell over, — we strolled still eastward, aiming at London Bridge; but missed it, and bewildered ourselves among many dingy and frowzy streets and lanes. I bore towards the right, however, knowing that that course must ultimately bring me to the Thames; and at last I saw before me ramparts, towers, circular and square, with battlemented summits, large sweeps and curves of fortification, as well as straight and massive walls and chimneys behind them (all a great confusion — to my eye), of ancient and more modern structure, and four loftier turrets rising in the midst; the whole great space surrounded by a broad, dry moat, which now seemed to be used as an ornamental walk, bordered partly with trees. This was the Tower; but seen from a different and more picturesque point of view than I have heretofore gained of it. Being so convenient for a visit, I determined to go in. At the outer gate, which is not a part of the fortification, a sentinel walks to and fro, besides whom there was a warder, in the rich old costume of Henry VIII.'s time, looking very gorgeous indeed, — as much so as scarlet and gold can make him.

. . . . . .

As J—— and I were not going to look at the Jewel-room, we loitered about in the open space, before the White Tower, while the tall, slender, white-haired, gentlemanly warder led the rest of the party into that apartment. We found what one might take for a square in a town, with gabled houses lifting their peaks on one side, and various edifices enclosing the other sides, and the great White Tower, — now more black than white, — rising venerable, and rather picturesque than otherwise, the most prominent object in the scene. I have no plan nor available idea of it whatever in my mind, but it seems really to be a town within itself, with streets, avenues, and all that pertains to human life. There were soldiers going through their exercise in the open space, and along at the base of the White Tower lay a great many cannon and mortars, some of which were of Turkish manufacture, and immensely long and ponderous. Others, likewise of mighty size, had once belonged to the famous ship Great Harry, and had lain for ages under the sea. Others were East-Indian. Several were beautiful specimens of workmanship. The mortars — some so large that a fair-sized man might easily be rammed into them — held their great mouths slanting upward to the sky, and mostly contained a quantity of rain-water. While we were looking at these warlike toys, — for I suppose not one of them will ever thunder in earnest again, — the warden reappeared with his ladies, and, leading us all to a certain part of the open space, he struck his foot on the small stones with which it is paved, and told us that we were standing on the spot where Anne Boleyn and Catharine Parr were beheaded. It is not exactly in the centre of the square, but on a line with one of the angles of the White Tower. I forgot to mention that the middle of the open space is occupied by a marble statue of Wellington, which appeared to me very poor and laboriously spirited.

Lastly, the warder led us under the Bloody Tower, and by the side of the Wakefield Tower, and showed us the Traitor's Gate, which is now closed up, so as to afford no access to the Thames. No; we first visited the Beauchamp Tower, famous as the prison of many historical personages. Some of its former occupants have left their initials or names, and inscriptions of piety and patience, cut deep into the freestone of the walls, together with devices — as a crucifix, for instance — neatly and skilfully done. This room has a long, deep fireplace; it is chiefly lighted by a large window, which I fancy must have been made in modern times; but there are four narrow apertures, throwing in a little light through deep alcoves in the thickness of the octagon wall. One would expect such a room to be picturesque; but it is really not of striking aspect, being low, with a plastered ceiling, — the beams just showing through the plaster, — a boarded floor, and the walls being washed over with a buff color. A warder sat within a railing, by the great window, with sixpenny books to sell, containing transcripts of the inscriptions on the walls.

We now left the Tower, and made our way deviously westward, passing St. Paul's, which looked magnificently and beautifully, so huge and dusky as it was, with here and there a space on its vast form where the original whiteness of the marble came out like a streak of moonshine amid the blackness with which time has made it grander than it was in its newness. It is a most noble edifice; and I delight, too, in the statues that crown some of its heights, and in the wreaths of sculpture which are hung around it.

. . . . .

November 12th. — This morning began with such fog, that at the window of my chamber, lighted only from a small court-yard, enclosed by high, dingy walls, I could hardly see to dress. It kept alternately darkening, and then brightening a little, and darkening again, so much that we could but just discern the opposite houses; but at eleven or thereabouts it grew so much clearer that we resolved to venture out. Our plan for the day was to go in the first place to Westminster Abbey; and to the National Gallery, if we should find time. . . . . The fog darkened again as we went down Regent Street, and the Duke of York's Column was but barely visible, looming vaguely before us; nor, from Pall Mall, was Nelson's Pillar much more distinct, though methought his statue stood aloft in a somewhat clearer atmosphere than ours. Passing Whitehall, however, we could scarcely see Inigo Jones's Banqueting-House, on the other side of the street; and the towers and turrets of the new Houses of Parliament were all but invisible, as was the Abbey itself; so that we really were in some doubt whither we were going. We found our way to Poets' Corner, however, and entered those holy precincts, which looked very dusky and grim in the smoky light. . . . . I was strongly impressed with the perception that very commonplace people compose the great bulk of society in the home of the illustrious dead. It is wonderful how few names there are that one cares anything about a hundred years after their departure; but perhaps each generation acts in good faith in canonizing its own men. . . . . But the fame of the buried person does not make the marble live, — the marble keeps merely a cold and sad memory of a man who would else be forgotten. No man who needs a monument ever ought to have one.

. . . . .

The painted windows of the Abbey, though mostly modern, are exceedingly rich and beautiful; and I do think that human art has invented no other such magnificent method of adornment as this.

. . . . .

Our final visit to-day was to the National Gallery,

where I came to the conclusion that Murillo's St. John was the most lovely picture I have ever seen, and that there never was a painter who has really made the world richer, except Murillo.

. . . . . .

November 12*th.* — This morning we issued forth, and found the atmosphere chill and almost frosty, tingling upon our cheeks. . . . . The gateway of Somerset House attracted us, and we walked round its spacious quadrangle, encountering many government clerks hurrying to their various offices. At least, I presumed them to be so. This is certainly a handsome square of buildings, with its Grecian façades and pillars, and its sculptured bas-reliefs, and the group of statuary in the midst of the court. Besides the part of the edifice that rises above ground, there appear to be two subterranean stories below the surface. From Somerset House we pursued our way through Temple Bar, but missed it, and therefore entered by the passage from what was formerly Alsatia, but which now seems to be a very respectable and humdrum part of London. We came immediately to the Temple Gardens, which we walked quite round. The grass is still green, but the trees are leafless, and had an aspect of not being very robust, even at more genial seasons of the year. There were, however, large quantities of brilliant chrysanthemums, golden, and of all hues, blooming gorgeously all about the borders; and several gardeners were at work, tending these flowers, and sheltering them from the weather. I noticed no roses, nor even rose-bushes, in the spot where the factions of York and Lancaster plucked their two hostile flowers.

Leaving these grounds, we went to the Hall of the Middle Temple, where we knocked at the portal, and, finding it not fastened, thrust it open. A boy appeared within, and the porter or keeper, at a distance, along the inner passage, called to us to enter; and, opening the door of the great hall, left us to view it till he should be at leisure to attend to us. Truly it is a most magnificent apartment; very lofty, — so lofty, indeed, that the antique oak-roof was quite hidden, as regarded all its details, in the sombre gloom that brooded under its rafters. The hall was lighted by four great windows, I think, on each of the two sides, descending half-way from the ceiling to the floor, leaving all beneath enclosed by oaken panelling, which, on three sides, was carved with escutcheons of such members of the society as have held the office of reader. There is likewise, in a large recess or transept, a great window, occupying the full height of the hall, and splendidly emblazoned with the arms of the Templars who have attained to the dignity of Chief-Justices. The other windows are pictured, in like manner, with coats of arms of local dignities connected with the Temple; and besides all these there are arched lights, high towards the roof, at either end full of richly and chastely colored glass, and all the illumination that the great hall had came through these glorious panes, and they seemed the richer for the sombreness in which we stood. I cannot describe, or even intimate, the effect of this transparent glory, glowing down upon us in that gloomy depth of the hall. The screen at the lower end was of carved oak, very dark and highly polished, and as old as Queen Elizabeth's time. The keeper told us that the story of the

Armada was said to be represented in these carvings, but in the imperfect light we could trace nothing of it out. Along the length of the apartment were set two oaken tables for the students of law to dine upon; and on the dais, at the upper end, there was a cross-table for the big-wigs of the society; the latter being provided with comfortable chairs, and the former with oaken benches. From a notification, posted near the door, I gathered that the cost of dinners is two shillings to each gentleman, including, as the attendant told me, ale and wine. I am reluctant to leave this hall without expressing how grave, how grand, how sombre, and how magnificent I feel it to be. As regards historical association, it was a favorite dancing-hall of Queen Elizabeth, and Sir Christopher Hatton danced himself into her good graces there.

We next went to the Temple Church, and, finding the door ajar, made free to enter beneath its Norman arches, which admitted us into a circular vestibule, very ancient and beautiful. In the body of the church beyond we saw a boy sitting, but nobody either forbade or invited our entrance. On the floor of the vestibule lay about half a score of Templars, — the representatives of the warlike priests who built this church and formerly held these precincts, — all in chain-armor, grasping their swords, and with their shields beside them. Except two or three, they lay cross-legged, in token that they had really fought for the Holy Sepulchre. I think I have seen nowhere else such well-preserved monumental knights as these. We proceeded into the interior of the church, and were greatly impressed with its wonderful beauty, — the roof springing, as it were, in a harmonious and accordant fountain, out of the clustered pillars that support its groined arches; and these pillars, immense as they are, are polished like so many gems. They are of Purbeck marble, and, if I mistake not, had been covered with plaster for ages until latterly redeemed and beautified anew. But the glory of the church is its old painted windows; and, positively, those great spaces over the chancel appeared to be set with all manner of precious stones, — or it was as if the many-colored radiance of heaven were breaking upon us, — or as if we saw the wings of angels, storied over with richly tinted pictures of holy things. But it is idle to talk of this marvellous adornment; it is to be seen and wondered at, not written about. Before we left the church, the porter made his appearance, in time to receive his fee, — which somebody, indeed, is always ready to stretch out his hand for. And so ended our visit to the Temple, which, by the by, though close to the midmost bustle of London, is as quiet as if it were always Sunday there.

We now went to St. Paul's. U—— and Miss Shepard ascended to the Whispering Gallery, and we, sitting under the dome, at the base of one of the pillars, saw them far above us, looking very indistinct, for those misty upper-depths seemed almost to be hung with clouds. This cathedral, I think, does not profit by gloom, but requires cheerful sunshine to show it to the best advantage. The statues and sculptures in St. Paul's are mostly covered with years of dust, and look thereby very grim and ugly; but there are few memories there from which I should care to brush away the dust, they being, in nine cases out of ten, naval and military heroes of second or third class merit. I really remember no literary celebrity admitted solely on that account, except Dr. Johnson. The Crimean war has supplied two or three monuments, chiefly mural tablets; and doubtless more of the same excrescences will yet come out upon the walls. One thing that I newly noticed was the beautiful shape of the great, covered marble vase that serves for a font.

From St. Paul's we went down Cheapside, and, turning into King Street, visited Guildhall, which we found in process of decoration for a public ball, to take place next week. It looked rather gewgawish thus gorgeous, being hung with flags of all nations, and adorned with military trophies; and the scene was repeated by a range of looking-glasses at one end of the room. The execrably painted windows really shocked us by their vulgar glare, after those of the Temple Hall and Church; yet, a few years ago, I might very likely have thought them beautiful. Our own national banner, I must remember to say, was hanging in Guildhall, but with only ten stars, and an insufficient number of stripes.

. . . . .

November 15th. — Yesterday morning we went to London Bridge and along Lower Thames Street, and quickly found ourselves in Billingsgate Market, — a dirty, evil-smelling, crowded precinct, thronged with people carrying fish on their heads, and lined with fish-shops and fish-stalls, and pervaded with a fishy odor. The footwalk was narrow, — as indeed was the whole street, — and filthy to travel upon; and we had to elbow our way among rough men and slatternly women, and to guard our heads from the contact of fish-trays; very ugly, grimy, and misty, moreover, is Billingsgate Market, and though we heard none of the foul language of which it is supposed to be the fountain-head, yet it has its own peculiarities of behavior. For instance, U——_tells me that one man, staring at her and her governess as they passed, cried out, "What beauties!"—another, looking under her veil, greeted her with "Good morning, my love!" We were in advance, and heard nothing of these civilities. Struggling through this fishy purgatory, we caught sight of the Tower, as we drew near the end of the street; and I put all my party under charge of one of the Trump Cards, not being myself inclined to make the rounds of the small part of the fortress that is shown, so soon after my late visit.

When they departed with the warder, I set out by myself to wander about the exterior of the Tower, looking with interest at what I suppose to be Tower Hill,—a slight elevation of the large open space into which Great Tower Street opens; though, perhaps, what is now called Trinity Square may have been a part of Tower Hill, and possibly the precise spot where the executions took place. Keeping to the right, round the Tower, I found the moat quite surrounded by a fence of iron rails, excluding me from a pleasant gravel-path, among flowers and shrubbery, on the inside, where I could see nursery-maids giving children their airings. Possibly these may have been the privileged inhabitants of the Tower, which certainly might contain the population of a large village. The aspect of the fortress has so much that is new and modern about it that it can hardly be called picturesque, and yet it seems unfair to withhold that epithet from such a collection of gray ramparts. I followed the iron fence quite round the outer grounds, till it approached the Thames, and in this direction the moat and the pleasure-ground terminate in a narrow graveyard, which extends beneath the walls, and looks neglected and shaggy with long grass. It appeared to contain graves enough, but only a few tombstones, of which I could read the inscription of but one; it commemorated a Mr. George Gibson, a person of no note, nor apparently connected with the place. St. Katharine's Dock lies along the Thames, in this vicinity; and while on one side of me were the Tower, the quiet gravel-path, and the shaggy graveyard, on the other were draymen and their horses, dock-laborers, sailors, empty puncheons, and a miscellaneous spectacle of life, — including organ-grinders, men roasting chestnuts over small ovens on the sidewalk, boys and women with boards or wheelbarrows of apples, oyster-stands, besides pedlers of small wares, dirty children at play, and other figures and things that a Dutch painter would seize upon.

I went a little way into St. Katharine's Dock, and found it crowded with great ships; then, returning, I strolled along the range of shops that front towards this side of the Tower. They have all something to do with ships, sailors, and commerce; being for the sale of ships' stores, nautical instruments, arms, clothing, together with a tavern and grog-shop at every other door; book-stalls, too, covered with cheap novels and song-books; cigar-shops in great numbers; and everywhere were sailors, and here and there a soldier, and children at the doorsteps, and women showing themselves at the doors or windows of their domiciles. These latter figures, however, pertain rather to the street up which I walked, penetrating into the interior of this region, which, I think, is Blackwall — no, I forget what its name is. At all events, it has an ancient and most grimy and rough look, with its old gabled houses, each of them the seat of some petty trade and business in its basement story. Among these I saw one house with three or four peaks along its front, — a second story projecting over the basement, and the whole clapboarded over. . . . . There was a butcher's stall in the lower story, with a front open to the street, in the ancient fashion, which seems to be retained only by butchers' shops. This part of London, having escaped the Great Fire, I suppose there may be many relics of architectural antiquity hereabouts.

At the end of an hour I went back to the Refreshment-room, within the outer gate of the Tower, where the rest of us shortly appeared. We now returned westward by way of Great Tower Street, Eastcheap, and Cannon Street, and, entering St. Paul's, sat down beneath the misty dome to rest ourselves. The muffled roar of the city, as we heard it there, is very soothing, and keeps one listening to it, somewhat as the flow of a river keeps us looking at it. It is a grand and quiet sound; and, ever and anon, a distant door slammed somewhere in the cathedral, and reverberated long and heavily, like the roll of thunder or the boom of cannon. Every noise that is loud enough to be heard in so vast an edifice melts into the great quietude. The interior looked very sombre, and the dome hung over us like a cloudy sky. I wish it were possible to pass directly from St. Paul's into York Minster, or from the latter into the former; that is, if one's mind could manage to stagger under both in the same day. There is no other way of judging of their comparative effect.

Under the influence of that grand lullaby, — the roar of the city, — we sat for some time after we were sufficiently rested; but at last plunged forth again, and went up Newgate Street, pausing to look through the iron railings of Christ's Hospital. The boys, however, were not at play; so we went onward, in quest of Smithfield, and on our way had a greeting from Mr. Silsbee, a gentleman of our own native town. Parting with him, we found Smithfield, which is still occupied with pens for cattle, though I believe it has ceased to be a cattle-market. Except it be St. Bartholomew's Hospital on one side, there is nothing interesting in this ugly square; though, no doubt, a few feet under the pavement there are bones and ashes as precious as anything of the kind on earth. I wonder when men will begin to erect monuments to human error; hitherto their pillars and statues have only been for the sake of glorification. But, after all, the present fashion may be the better and wholesomer. . . . .

November 16*th.* — Mr. Silsbee called yesterday, and talked about matters of art, in which he is deeply interested, and which he has had good opportunities of becoming acquainted with, during three years' travel on the Continent. He is a man of great intelligence and true feeling, and absolutely brims over with ideas, — his conversation flowing in a constant stream, which it appears to be no trouble whatever to him to keep up. . . . . He took his leave after a long call, and left with us a manuscript, describing a visit to Berlin, which I read to my wife in the evening. It was well worth reading. He made an engagement to go with us to the Crystal Palace, and came hither for that purpose this morning.

We drove to the London Bridge Station, where we bought return tickets that entitled us to admission to the Palace, as well as conveyance thither, for half a crown apiece. On our arrival we entered by the garden front, thus gaining a fine view of the ornamental grounds, with their fountains and stately pathways, bordered with statues; and of the edifice itself, so vast and fairy-like, looking as if it were a bubble, and might vanish at a touch. There is as little beauty in the architecture of the Crystal Palace, however, as was possible to be with such gigantic use of such a material. No doubt, an architectural order of which we have as yet little or no idea is to be developed from the use of glass as a building material, instead of brick and stone. It will have its own rules and its own results; but, meanwhile, even the present palace is positively a very beautiful object. On entering we found the atmosphere chill and comfortless, — more so, it seemed to me, than the open air itself. It was not a genial day; though now and then the sun gleamed out, and once caused fine effects in the glass-work of a crystal fountain in one of the courts.

We were under Mr. Silsbee's guidance for the day, ... and first we looked at the sculpture, which is composed chiefly of casts or copies of the most famous statues of all ages, and likewise of those crumbs and little fragments which have fallen from Time's jaw, — and half-picked bones, as it were, that have been gathered up from spots where he has feasted full, — torsos, heads and broken limbs, some of them half worn away as if they had been rolled over and over in the sea. I saw nothing in the sculptural way, either modern or antique, that impressed me so much as a statue of a nude mother by a French artist. In a sitting posture, with one knee over the other, she was clasping her highest knee with both hands; and in the hollow cradle thus formed by her arms lay two sweet little babies, as snug and close to her heart as if they had not yet been born, — two little love-blossoms, — and the mother encircling them and pervading them with love. But an infinite pathos and strange terror are given to this beautiful group by some faint bas-reliefs on the pedestal, indicating that the happy mother is Eve, and Cain and Abel the two innocent babes.

Then we went to the Alhambra, which looks like an enchanted palace. If it had been a sunny day, I should have enjoyed it more; but it was miserable to shiver and shake in the Court of the Lions, and in those chambers which were contrived as places of refuge from a fervid temperature. Furthermore, it is not quite agreeable to see such clever specimens of stage decoration; they are so very good that it gets to be past a joke, without becoming actual earnest. I had not a similar feeling in respect to the reproduction of mediæval statues, arches, doorways, all brilliantly colored as in the days of their first glory; yet I do not know but that the first is as little objectionable as the last. Certainly, in both cases, scenes and objects of a past age are here more vividly presented to the dullest mind than without such material facilities they could possibly be brought before the most powerful imagination. Truly, the Crystal Palace, in all its departments, offers wonderful means of education. I marvel what will come of it. Among the things that I admired most was Benvenuto Cellini's statue of Perseus holding the head of Medusa, and standing over her headless and still writhing body, out of which, at the severed neck, gushed a vast exuberance of snakes. Likewise, a sitting statue, by Michel Angelo, of one of the Medici, full of dignity and grace and reposeful might. Also the bronze gate of a baptistery in Florence, carved all over with relievos of Scripture subjects, executed in the most lifelike and expressive manner. The cast itself was a miracle of art. I should have taken it for the genuine original bronze.

We then wandered into the House of Diomed, which seemed to me a dismal abode, affording no possibility of comfort. We sat down in one of the rooms, on an iron bench, very cold.

It being by this time two o'clock, we went to the Refreshment-room and lunched; and before we had finished our repast, my wife discovered that she had lost her sable tippet, which she had been carrying on her arm. Mr. Silsbee most kindly and obligingly immediately went in quest of it, ... but to no purpose. . . . .

Upon entering the Tropical Saloon, we found a most welcome and delightful change of temperature among those gigantic leaves of banyan-trees, and the broad expanse of water-plants, floating on lakes, and spacious aviaries, where birds of brilliant plumage sported and sang amid such foliage as they knew at home. Howbeit, the atmosphere was a little faint and sickish, perhaps owing to the odor of the half-tepid water. The most remarkable object here was the trunk of a tree, huge beyond imagination, — a pine-tree from California. It was only the stripped-off bark, however, which had been conveyed hither in segments, and put together again beyond the height of the palace roof; and the hollow interior circle of the tree was large enough to contain fifty people, I should think. We entered and sat down in all the remoteness from one another that is attainable in a good-sized drawing-room. We then ascended the gallery to get a view of this vast tree from a more elevated position, and found it looked even bigger from above. Then we loitered slowly along the gallery as far as it extended, and afterwards descended into the nave; for it was getting dusk, and a horn had sounded, and a bell rung a warning to such as delayed in the remote regions of the building. Mr. Silsbee again most kindly went in quest of the sables, but still without success. . . . . I have not much enjoyed the Crystal Palace, but think it a great and admirable achievement.

November 19*th.* — On Tuesday evening Mr. Silsbee came to read some letters which he has written to his friends, chiefly giving his observations on Art, together with descriptions of Venice and other cities on the Continent. They were very good, and indicate much sensibility and talent. After the reading we had a little oyster-supper and wine.

I had written a note to ——, and received an answer, indicating that he was much weighed down by his financial misfortune. . . . . However, he desired me to come and see him; so yesterday morning I wended my way down into the city, and after various reluctant circumlocutions arrived at his house. The interior looked confused and dismal.

. . . . .

It seems to me nobody else runs such risks as a man of business, because he risks everything. Every other man, into whatever depth of poverty he may sink, has still something left, be he author, scholar, handicraftman, or what not; the merchant has nothing.

We parted with a long and strong grasp of the hand, and —— promised to come and see us soon. . . . .

On my way home I called at Trübner's in Paternoster Row. . . . . I waited a few minutes, he being busy with a tall, muscular, English-built man, who, after he had taken leave, Trübner told me was Charles Reade. I once met him at an evening-party, but should have been glad to meet him again, now that I appreciate him so much better after reading Never too Late to Mend.

December 6th. — All these days, since my last date, have been marked by nothing very well worthy of detail and description. I have walked the streets a great deal in the dull November days, and always take a certain pleasure in being in the midst of human life, — as closely encompassed by it as it is possible to be anywhere in this world; and in that way of viewing it there is a dull and sombre enjoyment always to be had in Holborn, Fleet Street, Cheapside, and the other busiest parts of London. It is human life; it is this material world; it is a grim and heavy reality. I have never had the same sense of being surrounded by materialisms and hemmed in with the grossness of this earthly existence anywhere else; these broad, crowded streets are so evidently the veins and arteries of an enormous city. London is evidenced in every one of them, just as a megatherium is in each of its separate bones, even if they be small ones. Thus I never fail of a sort of self-congratulation in finding myself, for instance, passing along Ludgate Hill; but, in spite of this, it is really an ungladdened life to wander through these huge, thronged ways, over a pavement foul with mud, ground into it by a million of footsteps; jostling against people who do not seem to be individuals, but all one mass, so homogeneous is the street-walking aspect of them; the roar of vehicles pervading me, — wearisome cabs and omnibuses; everywhere the dingy brick edifices heaving themselves up, and shutting out all but a strip of sullen cloud, that serves London for a sky, — in short, a general impression of grime and sordidness; and at this season always a fog scattered along the vista of streets, sometimes so densely as almost to spiritualize the materialism and make the scene resemble the other world of worldly people, gross even in ghostliness. It is strange how little splendor and brilliancy one sees in London, — in the city almost none, though some in the shops of Regent Street. My wife has had a season of indisposition within the last few weeks, so that my rambles have generally been solitary, or with J—— only for a companion. I think my only excursion with my wife was a week ago, when we went to Lincoln's Inn Fields, which truly are almost fields right in the heart of London, and as retired and secluded as if the surrounding city were a forest, and its heavy roar were the wind among the branches. We gained admission into the noble Hall, which is modern, but built in antique style, and stately and beautiful exceedingly. I have forgotten all but the general effect, with its lofty oaken roof, its panelled walls, with the windows high above, and the great arched window at one end full of painted coats of arms, which the light glorifies in passing through them, as if each were the escutcheon of some illustrious personage. Thence we went to the chapel of Lincoln's Inn, where, on entering, we found a class of young choristers receiving instruction from their music-master, while the organ accompanied their strains. These young, clear, fresh, elastic voices are wonderfully beautiful; they are like those of women, yet have something more birdlike and aspiring, more like what one conceives of the singing of angels. As for the singing of saints and blessed spirits that have once been human, it never can resemble that of these young voices; for no duration of heavenly enjoyments will ever quite take the mortal sadness out of it.

In this chapel we saw some painted windows of the time of James I., a period much subsequent to the age when painted glass was in its glory; but the pictures of Scriptural people in these windows were certainly very fine, — the figures being as large as life, and the faces having much expression. The sunshine came in through some of them, and produced a beautiful effect, almost as if the painted forms were the glorified spirits of those holy personages.

After leaving Lincoln's Inn, we looked at Gray's Inn, which is a great, quiet domain, quadrangle beyond quadrangle, close beside Holborn, and a large space of greensward enclosed within it. It is very strange to find so much of ancient quietude right in the monster city's very jaws, which yet the monster shall not eat up, — right in its very belly, indeed, which yet, in all these ages, it shall not digest and convert into the same substance as the rest of its bustling streets. Nothing else in London is so like the effect of a spell, as to pass under one of these archways, and find yourself transported from the jumble, mob, tumult, uproar, as of an age of week-days condensed into the present hour, into what seems an eternal sabbath. Thence we went into Staple Inn, I think it was, — which has a front upon Holborn of four or five ancient gables in a row, and a low arch under the impending story, admitting you into a paved quadrangle, beyond which you have the vista of another. I do not understand that the residences and chambers in these Inns of Court are now exclusively let to lawyers; though such inhabitants certainly seem to preponderate there.

Since then J—— and I walked down into the Strand, and found ourselves unexpectedly mixed up with a crowd that grew denser as we approached Charing Cross, and became absolutely impermeable when we attempted to make our way to Whitehall. The wicket in the gate of Northumberland House, by the by, was open, and gave me a glimpse of the front of the edifice within, — a very partial glimpse, however, and that obstructed by the solid person of a footman, who, with some women, were passing out from within. The crowd was a real English crowd, perfectly undemonstrative, and entirely decorous, being composed mostly of well-dressed people, and largely of women. The cause of the assemblage was the opening of Parliament by the Queen, but we were too late for any chance of seeing her Majesty. However, we extricated ourselves from the multitude, and, going along Pall Mall, got into the Park by the steps at the foot of the Duke of York's Column, and thence went to the Whitehall Gateway, outside of which we found the Horse Guards drawn up, — a regiment of black horses and burnished cuirasses. On our way thither an open carriage came through the gateway into the Park, conveying two ladies in court dresses; and another splendid chariot pressed out through the gateway, — the coachman in a cocked hat and scarlet and gold embroidery, and two other scarlet and gold figures hanging behind. It was one of the Queen's carriages, but seemed to have nobody in it. I have forgotten to mention what, I think, produced more effect on me than anything else, namely, the clash of the bells from the steeple of St. Martin's Church and those of St. Margaret. Really, London seemed to cry out through them, and bid welcome to the Queen.

December 7th. — This being a muddy and dismal day, I went only to the

BRITISH MUSEUM,

which is but a short walk down the street (Great Russell Street). I have now visited it often enough to be on more familiar terms with it than at first, and therefore do not feel myself so weighed down by the many things to be seen. I have ceased to expect or hope or wish to devour and digest the whole enormous collection; so I content myself with individual things, and succeed in getting now and then a little honey from them. Unless I were studying some particular branch of history or science or art, this is the best that can be done with the British Museum.

I went first to-day into the Townley Gallery, and so along through all the ancient sculpture, and was glad to find myself able to sympathize more than heretofore with the forms of grace and beauty which are preserved there, — poor, maimed immortalities as they are, — headless and legless trunks, godlike cripples, faces beautiful and broken-nosed, — heroic shapes which have stood so long, or lain prostrate so long, in the open air, that even the atmosphere of Greece has almost dissolved the external layer of the marble; and yet, however much they may be worn away, or battered and shattered, the grace and nobility seem as deep in them as the very heart of the stone. It cannot be destroyed, except by grinding them to powder. In short, I do really believe that there was an excellence in ancient sculpture, which has yet a potency to educate and refine the minds of those who look at it even so carelessly and casually as I do. As regards the frieze of the Parthenon, I must remark that the horses represented on it, though they show great spirit and lifelikeness, are rather of the pony species than what would be considered fine horses now. Doubtless, modern breeding has wrought a difference in the animal. Flaxman, in his outlines, seems to have imitated these classic steeds of the Parthenon, and thus has produced horses that always appeared to me affected and diminutively monstrous.

From the classic sculpture, I passed through an Assyrian room, where the walls are lined with great slabs of marble sculptured in bas-relief with scenes in the life of Sennacherib, I believe; very ugly, to be sure, yet artistically done in their own style, and in wonderfully good preservation. Indeed, if the chisel had cut its last stroke in them yesterday, the work could not be more sharp and distinct. In glass cases, in this room, are little relics and scraps of utensils, and a great deal of fragmentary rubbish, dug up by Layard in his researches, — things that it is hard to call anything but trash, but which yet may be of great significance as indicating the modes of life of a long-past race. I remember nothing particularly just now, except some pieces of broken glass, iridescent with certainly the most beautiful hues in the world, — indescribably beautiful, and unimaginably, unless one can conceive of the colors of the rainbow, and a thousand glorious sunsets, and the autumnal forest-leaves of America, all condensed upon a little fragment of a glass cup, — and that, too, without becoming in the least glaring or flagrant, but mildly glorious, as we may fancy the shifting hues of an angel's wing may be. I think this chaste splendor will glow in my memory for years to come. It is the effect of time, and cannot be imitated by any known process of art. I have seen it in specimens of old Roman glass, which has been famous here in England; but never in anything is there the brilliancy of these

Oriental fragments. How strange that decay, in dark places, and underground, and where there are a billion chances to one that nobody will ever see its handiwork, should produce these beautiful effects! The glass seems to become perfectly brittle, so that it would vanish, like a soap-bubble, if touched.

Ascending the stairs, I went through the halls of fossil remains, — which I care little for, though one of them is a human skeleton in limestone, — and through several rooms of mineralogical specimens, including all the gems in the world, among which is seen, not the Koh-i-noor itself, but a fac-simile of it in crystal. I think the aerolites are as interesting as anything in this department, and one piece of pure iron, laid against the wall of the room, weighs about fourteen hundred pounds. Whence could it have come? If these aerolites are bits of other planets, how happen they to be always iron? But I know no more of this than if I were a philosopher.

Then I went through rooms of shells and fishes and reptiles and tortoises, crocodiles and alligators and insects, including all manner of butterflies, some of which had wings precisely like leaves, a little withered and faded, even the skeleton and fibres of the leaves represented; and immense hairy spiders, covering, with the whole circumference of their legs, a space as big as a saucer; and centipedes little less than a foot long; and winged insects that look like jointed twigs of a tree. In America, I remember, when I lived in Lenox, I found an insect of this species, and at first really mistook it for a twig. It was smaller than these specimens in the Museum. I suppose every creature, almost, that runs or creeps or swims or flies, is represented in this collection of Natural History; and it puzzles me to think what they were all made for, though it is quite as mysterious why man himself was made.

By and by I entered the room of Egyptian mummies, of which there are a good many, one of which, the body of a priestess, is unrolled, except the innermost layer of linen. The outline of her face is perfectly visible. Mummies of cats, dogs, snakes, and children are in the wall-cases, together with a vast many articles of Egyptian manufacture and use, — even children's toys; bread, too, in flat cakes; grapes, that have turned to raisins in the grave; queerest of all, methinks, a curly wig, that is supposed to have belonged to a woman, — together with the wooden box that held it. The hair is brown, and the wig is as perfect as if it had been made for some now living dowager.

From Egypt we pass into rooms containing vases and other articles of Grecian and Roman workmanship, and funeral urns, and beads, and rings, none of them very beautiful. I saw some splendid specimens, however, at a former visit, when I obtained admission to a room not indiscriminately shown to visitors. What chiefly interested me in that room was a cast taken from the face of Cromwell after death; representing a wide-mouthed, long-chinned, uncomely visage, with a triangular English nose in the very centre. There were various other curiosities, which I fancied were safe in my memory, but they do not now come uppermost.

To return to my to-day's progress through the Museum; — next to the classic rooms are the collections of Saxon and British and early English antiquities, the earlier portions of which are not very interesting to me, possessing little or no beauty in themselves, and indicating a kind of life too remote from our own to be readily sympathized with. Who cares for glass beads and copper brooches, and knives, spear-heads, and swords, all so rusty that they look as much like pieces of old iron hoop as anything else? The bed of the Thames has been a rich treasury of antiquities, from the time of the Roman Conquest downwards; it seems to preserve bronze in considerable perfection, but not iron.

Among the mediæval relics, the carvings in ivory are often very exquisite and elaborate. There are likewise caskets and coffers, and a thousand other Old-World ornamental works; but I saw so many and such superior specimens of them at the Manchester Exhibition, that I shall say nothing of them here. The seal-ring of Mary, Queen of Scots, is in one of the cases; it must have been a thumb-ring, judging from its size, and it has a dark stone, engraved with armorial bearings. In another case is the magic glass formerly used by Dr. Dee, and in which, if I rightly remember, used to be seen prophetic visions or figures of persons and scenes at a distance. It is a round ball of glass or crystal, slightly tinged with a pinkish hue, and about as big as a small apple, or a little bigger than an egg would be if perfectly round. This ancient humbug kept me looking at it perhaps ten minutes; and I saw my own face dimly in it, but no other vision. Lastly, I passed through the Ethnographical Rooms; but I care little for the varieties of the human race, — all that is really important and interesting being found in our own variety. Perhaps equally in any other. This brought me to the head of one of the staircases, descending which I entered the library.

Here — not to speak of the noble rooms and halls — there are numberless treasures beyond all price; too valuable in their way for me to select any one as more curious and valuable than many others. Letters of statesmen and warriors of all nations, and several centuries back, — among which, long as it has taken Europe to produce them, I saw none so illustrious as those of Washington, nor more so than Franklin's, whom America gave to the world in her nonage; and epistles of poets and artists, and of kings, too, whose chirography appears to have been much better than I should have expected from fingers so often cramped in iron gauntlets. In another case there were the original autograph copies of several famous works, — for example, that of Pope's Homer, written on the backs of letters, the direction and seals of which appear in the midst of "the Tale of Troy divine," which also is much scratched and interlined with Pope's corrections; a manuscript of one of Ben Jonson's masques; of the Sentimental Journey, written in much more careful and formal style than might be expected, the book pretending to be a harum-scarum; of Walter Scott's Kenilworth, bearing such an aspect of straightforward diligence that I shall hardly think of it again as a romance; — in short, I may as well drop the whole matter here.

All through the long vista of the king's library, we come to cases in which — with their pages open beneath the glass — we see books worth their weight in gold, either for their uniqueness or their beauty, or because they have belonged to illustrious men, and have their autographs in them. The copy of the English translation of Montaigne, containing the strange scrawl of Shakespeare's autograph, is here. Bacon's name is in another book; Queen Elizabeth's in another; and there is a little devotional volume, with Lady Jane Grey's writing in it. She is supposed to have taken it to the scaffold with her. Here, too, I saw a copy, which was printed at a Venetian press at the time, of the challenge which the Admirable Crichton caused to be posted on the church doors of Venice, defying all the scholars of Italy to encounter him. But if I mention one thing, I find fault with myself for not putting down fifty others just as interesting, — and, after all, there is an official catalogue, no doubt, of the whole.

As I do not mean to fill any more pages with the British Museum, I will just mention the hall of Egyptian antiquities on the ground-floor of the edifice, though I did not pass through it to-day. They consist of things that would be very ugly and contemptible if they were not so immensely magnified; but it is impossible not to acknowledge a certain grandeur, resulting from the scale on which those strange old sculptors wrought. For instance, there is a granite fist of prodigious size, at least a yard across, and looking as if it were doubled in the face of Time, defying him to destroy it. All the rest of the statue to which it belonged seems to have vanished; but this fist will certainly outlast the Museum, and whatever else it contains, unless it be some similar Egyptian ponderosity. There is a beetle, wrought out of immensely hard black stone, as big as a hogshead. It is satisfactory to see a thing so big and heavy. Then there are huge stone sarcophagi, engraved with hieroglyphics within and without, all as good as new, though their age is reckoned by thousands of years. These great coffins are of vast weight and mass, insomuch that when once the accurately fitting lids were shut down, there might have seemed little chance of their being lifted again till the Resurrection. I positively like these coffins, they are so faithfully made, and so black and stern, — and polished to such a nicety, only to be buried forever; for the workmen, and the kings who were laid to sleep within, could never have dreamed of the British Museum.

There is a deity named Pasht, who sits in the hall, very big, very grave, carved of black stone, and very ludicrous, wearing a dog's head. I will just mention the Rosetta Stone, with a Greek inscription, and another in Egyptian characters which gave the clew to a whole field of history; and shall pretermit all further handling of this unwieldly subject.

In all the rooms I saw people of the poorer classes, some of whom seemed to view the objects intelligently, and to take a genuine interest in them. A poor man in London has great opportunities of cultivating himself if he will only make the best of them; and such an institution as the British Museum can hardly fail to attract, as the magnet does steel, the minds that are likeliest to be benefited by it in its various departments. I saw many children there, and some ragged boys.

It deserves to be noticed that some small figures of Indian Thugs, represented as engaged in their profession and handiwork of cajoling and strangling travellers, have been removed from the place which they formerly occupied in the part of the Museum shown to the general public. They are now in the more private room, and the reason of their withdrawal is, that, according to the Chaplain of Newgate, the practice of garroting was suggested to the English thieves by this representation of Indian Thugs. It is edifying, after what I have written in the preceding paragraph, to find that the only lesson known to have been inculcated here is that of a new mode of outrage.

December 8th. — This morning when it was time to rise, there was but a glimmering of daylight, and we had candles on the breakfast-table at nearly ten o'clock. All abroad there was a dense dim fog brooding through the atmosphere, insomuch that we could hardly see across the street. At eleven o'clock I went out into the midst of the fog-bank, which for the moment seemed a little more interfused with daylight; for there seem to be continual changes in the density of this dim medium, which varies so much that now you can but just see your hand before you, and a moment afterwards you can see the cabs dashing out of the duskiness a score of yards off. It is seldom or never, moreover, an unmitigated gloom, but appears to be mixed up with sunshine in different proportions; sometimes only one part sun to a thousand of smoke and fog, and sometimes sunshine enough to give the whole mass a coppery hue. This would have been a bright sunny day but for the interference of the fog; and before I had been out long, I actually saw the sun looking red and rayless, much like the millionth magnification of a new halfpenny.

I was bound towards Bennoch's; for he had written a note to apologize for not visiting us, and I had promised to call and see him to-day.

. . . . .

I went to Marlborough House to look at the English pictures, which I care more about seeing, here in England, than those of foreign artists, because the latter will be found more numerously and better on the Continent. I saw many pictures that pleased me; nothing that impressed me very strongly. Pictorial talent seems to be abundant enough, up to a certain point; pictorial genius, I should judge, is among the rarest of gifts. To be sure, I very likely might not recognize it where it existed; and yet it ought to have the power of making itself known even to the uninstructed mind, as literary genius does. If it exist only for connoisseurs, it is a very suspicious matter. I looked at all Turner's pictures, and at many of his drawings; and must again confess myself wholly unable to understand more than a very few of them. Even those few are tantalizing. At a certain distance you discern what appears to be a grand and beautiful picture, which you shall admire and enjoy infinitely if you can get within the range of distinct vision. You come nearer, and find only blotches of color and dabs of the brush, meaning nothing when you look closely, and meaning a mystery at the point where the painter intended to station you. Some landscapes there were, indeed, full of imaginative beauty, and of the better truth etherealized out of the prosaic truth of Nature; only it was still impossible actually to see it. There was a mist over it; or it was like a tract of beautiful dream-land, seen dimly through sleep, and glimmering out of sight, if looked upon with wide-open eyes. These were the more satisfactory specimens. There were many others which I could not comprehend in the remotest degree; not even so far as to conjecture whether they purported to represent earth, sea, or sky. In fact, I should not have known them to be pictures at all, but might have supposed that the artist had been trying his brush on the canvas, mixing up all sorts of hues, but principally white paint, and now and then producing an agreeable harmony of color without particularly intending it. Now that I have done my best to understand them without an interpreter, I mean to buy Ruskin's pamphlet at my next visit, and look at them through his eyes. But I do not think that I can be driven out of the idea that a picture ought to have something in common with what the spectator sees in Nature.

Marlborough House may be converted, I think, into a very handsome residence for the young Prince of Wales. The entrance from the court-yard is into a large, square central hall, the painted ceiling of which is at the whole height of the edifice, and has a gallery on one side, whence it would be pleasant to look down on a festal scene below. The rooms are of fine proportions, with vaulted ceilings, and with fireplaces and mantel-pieces of great beauty, adorned with pillars and terminal figures of white and of variegated marble; and in the centre of each mantel-piece there is a marble tablet, exquisitely sculptured with classical designs, done in such high relief that the figures are sometimes almost disengaged from the background. One of the subjects was Androcles, or whatever was his name, taking the thorn out of the lion's foot. I suppose these works are of the era of the first old Duke and Duchess. After all, however, for some reason or other, the house does not at first strike you as a noble and princely one, and you have to convince yourself of it by examining it more in detail.

On leaving Marlborough House, I stepped for a few moments into the National Gallery, and looked, among other things, at the Turners and Claudes that hung there side by side. These pictures, I think, are quite the most comprehensible of Turner's productions; but I must say I prefer the Claudes. The latter catches "the light that never was on sea or land" without taking you quite away from Nature for it. Nevertheless, I will not be quite certain that I care for any painter except Murillo, whose St. John I should like to own. As far as my own pleasure is concerned, I could not say as much for any other picture; for I have always found an infinite weariness and disgust resulting from a picture being too frequently before my eyes. I had rather see a basilisk, for instance, than the very best of those old, familiar pictures in the Boston Athenæum; and most of those in the National Gallery might soon affect me in the same way.

From the Gallery I almost groped my way towards the city, for the fog seemed to grow denser and denser as I advanced; and when I reached St. Paul's, the sunny intermixture above spoken of was at its minimum, so that the smoke-cloud grew really black about the dome and pinnacles, and the statues of saints looked down dimly from their standpoints on high. It was very grand, however, to see the pillars and porticos, and the huge bulk of the edifice, heaving up its dome from an obscure foundation into yet more shadowy obscurity; and by the time I reached the corner of the churchyard nearest Cheapside, the whole vast cathedral had utterly vanished, leaving "not a wrack behind," unless those thick, dark vapors were the elements of which it had been composed, and into which it had again dissolved. It is good to think, nevertheless, — and I gladly accept the analogy and the moral, — that the cathedral was really there, and as substantial as ever, though those earthly mists had hidden it from mortal eyes.

I found —— in better spirits than when I saw him last, but his misfortune has been too real not to affect him long and deeply. He was cheerful, however, and his face shone with almost its old lustre. It has still the cheeriest glow that I ever saw in any human countenance.

. . . . .

I went home by way of Holborn, and the fog was denser than ever, — very black, indeed more like a distillation of mud than anything else; the ghost of mud, — the spiritualized medium of departed mud, through which the dead citizens of London probably tread in the Hades whither they are translated. So heavy was the gloom, that gas was lighted in all the shop-windows; and the little charcoal-furnaces of the women and boys, roasting chestnuts, threw a ruddy, misty glow around them. And yet I liked it. This fog seems an atmosphere proper to huge, grimy London; as proper to London as that light neither of the sun nor moon is to the New Jerusalem.

On reaching home, I found the same fog diffused through the drawing-room, though how it could have got in is a mystery. Since nightfall, however, the atmosphere is clear again.

December 20th. — Here we are still in London, at least a month longer than we expected, and at the very dreariest and dullest season of the year. Had I thought of it sooner, I might have found interesting people enough to know, even when all London is said to be out of town; but meditating a stay only of a week or two (on our way to Rome), it did not seem worth while to seek acquaintances.

I have been out only for one evening; and that was at Dr. ——'s, who had been attending all the children in the measles. (Their illness was what detained us.) He is a homœopathist, and is known in scientific or general literature; at all events, a sensible and enlightened man, with an un-English freedom of mind on some points. For example, he is a Swedenborgian, and a believer in modern spiritualism. He showed me some drawings that had been made under the spiritual influence by a miniature-painter who possesses no imaginative power of his own, and is merely a good mechanical and literal copyist; but these drawings, representing angels and allegorical people, were done by an influence which directed the artist's hand, he not knowing what his next touch would be, nor what the final result. The sketches certainly did show a high and fine expressiveness, if examined in a trustful mood. Dr. —— also spoke of

Mr. Harris, the American poet of spiritualism, as being the best poet of the day; and he produced his works in several volumes, and showed me songs, and paragraphs of longer poems, in support of his opinion. They seemed to me to have a certain light and splendor, but not to possess much power, either passionate or intellectual. Mr. Harris is the medium of deceased poets, Milton and Lord Byron among the rest; and Dr. —— said that Lady Byron — who is a devoted admirer of her husband in spite of their conjugal troubles — pronounced some of these posthumous strains to be worthy of his living genius. Then the Doctor spoke of various strange experiences which he himself has had in these spiritual matters; for he has witnessed the miraculous performances of Hume, the American medium, and he has seen with his own eyes, and felt with his own touch, those ghostly hands and arms the reality of which has been certified to me by other beholders. Dr. —— tells me that they are cold, and that it is a somewhat awful matter to see and feel them. I should think so, indeed. Do I believe in these wonders? Of course; for how is it possible to doubt either the solemn word or the sober observation of a learned and sensible man like Dr. ——? But again, do I really believe it? Of course not; for I cannot consent to have heaven and earth, this world and the next, beaten up together like the white and yolk of an egg, merely out of respect to Dr. ——'s sanity and integrity. I would not believe my own sight, nor touch of the spiritual hands; and it would take deeper and higher strains than those of Mr. Harris to convince me. I think I *might* yield to higher poetry or heavenlier wisdom than mortals in the flesh have ever sung or uttered. Meanwhile, this matter of spiritualism is surely the strangest that ever was heard of; and yet I feel unaccountably little interest in it, — a sluggish disgust, and repugnance to meddle with it, — insomuch that I hardly feel as if it were worth this page or two in my not very eventful journal. One or two of the ladies present at Dr. ——'s little party seemed to be mediums.

I have made several visits to the picture-galleries since my last date; and I think it fair towards my own powers of appreciation to record that I begin to appreciate Turner's pictures rather better than at first. Not that I have anything to recant as respects those strange, white-grounded performances in the chambers at the Marlborough House; but some of his happier productions (a large landscape illustrative of Childe Harold, for instance) seem to me to have more magic in them than any other pictures. I admire, too, that misty, morning landscape in the National Gallery; and, no doubt, his very monstrosities are such as only he could have painted, and may have an infinite value for those who can appreciate the genius in them.

The shops in London begin to show some tokens of approaching Christmas; especially the toy-shops, and the confectioners', — the latter ornamenting their windows with a profusion of bonbons and all mannner of pygmy figures in sugar; the former exhibiting Christmas-trees, hung with rich and gaudy fruit. At the butchers' shops, there is a great display of fat carcases, and an abundance of game at the poulterers'. We think of going to the Crystal Palace to spend the festival day, and eat our Christmas dinner; but, do what we may, we shall have no home feeling or fireside enjoyment. I am weary, weary of London and of England, and can judge now how the old Loyalists must have felt, condemned to pine out their lives here, when the Revolution had robbed them of their native country. And yet there is still a pleasure in being in this dingy, smoky, midmost haunt of men; and I trudge through Fleet Street and Ludgate Street and along Cheapside with an enjoyment as great as I ever felt in a wood-path at home; and I have come to know these streets as well, I believe, as I ever knew Washington Street in Boston, or even Essex Street in my stupid old native town. For Piccadilly or for Regent Street, though more brilliant promenades, I do not care nearly so much.

December 27th. — Still leading an idle life, which, however, may not be quite thrown away, as I see some things, and think many thoughts.

The other day we went to Westminster Abbey, and through the chapels; and it being as sunny a day as could well be in London, and in December, we could judge, in some small degree, what must have been the splendor of those tombs and monuments when first erected there.

I presume I was sufficiently minute in describing my first visit to the chapels, so I shall only mention the stiff figure of a lady of Queen Elizabeth's court, reclining on the point of her elbow under a mural arch through all these dusty years; . . . . and the old coronation-chair, with the stone of Scone beneath the seat, and the woodwork cut and scratched all over with names and initials. . . . .

I continue to go to the picture-galleries. I have an idea that the face of Murillo's St. John has a certain mischievous intelligence in it. This has impressed me almost from the first. It is a boy's face, very beautiful and very pleasant too, but with an expression that one might fairly suspect to be roguish if seen in the face of a living boy.

About equestrian statues, as those of various kings at Charing Cross, and otherwhere about London, and of the Duke of Wellington opposite Apsley House, and in front of the Exchange, it strikes me as absurd, the idea of putting a man on horseback on a place where one movement of the steed forward or backward or sideways would infallibly break his own and his rider's neck. The English sculptors generally seem to have been aware of this absurdity, and have endeavored to lessen it by making the horse as quiet as a cab-horse on the stand, instead of rearing rampant, like the bronze group of Jackson at Washington. The statue of Wellington, at the Piccadilly corner of the Park has a stately and imposing effect, seen from far distances, in approaching either through the Green Park, or from the Oxford Street corner of Hyde Park.

January 3d, 1858. — On Thursday we had the pleasure of a call from Mr. Coventry Patmore, to whom Dr. Wilkinson gave me a letter of introduction, and on whom I had called twice at the British Museum without finding him. We had read his Betrothal and Angel in the House with unusual pleasure and sympathy, and therefore were very glad to make his personal acquaintance. He is a man of much more youthful aspect than I had expected, ... a slender person to be an Englishman, though not remarkably so had he been an American; with an intelligent, pleasant, and sensitive face, — a man very evidently of refined feelings and cultivated mind. . . . . He is very simple and agreeable in his manners; a little shy, yet perfectly frank, and easy to meet on real grounds. . . . . He said that his wife had proposed to come with him, and had, indeed, accompanied him to town, but was kept away. . . . . We were very sorry for this, because Mr. Patmore seems to acknowledge her as the real "Angel in the House," although he says she herself ignores all connection with the poem. It is well for her to do so, and for her husband to feel that the character is her real portrait; and both, I suppose, are right. It is a most beautiful and original poem, — a poem for happy married people to read together, and to understand by the light of their own past and present life; but I doubt whether the generality of English people are capable of appreciating it. I told Mr. Patmore that I thought his popularity in America would be greater than at home, and he said that it was already so; and he appeared to estimate highly his American fame, and also our general gift of quicker and more subtle recognition of genius than the English public. . . . . We mutually gratified each other by expressing high admiration of one another's works, and Mr. Patmore regretted that in the few days of our further stay here we should not have time to visit him at his home. It would really give me pleasure to do so. . . . . I expressed a hope of seeing him in Italy during our residence there, and he seemed to think it possible, as his friend, and our countryman, Thomas Buchanan Read, had asked him to come thither and be his guest. He took his leave, shaking hands with all of us because he saw that we were of his own people, recognizing him as a true poet. He has since given me the new edition of his poems, with a kind note.

We are now making preparations for our departure, which we expect will take place on Tuesday; and yesterday I went to our Minister's to arrange about the passport. The very moment I rang at his door, it swung open, and the porter ushered me with great courtesy into the anteroom; not that he knew me, or anything about me, except that I was an American citizen. This is the deference which an American servant of the public finds it expedient to show to his sovereigns. Thank Heaven, I am a sovereign again, and no longer a servant; and really it is very singular how I look down upon our ambassadors and dignitaries of all sorts, not excepting the President himself. I doubt whether this is altogether a good influence of our mode of government.

I did not see, and, in fact, declined seeing, the Minister himself, but only his son, the Secretary of Legation, and a Dr. P——, an American traveller just from the Continent. He gave a fearful account of the difficulties that beset a person landing with much luggage in Italy, and especially at Civitä Vecchia, the very port at which we intended to debark. I have been so long in England that it seems a cold and shivery thing to go anywhere else.

Bennoch came to take tea with us on the fifth, it being his first visit since we came to London, and likewise his farewell visit on our leaving for the Continent.

. . . . .

On his departure, J—— and I walked a good way down Oxford Street and Holborn with him, and I took leave of him with the kindest wishes for his welfare.

THE END.

Cambridge: Printed by Welch, Bigelow, & Co.

www.ingramcontent.com/pod-product-compliance
Lightning Source LLC
LaVergne TN
LVHW020116110826
845151LV00001B/176

* 9 7 8 1 4 2 5 5 4 2 6 5 8 *